Chinese–English Interpret
Intercultural Communica

Chinese and English are the world's largest languages, and the number of interpreter-mediated interactions involving Chinese and English speakers has increased exponentially over the last 30 years. This book presents and describes examples of Chinese–English interpreting across a large number of settings: conference interpreting; diplomatic interpreting; media interpreting; business interpreting; police, legal and court interpreting; and healthcare interpreting. Interpreters working in these fields face not only the challenge of providing optimal inter-lingual transfer, but also need to fully understand the discourse-pragmatic conventions of both Chinese and English speakers.

This innovative book provides an overview of established and contemporary frameworks of intercultural communication and applies these to a large sample of Chinese–English interpreted interactions. The authors introduce the Inter-Culturality Framework as a descriptive tool to identify and describe the strategies and footings that interpreters adopt. This book contains findings from detailed data with Chinese–English interpreters as experts not only in inter-lingual exchange, but cross-linguistic and intercultural communication. As such, it is a detailed and authoritative guide for trainees as well as practising Chinese–English interpreters.

Jim Hlavac is a senior lecturer in Translation and Interpreting Studies, Monash University, and a certified and practising interpreter and translator. He has authored or edited four books and has published widely in the fields of translation and interpreting studies, multilingualism, contact linguistics, intercultural communication, pragmatics and language maintenance/shift.

Zhichang Xu is a senior lecturer in the Linguistics and English Language programme of the School of Languages, Literatures, Cultures and Linguistics at Monash University and an associate editor for *English Today*. His research areas include world Englishes, applied linguistics, cultural linguistics, intercultural communication, language education, and self-translation studies.

Routledge Advances in Translation and Interpreting Studies

For more information about this series, please visit https://www.routledge.com/
Routledge-Advances-in-Translation-and-Interpreting-Studies/book-series/RTS

Chinese–English Interpreting and Intercultural Communication

Jim Hlavac and Zhichang Xu

Routledge
Taylor & Francis Group

LONDON AND NEW YORK

First published 2020 by Routledge

2 Park Square, Milton Park, Abingdon, Oxon OX14 4RN
605 Third Avenue, New York, NY 10017

Routledge is an imprint of the Taylor & Francis Group, an informa business

First issud in paperback 2021

Publisher's Note

The publisher has gone to great lengths to ensure the quality of this reprint
but points out that some imperfections in the original copies may be apparent.

British Library Cataloguing-in-Publication Data
A catalogue record for this book is available from the British Library

Library of Congress Cataloging-in-Publication Data
Names: Hlavac, Jim, author. | Xu, Zhichang, author.
Title: Chinese–English interpreting and intercultural communication/
    Jim Hlavac and Zhichang Xu.
Description: First. | New York : Routledge, 2020. | Series: Routledge
    studies in sociolinguistics | Includes bibliographical references and index.
Identifiers: LCCN 2019044287 (print) | LCCN 2019044288 (ebook) |
    ISBN 9781138669628 (hardback) | ISBN 9781315618111 (ebook)
Subjects: LCSH: Chinese language—Translating into English. | English
    language—Translating into Chinese. | Translating and interpreting—
    China—Social aspects. | Translating and interpreting—Cross-cultural
    studies.
Classification: LCC PL1277 .H57 2020 (print) | LCC PL1277 (ebook) |
    DDC 495.18/0221—dc23
LC record available at https://lccn.loc.gov/2019044287
LC ebook record available at https://lccn.loc.gov/2019044288

ISBN: 978-1-138-66962-8 (hbk)
ISBN: 978-1-03-217471-6 (pbk)
DOI: 10.4324/9781315618111

Typeset in Times New Roman
by Apex CoVantage, LLC

Contents

Figures

Tables

Acknowledgements

We would like to warmly thank David Xiong Yong (Wenzhou University) for his tireless and precise work as a visiting scholar to Monash University Translation and Interpreting Studies Program and for his research work including Chinese–English translation that contributed greatly to the collection of the data sample. We would like to thank the following students of the Monash University Master of Interpreting and Translation Studies Program, Nellie Hua Bi, Calvin Hsien-hao Liao and Kay Xianya Zhao for their contributions to the analysis of selected excerpts. We would lastly like to thank Gloria Xian Jiang for her work in performing English–Chinese translation and transliteration.

Abbreviations

AUSIT	Australian Institute of Interpreters and Translators
BT	back translation
CALD	culturally and linguistically diverse
ICF	Inter-Culturality Framework
LOTE	language other than English
SS	source speech
SL	source language
T&I	translation and interpreting
TS	target speech
TL	target language
UCT	uninterpreted Chinese turn

1 Introduction

Concepts, perspectives and frameworks for intercultural communication

This book is about Chinese–English interpreting and intercultural communication. It is about where, with whom and how Chinese–English interpreters work and how they interact with both Chinese and English speakers. We commence this book with an account given by a Chinese–English interpreter working with senior government officials from China on a formal visit to the offices of a senior government official in Australia:

> I can recall a situation where I was interpreting for a delegation of government officials visiting Australia from China. The Australian host, who was himself also a senior government official, welcomed the delegates warmly. At the start there were the formal introductions and the welcome issued to them very warmly by their Australian host. Following this there was some small talk to warm things up. Then the Australian senior government official started to talk about local business and commercial opportunities, and in doing so, he started to add some humourous asides to what he was saying. I can remember a couple of these and I can also remember that they came rather unexpectedly.
>
> I can remember that after we'd left the entrance hall, we were then shown into his large office. He pointed to the framed document hanging on the wall that recorded an important agreement signed by both Chinese and Australian government officials, and very proudly pointed out that the agreement had been in place for some 20 years. All of this the members of the Chinese delegation could fully understand or appreciate.
>
> We then left his office and moved to the meeting room next door. The host, the Australian senior government official, then went on to point out some details of the table at which they were all sitting. The table was circular and had an empty space in the middle. The Australian senior government official then pointed to a button just underneath the table top where he would normally sit and explained that when one of his government colleagues did not agree with him, he would press the button which would cause the colleague's chair to explode, killing him, just like in the film "Goldfinger".
>
> At this point the Australian host made a loud exploding sound and threw his hands up in the air to indicate the explosive force of the detonation. This noise and his gesture actually startled some of the Chinese guests. Clearly the Australian

host thought this was very funny and that the Chinese guests would get the joke and the background context. However, in my mind as the interpreter, I had no idea if they would "get" the joke or the context it referred to, and was very concerned that they would misinterpret what the Australian senior government official meant; I was worried that maybe they would take what he said literally.

I therefore decided to preface my interpretation into Chinese with the statement that "your Australian host has just told a joke" and then went on to interpret what he had said quite literally, including the final comment about "just like in Goldfinger". At this point I added "the movie" and also "邦德 007" (bāngdé 007 – Bond 007). As it turned out, once I mentioned that it was a movie and that it was a Bond movie, the Chinese delegates were actually able to place the context (to my surprise) and very politely laughed appropriately at their Australian host's joke. I remember feeling a great sense of relief that the telling of this joke did not backfire, so to speak.

In this recollection, the interpreter describes how he relayed speech between the two groups of speakers and used his judgement in how he 're-presented' some things from English into Chinese, drawing on his knowledge of appropriate communication norms in the cultures of each group of speakers. This is a regular activity performed daily by Chinese–English interpreters worldwide, and indeed by all interpreters who work not only between two linguistic systems but between two (or more) sets of discourse-pragmatic conventions.

This book gives an insight into both inter-lingual transfer and interpreter-mediated intercultural communication in the Chinese–English language pair. This book contains five chapters and is structured in the following way. Chapter 1 provides a state-of-the-art review of research and practice in intercultural communication. In particular, we explore what 'intercultural communication' means in the era of globalization. Chapter 2 looks at profiles and descriptions of Chinese and English speakers and the discourse-pragmatic conventions that are commonly practised by them. We look comparatively at the way both groups communicate and introduce the role of the interpreter as a linguistic mediator. Chapter 3 looks closely at interpreted interactions and describes the most common settings that they work in, focusing on Chinese–English language-transfer in these. Chapter 4 presents data from Chinese speakers and English speakers who use interpreting services to communicate with each other, and data from Chinese–English interpreters. This chapter provides multiple perspectives on a number of situational features that relate to intercultural communication. Chapter 5 provides an overview of the findings from all chapters, and lists the implications of these for both the field of Chinese–English interpreting and for intercultural communication.

1.1 Introduction

Intercultural communication emerged as a discipline in its own right in the second half of the twentieth century following the work of sociolinguists such as Dell Hymes and John Gumperz. It sought to place the study of language within the context of culture and society, and strong research streams have grown within it and alongside it, e.g. ethnography of communication, anthropological linguistics, cross-cultural discourse studies and cultural linguistics. Since the start of the new millennium, other developments have occurred that have further foregrounded the place of intercultural communication within linguistics and beyond. These developments are globalization, increased mobility and, most particularly, advances in technology that have vastly multiplied the opportunities for us to interact with verbal, written, signed or visual texts, synchronously or asynchronously. With these developments we need to keep in mind that the text's linguistic form, the linguistic repertoire of the author and the linguistic profile of the recipient may be in some cases recognizable, but in others most probably just assumed or perhaps negotiated. For an increasing number of people worldwide, and in an increasing number of people's communication domains, e.g. the workplace, social interactions, commercial transactions and leisure activities, the way that they engage with other interlocutors and texts can be characterized as 'intercultural communication'. For many people, "intercultural communication is now the default context of communication in everyday life" (Sharifian & Jamarani, 2013, p. 4). Such a 'revolution' has significant implications, and these implications apply not only to communicative interactions in which people engage with other interlocutors and texts directly, but also in mediated interactions where written translation or spoken or signed interpreting is the means by which these interactions occur.

Current research and contemporary frameworks of intercultural communication have generally not devoted a great deal of attention to mediated interactions, even though they present themselves as interactions which, by definition, feature speakers of different languages and cultural backgrounds interacting with each other. This has, in large part, been due to researchers' keen interest in how participants directly negotiate with other interlocutors and texts in an un-relayed way, perhaps also due to the concern that the interpreter may be seen as the key protagonist who addresses and manages features of intercultural communication exclusively. As such, this book is a contribution to bringing interpreting to intercultural communication, and to bringing intercultural communication to interpreting studies. In so doing, we hope to achieve the following in this book:

1) build on existing approaches and theoretical frameworks, and apply analytical tools to examine intercultural communication in interpreter-mediated interactions;
2) examine the different forms and dynamics that are present in mediated communication interactions and how features pertaining to intercultural communication are negotiated, re-presented, re-directed or 'contained' (in a limiting sense);
3) to re-visit and extend our notions of 'competence', e.g. intercultural competence, multi-dialectal or multi-varietal competence, symbolic competence, performative competence, meta-cultural competence and translanguaging competence; and

4)   to propose a framework, i.e. the Inter-Culturality Framework, which may account for the nuances, subtleties and increasing complexities of interpreter-mediated intercultural communication, particularly among Chinese speakers and English speakers.

The language pair that this book focuses on is Chinese and English. As is well known, there has been an enormous expansion in the relations between China and the outside world over the last 40 years, with both predominantly Anglophone countries as well as non-Anglophone countries. There has been a burgeoning rise in relations – economic, trade, cultural and not least linguistic – between China and the English-speaking world, and the volume of communication occurring between Chinese and English speakers, whether through the use of the other's language to communicate or through translation and interpreting, is enormous. The Chinese–English language pair is likely to be one of the most heavily represented, if not the most represented of all language pairs in the area of inter-lingual transfer. Yet it has only been in recent years that the mediation of these exchanges between these two large languages and groups of speakers provided via translation or interpreting has started to attract some attention. As stated, one of the goals of this book is to provide a contemporary conceptualization of intercultural communication with an application to one of the most common and yet understudied types of interactions between Chinese and English speakers: communication mediated through interpreting.

This book firstly provides a description of spoken and discourse-pragmatic features that characterize the communicative features of speakers of both languages. This book moves beyond the twentieth century notion of 'native-speakers' as the basis of investigation and examines speakers of both languages, Chinese and English, as first-, second- or subsequent-language speakers. A majority of the world's English speakers speak it as their second- or subsequent-language. In a similar way, many of the world's Chinese speakers speak this language not as their first, but as a second or subsequent language. Notion of 'Chinese speakers' and 'English speakers' will be unpacked further in Chapter 2. This book provides a discussion of intercultural communication resting on a contemporary analysis of discourse that looks at not only the discourse-pragmatic features that speakers bring with them to an interaction, but how interactional features and discourse are enacted and negotiated.

Analysis of spoken, pragmatic and paralinguistic features is provided within a framework that comprises five major areas or theories. These include:

1)   traditional notions of speech acts, discourse and politeness;
2)   macro-cultural perspectives of high-vs-low context cultures (e.g., Hall, 1964), and dimensions of culture (e.g., Hofstede, 1994);
3)   emerging paradigms of world Englishes, English as a lingua franca, and English and Chinese as an international language;
4)   cultural linguistics, intercultural communication, and intercultural pragmatics; and

5) interpreting studies (Seleskovitch, 1978; Pöchhacker, 2006, 2012, 2016; Wadensjö, 1998), discourse of interpreters and role-relationships with interlocutors (Mason, 2009; Rudvin, 2004; Rudvin and Tomassini, 2011).

Discussion then moves to interactions between Chinese and English speakers that are mediated through interpreters. Such interactions, although very common in areas as diverse as diplomacy and business to healthcare and the legal field, have only until recently started to receive attention in applied linguistics or translation studies. Empirical data, consisting of both quantitatively and qualitatively focused samples, are presented from Chinese speakers, English speakers and Chinese–English interpreters from a multi-party perspective. Data are presented on how each group of speakers describes their own discourse-pragmatic features, the discourse-pragmatic features of the other groups of speakers, and in interactions with interpreters. Data are provided on interpreters, together with findings from in-depth interviews with them as experts not only in inter-lingual exchanges, but cross-linguistic and intercultural communication. This book therefore applies contemporary theories to the interactions between speakers of the world's two largest languages and provides a practical analysis of speakers' interactions, attitudes and reported behaviour. This book is therefore of relevance for those working in fields such as translation studies, linguistics, pedagogy, cultural studies and intercultural communication. This book seeks to help establish and strengthen the 'nexus' between relevant state-of-the-art theories on communication and mediation between speakers of different languages and grounded practices in particular sectors of multilingual and multicultural societies, e.g., healthcare, teaching, law and social services.

This book presents contemporary theories on intercultural communication between Chinese and English speakers. It moves beyond purely theoretical or hypothetical discussions of intercultural communication to apply these to the situation of real speakers. These include a data sample of 82 informants (25 Chinese- and 24 English speakers, and 33 Chinese–English interpreters). It examines informants' reported behaviour and perceptions of specific features in communicative interactions, such as introductory and leave-taking protocols; physical presence, body language; information elicitation; problem-stating; phatic functions of language and affective reactions; speech modification in the interpreted interaction; perceptions of interpreters as cross-cultural experts. Thus this book makes the connection between theory and practice, and presents to the reader multiple perspectives of interactions between Chinese and English speakers, as well as those including both groups of speakers together with Chinese–English interpreters. This book focuses on Chinese–English interpreters who are not only highly proficient in inter-lingual transfer, but also intercultural experts who are in a unique position to report on features of Chinese speakers and English speakers in general, and specifically to the features of mediated encounters. This feature underlines the interdisciplinary character of the book's focus which will be informed by a variety of frameworks and approaches. The book provides the reader with a state-of-the-art description of the concepts and perspectives that are closely involved in intercultural communication and interpreting, related to Chinese and English speakers. The book contains five chapters. Including:

1) Introduction: Concepts, perspectives and frameworks for intercultural communication;
2) Mediated intercultural communication involving Chinese and English speakers;
3) The interpreted interaction;
4) Chinese–English interpreter-mediated interactions; and
5) Findings and implications for intercultural communication and for Chinese–English interpreting.

Chapter 1 provides a review of research and practice in intercultural communication. In particular it explores what 'intercultural communication' means in the era of globalization. In addition, this chapter reviews a number of major concepts and theories of intercultural communication. A model for understanding intercultural communication in mediated interactions is proposed towards the end of the chapter, i.e. the Inter-Culturality Framework (ICF), followed by a conclusion summarizing the chapter.

Chapter 2 explores intercultural communication that primarily involves Chinese and English speakers. This chapter focuses on intercultural pragmatics of Chinese and English speakers and mediated intercultural communication practices through Chinese–English interpreters in the current globalized world. Drawing critically on traditional as well as up-to-date research on intercultural communication, for example, Hymes' SPEAKING model, Hall's high and low context cultures, Hofstede's dimensions of culture, and face and maxims of politeness, as well as the Inter-Culturality Framework (ICF) we have developed in Chapter 1, this chapter explores the extent to which intercultural communication among Chinese and English speakers can be effectively mediated through Chinese–English interpreters in domain-related interactions, e.g. healthcare, and legal service settings.

Chapter 3 explores interpreted interactions involving Chinese speakers, English speakers and Chinese–English interpreters across a range of settings. The interpreted interaction is a situation *par excellence* to examine intercultural discourse and agency and to examine examples of reported behaviour in intercultural settings. Speakers bring their own discourse-pragmatic norms of intra-cultural and inter-cultural communication to the interaction, knowing that at least one interlocutor (the interpreter) will have some shared cultural knowledge, while the other (or 'allophone' speaker) is unlikely to share this knowledge. At the same time the different intercultural schemas that speakers (and interpreter) may hold still share a common feature: the desire to perform a communicative interaction, via linguistic mediation.

Chapter 4 presents the perspectives of speakers and interpreters, in the first place as separate groups and then comparatively. The perspectives are based on empirical and qualitatively based data from Chinese speakers, English speakers and Chinese–English interpreters. The features that are represented in speakers' and interpreters' perspectives include self-introduction, role explanation, pre-interactional briefing, physical proximity, small talk, body language, facial expressions, and paralinguistic markers, presentation and elicitation of information, leave taking and discursive directness. In regard to discursive directness, we elicit responses on Chinese and English speakers' performance of speech acts such as explanations, answers to questions, requests, complaints/criticisms, compliments, and in interpretations of these speech acts into the other language. We focus on the following features specific to interpreter-mediated interactions: role explanation, pre-interaction verbal contact or briefing, metalinguistic awareness of interpreted speech and of the form of target speech.

Chapter 5 reports and summarizes major findings of the research. The 'social turn' in Interpreting (and Translation) Studies from the start of the twenty-first century has resulted in still only few large-scale or qualitative studies that examine intercultural communication as a prominent feature in interpreted interactions. Specific to the language pair of Chinese and English, the discourse-pragmatic norms and intercultural strategies of Chinese–English interpreters are an under-researched area, as the attributes of this group of linguistic mediators have been examined mostly in relation to linguistic message transfer only. Aspects relating to intercultural communication have, in general, not been addressed in such detail, or in many instances, not addressed at all. Findings are presented employing the Inter-Culturality Framework (ICF) analysis to the data sample. This framework and the in-depth discussion of intercultural features in a hitherto lesser-researched area move a contemporary understanding of intercultural communication forward.

1.2   Revisiting intercultural communication

The first two decades of the new millennium have featured unprecedented globalization and an increase in intercultural communication alongside the spread of English and Chinese across the globe, albeit via different routes and means. In the case of English, it was through colonization, migration and globalization, and in the case of Chinese, through diasporization and globalization. We understand the process of diasporization as an ongoing ethnification and reconfiguration of transnational diasporic connections through continuing mobility, migration, return and/or re-migration. The wide use of social media, e.g. blogs, Facebook, Twitter, Instagram and WeChat, and the increasing mobility of people and the contact of languages and cultures have added new dimensions to intercultural communication. Some make the contention that there is currently a "revolution in the contexts and contents of intercultural communication" (Sharifian and Jamarani, 2013, p. 4). Globalization and technological advances have brought people physically and virtually closer to one another across cultures, countries, and continents. At the same time, relevant research is needed regarding domain-related mediated interactions among people of different linguistic and cultural backgrounds, e.g. intercultural communication through mediated interpreting in legal and healthcare services. For the majority of people who shift between communities or communicate online through social media across cultures, intercultural communication takes place on a daily basis. Although people have been communicating inter-culturally for centuries, and research on intercultural communication has been ongoing for decades, it is still of worth to revisit the fundamental notions and concepts of language, culture, interculturality and intercultural communication to move our understanding and practice forward.

Intercultural communication has always been something of an enigma for a number of reasons. First, the essential notions and concepts involved in inter-cultural communication, e.g. language and culture, are notoriously fluid in terms of their definitions and applications. Second, instances of intercultural commu-nication and circumstances in which intercultural communication takes place vary massively so that any attempts at generalizing guiding principles may end up being simplifying, stereotyping or over-generalizing language and culture. Third, intercultural communication research is interdisciplinary in nature, and it involves, to name just a few disciplines, anthropology, ethnography of communi-cation, applied linguistics, cognitive linguistics, cultural linguistics, pragmatics, psychology, education, and philosophy. Last but not least, new theories, frame-works and models, and above all, new notions and concepts regarding intercul-tural communication have been emerging on a constant basis, and those theories as well as concepts do not necessarily cohere well with one another.

In the following sections we revisit constituent components of intercultural communication, namely language, culture, and interculturality, with an intention to set up a framework for analyzing empirical data regarding mediated intercul-tural communication in domain-related settings, e.g. healthcare and legal services.

1.2.1   Language

Language is a system of signs, and signs always refer to other signs, existing only in relation to one another. This system of signs is what we use primarily to conduct our social lives, including communication with others, and also with ourselves. A language has both lexical and non-lexical aspects as far as 'communication' is concerned. Communication through lexical forms refers to the words we use to communicate a message; and forms of non-lexical communication refer aspects of communication other than the words themselves. In addition, there is also a distinc-tion between verbal and non-verbal communication. Verbal communication refers to vocal aspects of communication, i.e. communication by mouth; non-verbal com-munication refers primarily to written communication with literally no vocal char-acteristics (see Figure 1.1). An example showing the differences between verbal and non-verbal communication is when someone says "I do not have any problem with you!" while his or her non-verbal cues, e.g. avoiding eye-contact, looking anxious, and having closed body language, may convey a different 'message'.

There are many branches of linguistics that involve intercultural communica-tion, e.g. applied linguistics, sociolinguistics, psycholinguistics, cognitive linguis-tics, corpus linguistics, second language acquisition, and cultural linguistics. The relationship among language, humanity and culture has always been a complex issue, and it has attracted the attention of many researchers. One of the notions

	Lexical	*Non-lexical*
Verbal	Spoken words	**Paralinguistic features**, including voice quality, rate, pitch, volume, and speaking style, and prosodic features, such as rhythm, intonation, and stress
Non-verbal	Written words	**Kinesics**: body language, e.g. oculesics: eye contact (actions of looking while talking and listening, frequency of glances, patterns of fixation, pupil dilation, and blink rate)
		Haptics: contact (or the absence thereof) with others
		Proxemics: distance, or space around the body
		Chronemics: the use of time
		Presentation cues: emoticons

Figure 1.1 The lexical/non-lexical and verbal/non-verbal interpersonal communication matrix

about the relationship is 'linguistic relativity', which is the idea that "different people speak differently because they think differently, and that they think differently because their language offers them different ways of expressing the world around them" (Kramsch, 1998, p. 11). As far as intercultural communication is concerned, this linguistic relativity view posits that our language determines the way we communicate, and cultural differences are relative to linguistic meanings and norms. Understanding others who have a different linguistic or cultural heritage "does not depend on structural equivalences but on common conceptual systems, born from the larger context of our experience" (Kramsch, 1998, p. 13). This is particularly true when non-verbal messages and pragmatic norms are communicated through mediated interpreting across cultures.

One of the current perspectives in intercultural communication is to view language as discourse. Language is not a "closed linguistic system of symbolic forms and semantic meanings enshrined in grammars and dictionaries, but a living cultural and historical social semiotic, or meaning-making system that links text and social context in multiple ways" (Kramsch, 2013, p. 24). Language is also viewed as cultural practice, communicative practice, social practice and discursive practice. Discursive practice addresses the processes by which cultural meanings are produced and understood and culturally meaningful behaviours are conducted in actual situations. In this book, we view language and its associated non-verbal behaviour through mediated communication, such as interpreting, as an instantiation of intercultural communication.

1.2.2 Culture

'Culture' is a slippery term. The paradox of 'culture' is that, many people define it, but they also admit that it is difficult, if not entirely impossible, to define. The notion of culture originates in anthropology, yet it is also a term that is half-abandoned in this very field of research. Prof. Michael Agar, a practitioner and researcher in intercultural communication and anthropology recounted the following anecdote:

> A few years ago, at the International Pragmatics Association meetings in Antwerp, I stood in the hall and talked with my old teacher, John Gumperz. A colleague came up and said, 'You know, this is really an interesting meeting. But how do you tell who the anthropologists are?' Gumperz smiled and answered, 'It's easy. They're the ones who never use the word *culture*'.
>
> (Agar, 1994, p. 224)

The term 'culture' remains hard to define. As with the term 'language', culture is not a closed system of meanings either. "All cultures are works in progress, moving targets, and it is this understanding itself that liberates us from essentialized conceptualizations of culture" (Szalay, 1981, p. 242). Szalay also addresses the frequently encountered conceptualization of culture as something tangible.

> The problem with the word 'culture' as it has been used in anthropology, sociology, and in everyday life, it has been pointed out, is that it is used as a noun, conceived of as something 'solid,' an essential set of traits or characteristics of certain people or groups, something people 'have' rather than something they 'do'.
>
> (Szalay, 1981, p. 237)

One of the first researchers to look at the presence and form of discourse and pragmatic features across languages in a comparative approach was Hofstede (1994). He defines culture as the "collective programming of the mind which distinguishes the members of one group or category of people from another" (Hofstede, 1994, p. 5). A more recent definition of culture is proposed by Spencer-Oatey (2008), who has worked extensively on features of communication amongst both Chinese and English speakers:

> culture is a fuzzy set of basic assumptions and values, orientations to life, beliefs, policies, procedures and behavioural conventions that are shared by a group of people, and that influence (but do not determine) each member's behaviour and his/her interpretations of the 'meaning' of other people's behaviour.
>
> (Spencer-Oatey, 2008, p. 3)

It can be observed that all of these definitions list tangible and/or intangible aspects of what 'culture' implies, however, we view culture as a process. We are interested in 'how' culture is constructed and co-constructed, and practiced in mediated contexts, such as domain related intercultural communication through interpreters.

Dynamic as culture is, it is generally perceived as having two subcategories: 'subjective culture' (an individual's personal identity and life projects), and 'objective culture' (the objectivity of social circumstances). More recently, Kecskes (2013, p. 47) specifies the distinction as follows: subjective culture is "the psychological feature of culture, including assumptions, values, beliefs, and patterns of thinking' and objective culture includes "the institutions and artifacts of culture, such as its economic system, social customs, political structures, processes, arts, crafts, and literature".

No matter how we define and perceive 'culture', we generally accept that cultural knowledge is ambiguous, flexible, and negotiable, and that cultures can hardly be compared without biases. Therefore, we have to be careful when we attempt to make comparisons between cultures. Scollon, Scollon, and Jones (2012, p. 277) caution that "there is hardly any dimension on which you could compare 'cultures' and with which one 'culture' could be clearly and unambiguously distinguished from another".

1.2.3 *Interculture and interculturality*

Interculture is a 'culture' in itself, and it refers to a specific contact situation or a context involving more than one culture, or one set of cultural conceptualizations. Interculturality is the interaction of people from different linguistic and cultural backgrounds using linguistic means that demonstrate their cultural knowledge and understanding.

The prefix 'inter-' of interculture implies the intermediate or in-between nature of the contact situation. In this sense, mediated intercultural communication through interpreters, e.g., in healthcare settings, can be characterized by interculturality in professional contexts. Koole and ten Thijie (2001, p. 575) define interculture as

> an intermediate culture which shares properties of both home culture and host culture, independent of whether those properties are shared between the cultures-in-contact . . . In this respect, interculture is concerned with the dynamics of culture contact *par excellence*.

They also point out that "intercultures do not necessarily remain 'inter'-cultures, but may end up being incorporated into the dominant culture" (Koole & ten Thijie, 2001, p. 585).

Kecskes (2013, p. 39) regards 'intercultures' as "situationally emergent and co-constructed phenomena that rely on relatively definable cultural models and norms, as well as situationally evolving features". Therefore, "interculturality has both relatively normative and emergent components". According to Kecskes (2013, p. 39),

> intercultures are usually *ad hoc* creations. They are generated in a communicative process in which cultural norms and models brought into the interaction from the prior experience of interlocutors blend with features created *ad hoc* in the interaction in a synergetic way. The result is intercultural discourse

in which there is mutual transformation of knowledge and communicative behaviour rather than transmission.

The notion of intercultural discourse is an important one, and it will be discussed in more detail later in this chapter. In addition, it is important to understand that interculturality embodies mutual 'transformation' of cultural knowledge and behaviour, rather than 'transmission' of cultural knowledge and behaviour.

Interculturality has increasingly become a key notion in the current era of globalization, where interculture has become the norm whereas monolingual and monocultural societies are rare species. Interculturality renders benefits to both individuals and societies in terms of cultural diversity, enrichment and creativity. However, it may also be problematic when instances of linguistic imperialism, racism and xenophobia occur. One of the implications of understanding the notion of interculturality is the acquisition of skills to further the development of intercultural competence among interlocutors, including interpreters, to achieve effective intercultural communication.

Leclercq (2003, p. 9) defines interculturality as "the set of processes through which relations between different cultures are constructed" whereby "the aim is to enable groups and individuals who belong to such cultures within a single society or geo-political entity to forge links based on equity and mutual respect". Jackson (2014, p. 374) defines interculturality as "the forging of respectful, equitable links between individuals and groups from different cultural (and linguistic) backgrounds". In light of the definitions and illustrations of 'interculturality', we understand it as a sphere or a contact zone of multiple cultures where people of different linguistic and cultural backgrounds interact, communicate and negotiate meaning through linguistic and paralinguistic measures for intercultural communication.

1.2.4   Communication

The field of communication studies ranges from social sciences to humanities, involving primarily sociology, anthropology, psychology, ethnography, economics, political science, rhetoric studies, discourse analysis, semantics, pragmatics of politeness, face, and speech acts, translation and interpreting, applied linguistics, cognitive linguistics and cultural linguistics. Communication studies is a discipline that is inter-dependent on the advances in technology, media and globalization studies, and it intersects with applied journalism, public relations, healthcare, organizational and environmental studies. Over the past decades, communication studies has also taken up new directions such as mediated communication, e.g. electronically mediated communication and translator/interpreter mediated communication.

The rise of the discipline of 'intercultural communication' occurred around the middle of the twentieth century. American anthropologist Edward T. Hall has been regarded as one of the founders of the field of intercultural communication. He was one of the anthropologists alongside a number of linguists employed to help the U.S Foreign Service Institute to train their Foreign Service Officers. Hall (1964, p. 155) applied a linguistic model for analysis of culture, and points out that "the great strengths of linguistics are that it has distinguished between *etic* and *emic* events, and has been able to handle greater and greater complexity". *Etic* and *emic* events are intercultural interaction occurrences that involve the so-called cultural 'outsiders' and cultural 'insiders'. An *etic* event is an event where there is a cultural outsider looking in. An example of this would be, a Chinese speaker and researcher going to visit an English speaking community to observe their cultural norms through interacting with the people of the community. An *emic* event is an event where a culture 'insider' participates in the interactions among people of his or her linguistic and cultural backgrounds to focus on the intrinsic cultural practices that are generally taken for granted by the members of the community. The main purpose of an *emic* perspective is to provide in-depth insights about how a cultural insider understands or interprets the cultural norms and rituals of the community. Interpreted interactions offer rich examples of *etic* and *emic* perspectives, where interlocutors encounter each other, as linguistic discordance and the act of linguistic mediation typically heightens these perspectives. At the same time the interpreter who has knowledge of and expertise in the cultural practices of both groups is usually seen as a ratified 'insider' of both groups.

In the brief history of intercultural communication research, one of the traditions following the work of sociolinguists in the 1980s, e.g. Dell Hymes and John Gumperz, was to place the study of language within the context of culture and society, i.e. the ethnography of communication, or culturally distinctive means of communication. A significant contribution of the Hymes and Gumperz tradition is the continuing development and focus on the emic or the insider's perspectives in relation to the etic or the outsider's perspectives. Traditionally the *etic* and *emic* were approaches that represented two sides of the epistemological and methodological divides. The *etic* approach is more quantitative-oriented, involving large samples, and it is adopted for comparative research across languages and cultures, whereas the *emic* approach focuses more on the perspectives and interpretations of relatively small groups of individuals (Dewaele, 2015, p. 358). This book explores intercultural communication in mediated interpreting settings from a mixed *emic* and *etic* approach, consisting of *emic* reflections by Chinese speakers and English speakers, as well as *etic* perceptions of each other's groups. The Chinese–English interpreter group has a mixed orientation towards cultural practices, reflections and perspectives through its dual affiliations to both groups of speakers, and towards a third group which is an occupationally based one.

By the mid-1990s further analyses on intercultural communication were developed. In an attempt to distinguish various types of data sets based on whether the predominant code used in communication was also the L1 of one of the interlocutors, or whether it was a shared lingua franca and so on, Clyne (1994) classified intercultural communication studies into three categories: 1) contrastive approach; 2) interlanguage approach; and 3) interactive intercultural approach. The 'contrastive approach' mainly compares communicative discourse across cultures. The 'interlanguage approach' examines how learners of a language or non-native speakers communicate across cultures in their second or subsequent language(s). The 'interactive approach' focuses on the interaction between people of different linguistic and cultural backgrounds in a language that serves as a lingua franca. In addition, we propose that there is a fourth approach, which is a 'mediated approach'. This approach explores intercultural communication through mediation. Such mediation involves both interpreters and translators in formal and less formal contexts, and various platforms of social media in virtual communication environments.

Since the beginning of the twenty-first century there has been a "revolution in the contexts and contents of intercultural communication" (Sharifian & Jamarani, 2013, p. 4). Such a 'revolution' calls for the following: 1) advancing our known approaches and theoretical frameworks, and developing analytical tools that are applicable to the study of intercultural communication; 2) forms of face-to-face and mediated intercultural communication through translation/interpreting and social media need to be explored; 3) basic notions and concepts of language, culture, and interculture need to be re-examined; 4) new types of 'competence', e.g. intercultural competence, multi-dialectal/multi-varietal competence, symbolic competence, performative competence, meta-cultural competence and translanguaging competence, need to be considered and explored.

1.2.5   *Intercultural communication*

Depending on how culture is defined, 'intercultural communication' may refer to "the meeting of two cultures or two languages across the political boundaries of nation-states" on the assumption of 'one nation-one culture-one language', and it may also refer to "communication between people from different ethnic, social, gendered cultures within the boundaries of the same national language" (Kramsch, 1998, p. 81).

Kecskes (2013) views intercultural communication as a space for the construction and co-construction of intercultures, from socially and contextually situated meanings as well as those that are informed by relatively definable cultural models that characterize speech communities. Kecskes (2013, p. 40) has associated the notion of a 'third space' with 'intercultures'.

> In emerging intercultures, encyclopedic knowledge represents the relatively definable cultural models and norms that the interlocutors bring into the communicative situation based on their prior experience. This individual prior knowledge blends with the knowledge and information emerging from the actual situational context, and this blend creates a third space that we call intercultures.
>
> (Kecskes, 2013, p. 40)

There are obvious parallels to Kecskes' statement about 'intercultures' and Clyne's 'interactive intercultural approach'. It is important to note that intercultural communication can be different from the notion of 'cross-cultural communication', although both involve people from more than one cultural and linguistic background, these two notions can sometimes be used interchangeably. According to Bowe, Martin, and Manns (2014, p. 3), 'cross-cultural communication' and 'intercultural communication' are different in that research on cross-cultural communication typically compares communication practices of one language/cultural group with another, i.e. analogous to Clyne's 'contrastive approach', while studies on intercultural communication focus on features of the shared communication between speakers from different language/cultural backgrounds. However, they also recognize that cross-cultural communication and intercultural communication are often used as synonyms and that studies using either designation very commonly focus on the same phenomena: cultural expectations, social relations and the purpose of the communication.

1.2.6 Competence for intercultural communication

The previous section has proposed further categories of competence that we need and describe. In this section we focus more closely on 'competence' for intercultural communication. Xu (2013, pp. 3–8) has summarized the current conceptualizations of globalization, including globalization as mobility, cultural blending, local functionality, super-diversity and heterogeneity. Mobility in terms of globalization refers to the global flow of people, commodities, services and ideologies. Such unprecedented mobility creates new contexts for intercultural communication, which are characterized as being mobile and dynamic, blended with multiple languages and cultures, location-based, super-diverse and heterogeneous by nature. Such contexts require interlocutors as well as interpreters to acquire new competence so as to engage in mediated intercultural communication successfully. Traditional types of competence include linguistic competence (cf. Noam Chomsky) and communicative competence (cf. Dell Hymes). Over the decades, new types of competence, particularly for mediated intercultural communication, have been conceptualized and explored. These include 'intercultural communicative competence' (Byram, 1989, 1997), multidialectal competence (Canagarajah, 2006), semiotic competence (Van Lier, 2004), performative competence (Canagarajah, 2013b), metacultural competence (Sharifian, 2013; Sharifian & Jamarani, 2013) and translanguaging competence, as outlined in the following paragraphs.

Intercultural communicative competence (ICC) refers generally to subtle and complex abilities to communicate effectively and appropriately in a variety of intercultural contexts or situations. It builds on Hymes' (1972) communicative competence, and it involves not only language abilities, but appropriate attitudes, knowledge and skills, pertinent to intercultural communication. We briefly digress to revisit Hymes' (1972) 'communicative competence' before elaborating on intercultural communicative competence. Hymes' communicative competence comprises grammatical competence, sociolinguistic competence, discourse competence and strategic competence. Grammatical competence refers to a sufficient command of the language being adopted for communication; sociolinguistic competence refers to the ability to produce appropriate utterances or sentences in different sociolinguistic contexts; discourse competence refers to the ability to achieve cohesion in language form and coherence in linguistic and sociocultural meaning; and strategic competence refers to the awareness and use of appropriate verbal and nonverbal communication strategies in human interaction.

In addition to Hymes' communicative competence a model of 'communicative ability' was proposed by van Ek (1986, p. 35). This model comprises six competences, together with autonomy and social responsibility. These include *linguistic competence*, "the ability to produce and interpret meaningful utterances which are formed in accordance with the rules of the language concerned and bear their conventional meaning" (p. 39); *sociolinguistic competence*, "the awareness of ways in which the choice of language forms . . . is determined by such conditions as setting, relationship between communication partners, communicative intention" (p. 41); *discourse competence*, "the ability to use appropriate strategies in the construction and interpretation of texts" (p. 47), and *strategic competence*; when communication is difficult we have to find ways of "getting our meaning across" or of "finding out what somebody means", such as rephrasing, asking for clarification (p. 55); *socio-cultural competence*, i.e. "every language is situated in a sociocultural context and implies the use of a particular reference frame which is partly different from that of the foreign language learner" (p. 35); and *social competence*, which involves "both the will and the skill to interact with others, involving motivation, attitude, self-confidence, empathy and the ability to handle social situations" (p. 65). Linguistic competence is heavily foregrounded as an important attribute in interpreting testing and training (Ruiz Rosendo & Diur, 2017; Tzou, Eslami, & Chen, 2011; Fan, 2012) while others such as discourse competence (Clifford, 2001; Hild, 2015) and also strategic competence (Rennert, 2010; Chabasse & Kader, 2014; Russo, 2014) are afforded attention in studies on interpreting pedagogy and performance. But the three remaining competences – sociolinguistic, socio-cultural and social – tend to receive less attention, notwithstanding the work of Wadensjö (1998), Rudvin (2004), Mason (2009) and others.

Building on communicative competence, Byram (1997) theorizes intercultural communicative competence as comprising attitudes, knowledge and skills. Such 'attitudes' include curiosity and openness, readiness to suspend disbelief about other cultures and belief about one's own without being judgmental. The required 'knowledge' is "of social groups and their products and practices in one's own and in one's interlocutor's country, and of the general processes of societal and individual interaction" (Byram, 1997, p. 51). In addition, Byram (1997) suggests that essential skills for intercultural communication include those of inferring and relating, discovery and interaction, and critical cultural awareness and political education. To be more specific, skills of inferring and relating refer to the "ability to interpret a document or event from another culture, to explain it and relate it to documents from one's own"; skills of discovery and interaction refer to the "ability to acquire new knowledge of a culture and cultural practices and the ability to operate knowledge, attitudes and skills under the constraints of real-time communication and interaction"; and skills of critical cultural awareness and political education refer to the "ability to evaluate critically and on the basis of explicit criteria perspectives, practices and products in one's own and other cultures and countries" (Byram, 1997, p. 51).

The first decade of the twenty-first century witnessed a paradigm shift in the use of English as a lingua franca for intercultural communication. Alongside other major languages, such as Chinese, Spanish, Hindi, Arabic, Portuguese and Russian, English has become more salient for intercultural communication in that the numbers of second and subsequent language speakers are *greater* than the numbers of speakers who use it as their first language. An estimated 80% of verbal intercultural communication in English involves English used by those who are second or subsequent language speakers of the language. This poses new challenges for people to develop multidialectal and multi-varietal competence, because English is no longer a monolithic entity, but a pluricentric language, consisting of different 'Englishes'. In this super-diverse context, Canagarajah (2006) points out that people constantly shuttle between different varieties and communities, and that one needs the capacity to negotiate diverse varieties to facilitate communication. Understanding new varieties has become part of what Canagarajah (2006, p. 233) terms as 'multidialectal competence'.

Apart from the aforementioned competences, Kramsch (1998, p. 81) points out that intercultural communication requires the ability or competence to "understand someone else's culture while retaining one's own" or more generally to "mediate between several languages and cultures". Both of these definitions apply to interpreters in relation to interpreter-mediated intercultural communication. Kramsch (2008, p. 400) comments that

> social actors in multilingual settings, even if they are non-native speakers of the languages they use, seem to activate more than a communicative competence that would enable them to communicate accurately, effectively and appropriately with one another. They seem to display a particularly acute ability to play with various linguistic codes and with the various spatial and temporal resonances of these codes.

All of these mentioned competences are attributes that interpreters are required to possess.

Canagarajah (2013b, p. 85) proposes a 'performative competence' based on his research regarding translingual practice among skilled multilingual immigrant speakers in 'contact zones'. He points out that:

> [i]n the contact zones, interactants can communicate through heterogeneous codes and diverse norms because they adopt negotiation strategies to co-construct meaning. They also learn new repertoires as they communicate, engaged as they are in practice-based learning. . . . It emerged that what makes such communication possible is not a competence for form but a competence for practice.

> (Canagarajah, 2013b, p. 85)

A relevant term here is 'negotiation strategies' that relates to the dynamic and interactive character of 'contact zone' interactions which are in many ways analogous to linguistically mediated interactions. Canagarajah defines performative competence as "a procedural knowledge, not a propositional knowledge", and he describes this procedural knowledge as involving the following practices: starting from one's own positionality; negotiating on equal terms; focusing on practices, not form; co-constructing rules and terms of engagement; being responsive to joint accomplishment of goals, and reconfiguring one's norms and expanding one's repertoire. According to Canagarajah (2013b, p. 88), this type of knowledge can be developed in and through practice, shaping both cognition and form in terms of one's ongoing experiences. Multilingual interlocutors adopt dynamic and reciprocal strategies to respond strategically to unexpected interlocutors and spaces with diverse norms in contact zones.

Multilinguals in contact zones develop their performative competence through "suitable *frame* and *footing* for the context of communication" (Canagarajah, 2013b, p. 86). According to Canagarajah (2013b, pp. 87–88), this competence enables multilingual interlocutors not to master one language system at a time but to develop an "integrated repertoire of codes". Multilingual interlocutors focus on developing their language awareness or metalinguistic competence that enables them to deal with issues they encounter in contact situations. "In contexts where norms are always new, diverse, and unpredictable, such metalinguistic competence helps them to decode the interlocutor's norms on the spot as they engage in communication". In this form of competence, what is emphasized is "the repertoire – the way the different language, resources constitute an integrated and ever widening competence" (Canagarajah, 2013b, pp. 87–88).

The rise of cultural linguistics as a field of research has provided new tools and frameworks for understanding intercultural communication on a global scale. Cultural linguistics (Sharifian, 2011) refers to a branch of linguistics that explores the relationship between language, culture, and conceptualization. Cultural linguistics examines how various features of language encode cultural conceptualizations. The main analytical tools of cultural linguistics are cultural schemas, cultural categories, and cultural-conceptual metaphors, collectively referred to as cultural conceptualizations and "from the perspective of cultural linguistics, during intercultural communication, interlocutors draw on their cultural conceptualizations in constructing, interpreting, and negotiating intercultural meanings" (Sharifian & Jamarani, 2013, p. 7). The notion of 'cultural conceptualizations' is introduced as an analytical framework to decode cultural and intercultural communication phenomena. It is a cover term that refers to fundamental cultural cognitive processes. One of the cultural conceptualizations is cultural schema, and there are different types of cultural schema, including *event schema*, e.g. the expected routines of visiting a doctor in a healthcare setting, *role schema*, e.g. expected behaviours from people in particular social positions, such as a doctor, an interpreter, and a patient, *proposition schema*, i.e. cultural models of thought and behaviour, e.g. the cultural belief that Chinese are descendants of dragons.

Drawing on the framework of cultural conceptualizations, Sharifian (2013, p. 8) proposes the notion of 'metacultural competence', and he defines it as a "competence that enables interlocutors to communicate and negotiate their cultural conceptualizations during the process of intercultural communication". There are three components in metacultural competence: 1) conceptual variation awareness, 2) conceptual explication strategies and 3) conceptual negotiation strategies. Cultural variation awareness is "the awareness that one and the same language could be used by different speech communities to encode and express their respective cultural conceptualizations" (Sharifian, 2013, pp. 8–9). Cultural explication strategies comprise a conscious effort to clarify relevant conceptualizations that people from different cultures may not be familiar with (Sharifian, 2013, p. 9). Intercultural negotiation strategies are strategies that participants adopt to negotiate intercultural meanings, or to seek conceptual clarifications when participants feel that "there might be more behind the use of a certain expression than is immediately apparent" (Sharifian, 2013, p. 9).

In order to develop meta-cultural competence for intercultural communication, Xu (2017, p. 711) suggests three steps that intercultural interlocutors may consider taking. These are:

(a) Acknowledging the paradigm shift in relation to the current use and users of English. English has become pluricentric, and it is increasingly used as a lingua franca. The majority of English users are multilingual speakers of English, and the default context for intercultural communication involves speakers of different world Englishes.

(b) Anticipating different cultural conceptualizations that are embedded in English when using English as an international language for intercultural communication. It is the different cultural conceptualizations enacted and indexed by speakers when interacting with each other that endow many English (as a lingua franca) language interactions as culturally diverse in a truly global way. This leads to interlocutors viewing English as an international language in a more profound sense than any other language.

(c) Acquiring and accomplishing new literacy, proficiency and competence to engage in intercultural communication in English as an international language. This entails sufficient exposure to world Englishes, increasing familiarity with different cultural conceptualizations and effective use of strategies to (co-)construct, explain and (re-)negotiate meaning across cultures.

Another competence that is relevant to mediated intercultural communication through interpreters involves some more recent developments in applied linguistics, regarding notions such as 'languaging', 'translanguaging' and 'translanguaging space'. We propose a 'translanguaging competence' as part of the conceptual framework for the purpose of analyzing our interpreter-mediated intercultural communication data throughout the book.

Translanguging is understood as a repertoire-based communicative act among bilinguals and multilinguals, and it refers to the flexible use of linguistic resources by bilinguals and multilinguals as they make sense of their worlds (García, 2009). It is a process of 'making meaning, shaping experiences, gaining understanding and knowledge through the use of two languages' (Baker, 2011, p. 288). It is 'transformative in nature; it creates a social space for the multilingual language user by bringing together different dimensions of their personal history, experience and environment' (Li, 2011, p. 1223). More recently, Li (2018, p. 9) approaches translanguaging as a 'practical theory of language'. According to Li (2018, p. 22),

> Translanguaging reconceptualizes language as a multilingual, multisemiotic, multisensory, and multimodal resource for sense- and meaning-making, and the multilingual as someone who is aware of the existence of the political entities of named languages and has an ability to make use the structural features of some of them that they have acquired.

Li (2018, p. 23) has taken a step further in proposing a 'translanguaging space' as

> a space that is created by and for translanguaging practices, and a space where language users break down the ideologically laden dichotomies between the macro and the micro, the societal and the individual, and the social and the psychological through interaction. A translanguaging space allows language users to integrate social spaces (and thus 'linguistic codes') that have been formerly separated through different practices in different places.

In addition, according to Li (2018, p. 23),

> translanguaging underscores multilinguals' creativity – their abilities to push and break boundaries between named languages and between language varieties, and to flout norms of behavior including linguistic behavior, and criticality – the ability to use evidence to question, problematize, and articulate views.

Zhu, Li, and Jankowicz-Pytel (2019) argue that "the concept of translanguaging has opened up new ways of understanding human communication and social action", and that "the translanguaging approach to human social interaction as intersection of multiple linguistic and semiotic systems enables us to look more closely at the role of embodied repertoires". In line with the current understanding of languaging, translanguaging and translanguaging space, we understand that a translanguaging competence involves dynamic, embodied and mediated linguistic and cultural repertoires of multilingual users when they make sense of their worlds through languaging as an act and process of sense- and meaning-making across cultures.

In the following section we propose an adapted framework for intercultural communication research based on existing and new developments in the relevant disciplines that contribute to intercultural communication studies and practices.

1.3 A framework for intercultural communication research

Our framework for mediated intercultural communication research focuses on 'inter-culturality', and it draws on existing theoretical and practical frameworks regarding intercultural communication research and practice over the past decades (e.g. Agar, 1991, 1994; Clyne, 1994; Hymes, 1972; Zhu et al., 2019). We label the framework the 'Inter-Culturality' framework (ICF), and it is primarily based on the perceptions of variation and diversity rather than homogeneity of language and culture. Within this ICF framework **intercultural discourse** comprises the intercultural frames and intercultural models; whereas **intercultural agency** comprises intercultural schemas and intercultural strategies (see Figure 1.2). The way we understand intercultural discourse and intercultural agency is that the former is more socio-cultural context oriented and the latter is more behavioural and interactional concerning intercultural interlocutors (including interpreters) at individual or group levels. The ICF maps social and linguistic intercultural discourse onto the agency of individual participants who engage in intercultural communication. It is about how the intercultural landscape interacts with the intercultural 'mindscape' (Xu, Leung, Hall, Jafari, & Pour, 2019, p. 207) in an era of changing techno-scape and media-scape. The ICF framework consists of a further four key elements or concepts: intercultural **frames**, intercultural **schemas**, intercultural **models,** and intercultural **strategies**. The way we conceptualize these intercultural concepts is based on relevant literature in intercultural communication studies, and it is also related to our own interpretations as researchers and practitioners in intercultural communication and interpreting practices. Among these four concepts, intercultural frames and intercultural schemas are leaning towards abstracted concepts and notions, whereas intercultural models and intercultural strategies are manifestations and instantiations.

In the following sections we elaborate on the Inter-Culturality Framework (ICF) and unpack the major components that constitute it.

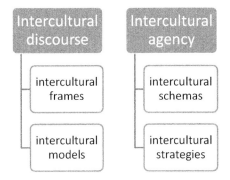

Figure 1.2 The Inter-Culturality Framework (ICF)

1.3.1   Intercultural discourse

Previous research has already explored the notion of 'intercultural discourse'. Clyne (1994, pp. 48–49) defines intercultural discourse as being about "cultural variation in the incidence of particular speech acts and the way in which they are performed". So, Clyne's view is that intercultural discourse is about speech acts in action. According to Clyne (1994, pp. 48–49), most of the intercultural interactions comprise "realizations of several connected and interdependent speech acts by some or all of the participants" and "most speech acts are ambiguous and multi-functional". Koole and ten Thijie (2001, p. 575) define intercultural discourse as the "discourse in which the practices are constructed and enacted by participants in the interaction; the concept stresses the character of the interactional process as a here-and-now accomplishment of the participants". For Kiesling and Paulston (2005, p. xii), intercultural discourse is about "the study of how language use varies from culture to culture, and how knowledge of these differences can be put to work to help understand differences and dominance relations between cultures".

We propose that intercultural discourse is about establishing a discursive common ground for intercultural communication. It is a shared discourse of cultural knowledge and experience, which is co-constructed and re-negotiated as the actual interaction between people of different linguistic and cultural backgrounds takes place. It encompasses two parts: the level of 'intercultural frames', and the level of 'intercultural models', which will be elaborated as follows.

1.3.1.1   Intercultural frames

The intercultural frames are about units of context in which intercultural communication occurs. Such units of context involve what Hymes (1972) coined as the SPEAKING acronym, including scene/setting, participants, ends, act sequence, key, instrumentalities, norms, and genre. Specifically, these terms are understood as follows: Setting and Scene – the time and place of a speech act and, in general, to the physical circumstances; Participants – speaker and audience; Ends – purposes, goals, and outcomes; Act Sequence – form and order of the event; Key – clues that establish the 'tone, manner or spirit' of the speech act; Instrumentalities – forms and styles of speech; Norms – social rules governing the event and the participants' actions and reaction; Genre – the kind of speech act or event.

In terms of intercultural frames, we follow Agar (1991, p. 176) regarding his definition of 'frames', i.e. "structures of interrelated expectations into which a particular expression fits". According to Agar (1991, p. 176), "frames provide a context in terms of which an expression makes sense, knowledge in terms of which the expression can be discussed". We understand that a cultural frame of reference is an existing notion in intercultural studies, e.g. high context culture and low context culture, and collectivist vs. individualistic cultures. According to Agar (1994, pp. 231–232), "frames run from dictionary definitions through speech acts and conversational style up to history, political economy and basic ideas about how things are". However, the notion of 'intercultural frames' has rarely been explored and employed. Our understanding of intercultural frames is that they develop from intercultural encounters, and they also serve as a referent of respective cultures. Intercultural interlocutors may have their own formerly taken-for-granted frames without much of their own awareness, however, when they start interacting with one another, intercultural frames emerge and affect the way in which interlocutors interact with one another. Intercultural frames can be historical frames, economic and political frames, geographical frames as well as linguistic and cultural frames. Some frames can be shared interculturally, such as academic frames and business frames, but other frames are different across cultures, such as linguistic and cultural frames. Cultural differences are tied into these intercultural frames. Raising awareness of intercultural frame may enable interlocutors to interpret intercultural differences in more constructive and effective ways and to cope with difficulties or even conflicts as they occur in mediated intercultural communication. In more recent research, Zhu (2014, pp. 127–128) proposes that frames are "interactional devices used by conversation participants to define the boundary of an event and foreground the contextual information in interactions. Shared frames are central to creating the conditions for shared interpretations". This shows how important it is to be aware of intercultural frames and to develop and consider intercultural frames for effective mediated intercultural communication.

1.3.1.2 *Intercultural models*

As stated in section 1.2, there were early models developed in the 1980s for intercultural communication, e.g., Szalay's (1981, p. 138) 'process' model, and Imahori and Lanigan's (1989, p. 278) 'relational' model. The process model views intercultural communication as a 'process', involving communicator A and communicator B, who are people from different cultural backgrounds. In this model Szalay (1981) uses the term 'translating' in a metaphoric sense, not referring directly to the practice of inter-lingual transfer, although the analogy itself is suggestive of the transfer processes that interpreters perform almost contemporaneously. According to Szalay (1981), the difference in languages and cultures between the two communicators

> forces us to include a translation step into the model of the intercultural communication process. This step involves the switch from one language to another in which communicator A's message is translated into the code system or language of communicator B. This switching from one language to another may take place before or after the message is sent. Translation involves finding equivalent codes in the second language which make it possible to convey the same idea which was originally encoded in the first language. In some instances this translation is easily accomplished; in others it poses some problems. There is another type of translation problem which is more basic and yet is more frequently overlooked. This involves differences in cultural meanings.
>
> (Szalay, 1981, p. 138)

The 'process' model can be explained as follows: communicator A encodes his/her thought/content and transmits or code-switches it through a 'translation' process to code B, involving or not involving a translator. Communicator B then decodes the message and constructs a thought/content. He/she responds by encoding code B and transmits or code-switches it to code A. Communicator A receives it, decodes it and constructs another thought/content.

In comparison the 'relational' model views intercultural communication as a shared endeavour with 'appropriate level of motivation, knowledge, and skills of both the sojourner and the host national in regards to their relationship, leading to an effective relational outcome' (Imahori & Lanigan, 1989, p. 277). This relational model has two major components: a sojourner and a host-national. Each dyadic member conceptually possesses three major elements contributing to relational outcome; that is, competence, experience, and goal (Imahori & Lanigan, 1989, p. 277).

Both process and relational models contribute to our understanding of intercultural communication. However they are based on a stereotypical premise that intercultural communication takes place between a native speaker (communicator B in the process model, or a host-national in the relational model) and a non-native speaker (communicator A or a sojourner). In fact, current intercultural communication has largely become a default context, and it involves speakers of many different languages. Even amongst speakers of the same particular language, e.g. English, there are speakers of different varieties of English. This will be further discussed in Chapter 2. English, in this case, is used as a lingua franca among people of different first language and culture backgrounds. Neil (1997, p. 8) puts forward a "model of collaborative intercultural discourse", in which "a repertoire of discourse strategies including turn-sharing, repetition, and clarification is employed by speakers regardless of ethnolinguistic background or linguistic ability, when they are interacting interculturally".

Intercultural models are jointly established among participants of intercultural communication on the basis of intercultural knowledge, goals, values, perceptions, emotional states and actions in different intercultural contexts. Kecskes (2013, p. 48) defines an intercultural model as "a set of context-based action plans, including judgements of the formality of the situation, what is the most appropriate things to do". When participants of intercultural communication routinely and repeatedly do things together, they usually develop some standardized way of doing. "These shared action plans may emerge as (inter)cultural models" (Kecskes, 2013, p. 48).

We acknowledge that intercultural models are abstractions and processes based on prior intercultural experience, and we also acknowledge the various definitions of previous researchers regarding intercultural models. For our research we propose that intercultural models are cognitive patterns that develop from different types of intercultural inputs, such as explicit instruction, daily activity, communication, observation and practice. Intercultural models become a part of interlocutors' cognitive resources, and they influence their worldview and behaviour, as well as how they interpret and react to other people's behaviour, information and situations.

1.3.2   *Intercultural agency*

Agency is a notion derived from sociology. In social sciences, agency is the capacity of individuals to act on their own free will. It stands in relation to social structure, such as social class, religion, gender, ethnicity etc., which may determine or limit individuals' agency. Agency operates closely through individuals' cognitive structures, i.e. mindset, that are formed through their experiences and perceptions of their worlds.

Intercultural agency involves the awareness of explicit and implicit power and inequality in multicultural societies, and the (re-)negotiation of the valuation and status of language use in intercultural discourse. Intercultural communication, particularly mediated intercultural communication through interpreters, involves 'agentive negotiations in intercultural rhetoric' (Canagarajah, 2013a, p. 204).

Intercultural agency helps unpack how micro- and macro-level linguistic and cultural relations operate through individuals in a multicultural society involving intercultural schemas and strategies. In addition, intercultural agency involves ongoing negotiation of cultural identities, norms and trajectories of actions in response to an intercultural context. We propose that intercultural agency is enacted through intercultural schemas and intercultural strategies, which will be elaborated ahead.

1.3.2.1   *Intercultural schemas*

Schemas, according to Rumelhart (1975) and van Dijk (1977), are socially constructed patterns of communicative behaviour available to the interlocutors from the experience and knowledge they bring to the encounter, e.g. how a patient communicates with a doctor from a different linguistic and cultural background. Schemas are naturally developed mechanisms in our brain which help us predict what is to be expected and how to act or respond appropriately in certain cultural circumstances or contexts. Clyne (1994, p. 7) refers to a schema as the "awareness, purposes/ends, relevant past experience (internal reaction: relevant schemata are activated, including what language to choose, what to say and how to say it, what norms to follow)". "Cultural schemas are conceptual structures that enable an individual to store perceptual and conceptual information about his or her culture and interpret cultural experiences and expressions" (Malcolm & Sharifian, 2002, p. 170).

In terms of cultural schema types, Nishida (1999, pp. 757–759) summarizes eight primary types for generating human behaviour for social interactions. These eight schemas are also referred to as Primary Social Interaction (PSI) schemas, including 1) fact-and-concept schemas: pieces of general information about facts and concepts; 2) person schemas: knowledge about different types of people, which includes their personality traits. In some instances person schemas are linked to stereotypes or prejudice; 3) self schemas: people's knowledge about themselves, i.e., how they see themselves and how others see them; 4) role schemas: knowledge about social roles which denote sets of behaviours that are expected of people in particular social positions; 5) context schemas: information about the situation and appropriate setting of behavioural parameters; 6) procedure schemas: knowledge about the appropriate sequence of events in common situations; 7) strategy schemas: knowledge about problem-solving strategies; and 8) emotion schemas: information about affect and evaluation stored in long-term memory which is accessed when other schemas are activated. These schemas are constructed in social interactions throughout one's life. The relationship between these types of schemas and intercultural communication, particularly mediated intercultural communication is that these schemas can be acknowledged and activated throughout intercultural encounters, e.g., interlocutors may have different role schemas of what an interpreter can or cannot do, in relation to their roles from intercultural perspectives. There can also be strategy schemas that are adopted differently between monolingual speakers and bilingual or multilingual speakers, and it is important that interlocutors and interpreters are made aware of the strategies commonly adopted or available.

Research on cultural schemas, as illustrated, may lay a solid foundation for the proposal of 'intercultural schemas'. Acknowledging various types of cultural schemas, the concept of 'intercultural schemas' helps highlight the changing and dynamic nature of cultural schema development, maintenance and operation. It also focuses on intercultures, rather than particular cultures *per se*. We propose that intercultural schemas are mental representations or conceptual structures developed through intercultural encounters among people of different linguistic and cultural backgrounds. Intercultural schemas represent and embody ongoing schema (re-)negotiations and (re-)conceptualizations across cultures.

1.3.2.2   Intercultural strategies

Intercultural strategies involve a plethora of strategies for intercultural communication. Research on communication strategy has been ongoing for the past decades. There are two major approaches to communication strategy studies. One is derived from Second Language Acquisition (SLA), focusing on the strategies language learners adopt to communicate with native speakers of the chosen language. The other is related to more current English as a Lingua Franca (ELF) research, which focuses on the interaction among speakers of different linguistic and cultural backgrounds using a chosen language as a lingua franca. Færch and Kasper (1983, p. 36) define communication strategy as "potentially conscious plans for solving what to a participant in a communicative exchange presents itself as a problem in reaching a particular communicative goal".

The ELF approach to communication strategy is more of an interactional orientation. It focuses on the interaction and negotiation of meaning among speakers of different linguistic and cultural backgrounds, irrespective of the native-ness or non-native-ness of their use of the chosen lingua franca. Strategies for ELF communication are not primarily adopted to overcome difficulties or problems. Instead they can also be adopted to enhance intercultural communication, or to boost the effectiveness of intercultural communication, through meaning making and negotiation. They can refer to pre-emptive strategies where experienced communicators pre-empt potential issues with communication and adopt necessary measures to cope with them beforehand. For example, speakers for ELF communication tend to use pro-active strategies to enhance communicative effectiveness (Mauranen, 2007) and they employ strategies to both pre-empt and resolve communication difficulties (Kaur, 2010, 2011; Björkman, 2011).

Communication studies have experienced a shift over the past decades to ELF paradigms focusing on mutual accommodation among speakers of different varieties of the language as a lingua franca. Dörnyei and Scott (1997, pp. 188–194) have summarized an inventory of strategic language devices, based on previous research on communication strategy taxonomies. We understand that the majority of these strategic language devices can be located in interpreter-mediated intercultural communication practices. As such, they represent features that can be used as descriptive or explanatory markers for interpreter performance. These strategic language devices, when adopted by interlocutors and interpreters for mediated intercultural communication, may develop into intercultural strategies that this section elaborates on. Here is a list of the 'strategic language devices'. More details regarding definitions and examples of these devices can be found in Dörnyei and Scott (1997, pp. 188–194). The 'strategic language devices' include: 1) *message abandonment;* 2) *message reduction or topic avoidance;* 3) *message replacement;* 4) *circumlocution or paraphrase;* 5) *approximation;* 6) *use of all-purpose words;* 7) *word-coinage;* 8) *restructuring;* 9) *literal translation or transfer;* 10) *foreignizing;* 11) *code switching or language switch;* 12) *use of similar-sounding words;* 13) *mumbling;* 14) *omission;* 15) *retrieval;* 16a) *self-repair;* 16b) *other-repair;* 17) *self-rephrasing;* 18) *over-explicitness or waffling;* 19) *mime or nonlinguistic/paralinguistic strategies;* 20) *use of fillers;* 21a) *self-repetition;* 21b) *other-repetition;* 22) *feigning understanding;* 23) *verbal strategy markers;* 24a) *direct appeal for help;* 24b) *indirect appeal for help;* 25) *asking for repetition;* 26) *asking for clarification;* 27) *asking for confirmation;* 28) *guessing;* 29) *expressing non-understanding;* 30) *interpretive summary;* 31) *comprehension check;* 32) *own-accuracy check;* 33) *responses: repeat, repair, rephrase, expand, confirm.*

The strategies are largely adopted by L2 speakers of a language, and increasingly used by ELF speakers. They form a significant number of the intercultural strategies as they are commonly adopted for intercultural communication and interpreter-mediated intercultural communication. Another intercultural strategy is empathy. According to Szalay (1981),

> [c]ommunicators in intercultural situations perhaps should adopt a different strategy, carefully define the communication event, take into account the setting and context, establish the nature of the common task and make judgements about the communication in progress with respect to the common domain rather than to internal similarities between communicators. This strategy is empathy.
>
> (p. 139)

It is worth noting that 'intercultural strategies' may not only contain the actual strategies or strategic language devices, but they also involve the awareness and open-mindedness of the interlocutors and interpreters in mediated intercultural communication, in the sense that they become open to negotiation, understanding and respectful of different cultural values, norms, conventions, histories, and practices.

1.4   Inter-Culturality Framework (ICF) and interpreting

Having elaborated on the Inter-Culturality Framework (ICF), we are aware of the need to foreground that speakers'/interlocutors'/participants' intercultural frames and schemas are not 'suspended' or 'rendered superfluous' by the presence of the interpreter, who is often seen not only as a linguistic mediator, but also an intercultural mediator. Instead the addition of an interpreter to an interaction results in a re-alignment of the constellation of features that pertain to intercultural situations, such that speakers' agency manifested as intercultural schemas and strategies are enacted or practised towards and negotiated with an additional interlocutor, who in a primary sense provides language transfer of the referential content to others who lack proficiency in the language of the source speech (i.e. 'allophone speakers').

The allophone nature of the interaction means that the source language speaker may activate or adopt a number of intercultural schemas and strategies. These may range from non-engagement via eye contact avoidance, proxemics or other paralinguistic markers with the target language hearer and indirect imperatives addressed to the interpreter but meant for the target language hearer (e.g. "Tell her that she needs to . . .") to engagement via paralinguistic and other markers as well as use of direct speech (e.g. "You need to . . .") to the target language hearer relayed by the interpreter, as end-points of a continuum. Speakers and hearers can adopt constellations along these continua and there can be shifts in focus and engagement that are reflective of interlocutors' negotiation of meaning and the performance of the interaction, e.g. circumlocution or paraphrase, restructuring, over-explicitness, feigning understanding (Dörnyei & Scott, 1997, pp. 188–194). Intercultural interactions occur all the time, but interpreter-mediated interactions are much less frequent, and allophone speakers' knowledge of how to negotiate and structure an interpreted interaction is much more variable, as is their familiarity with the changing roles of the interpreter, which will be further elaborated in Chapter 2.

The interpreter-mediated interaction is not a 'vacuum' that exists outside or without relation to monolingual or ELF interactions. Interlocutors bring to them their own experience, knowledge and conventions of discursive practices, and may typically attempt to negotiate for these to be replicated in an interpreter-mediated interaction. Therefore, interactional management is typically required from the interpreter, in introducing themselves to others as the interpreter, giving a brief explanation of their role and how they will work with others. The self-introduction and role explanation is itself part of the interpreter-mediated interaction even where these usually involve monolingual exchanges with each of the interlocutors/parties. Here, interpreters activate or employ schemas and strategies to negotiate understandings of individual roles and role-relationships amongst interlocutors, voice, floor-holding, the re-presenting of talk to others, and to clarify situational (e.g. seating arrangements, turn-taking), logistic (e.g., audibility, line of vision) and protocol features (e.g. assurances of confidentiality, impartiality). This is a 'textbook' description of the interpreter-mediated interaction. The unfolding of intercultural and inter-lingual interactions reflects all participants' negotiation of their intercultural frames and models. This will be taken up further in Chapters 3 and 4.

1.5   Conclusion

In this chapter we have introduced what this volume is about by providing a description of the five major chapters. We have revisited a number of fundamental concepts such as language, culture, interculture and interculturality, communication and intercultural communication. In addition, we have proposed a framework, namely the Inter-Culturality Framework (ICF) for understanding intercultural communication research, particularly intercultural communication through the mediation of interpreters. The ICF comprises intercultural discourse and intercultural agency. The former consists of intercultural frames and intercultural models, and the latter consists of intercultural schemas and intercultural strategies. In the next chapter, we explore mediated intercultural communication that primarily involves Chinese and English speakers, and Chinese–English interpreters. We focus on intercultural pragmatics of Chinese and English speakers, and mediated intercultural communication practices employed by Chinese–English interpreters. Drawing critically on traditional as well as more recent research studies on intercultural communication, as well as the Inter-Culturality Framework that we have developed in this chapter, we explore the extent to which intercultural communication among Chinese and English speakers can be effectively mediated through Chinese–English interpreters in domain-specific interactions.

References

Agar, M. (1991). The biculture in bilingual. *Language in Society*, *20*, 167–181. https://doi.org/10.1007/978-1-349-25582-5_36

Agar, M. (1994). The intercultural frame. *International Journal of Intercultural Relationship*, *18*(2), 221–237. https://doi.org/10.1016/0147-1767(94)90029-9

Baker, C. (2011). *Foundations of bilingual education and bilingualism*. Bristol, New York and Ontario: Multilingual Matters.

Björkman, B. (2011). Pragmatic strategies in English as an academic lingua franca: Ways of achieving communicative effectiveness. *Journal of Pragmatics*, *43*, 950–964.

Bowe, H., Martin, K., & Manns, H. (2014). *Communication across cultures: Mutual understanding in a global world* (2nd ed.). Melbourne: Cambridge University Press.

Byram, M. (1989). *Cultural studies in foreign language education.* Clevedon: Multilingual Matters.

Byram, M. (1997). *Teaching and assessing intercultural communicative competence.* Clevedon: Multilingual Matters.

Canagarajah, S. (2006). Changing communicative needs, revised assessment objectives: Testing English as an international language. *Language Assessment Quarterly, 3*(3), 229–242. https://doi.org/10.1207/s15434311laq0303_1

Canagarajah, S. (2013a). Agency and power in intercultural communication: Negotiating English in translocal spaces. *Language and Intercultural Communication, 13*(2), 202–224. https://doi.org/10.1080/14708477.2013.770867

Canagarajah, S. (2013b). Theorizing a competence for translingual practice at the contact zone. In S. May (Ed.), *The multilingual turn: Implications for SLA, TESOL, and bilingual education* (pp. 78–102). New York and London: Routledge.

Chabasse, C., & Kader, S. (2014). Putting interpreting admissions exams to the test. *Interpreting, 16*(1), 19–33. https://doi.org/10.1075/intp.16.1.02cha

Clifford, A. (2001). Discourse theory and performance-based assessment: Two tools for professional interpreting. *Meta, 46*(2), 365–378. https://doi.org/10.7202/002345ar

Clyne, M. (1994). *Intercultural communication at work: Cultural values in discourse.* Cambridge and New York: Cambridge University Press.

Dewaele, J. (2015). Culture and emotional language. In F. Sharifian (Ed.), *The Routledge handbook of language and culture* (pp. 357–370). Oxford: Routledge.

Dörnyei, Z., & Scott, M. L. (1997). Communication strategies in a second language: Definitions and taxonomies. *Language Learning, 47*(1), 173–210. https://doi.org/10.1111/0023-8333.51997005

Fan, D. (2012). Interpreters' views on the necessary aptitudes of the interpreter. *Compilation and Translation Review, 5*(2), 117–151.

Færch, C., & Kasper, G. (1983). Plans and strategies in foreign language communication. In C. Færch & G. Kasper (Eds.), *Strategies in interlanguage communication* (pp. 20–60). London: Longman.

García, O. (2009). *Bilingual education in the 21st century.* Oxford: Wiley Blackwell.

Hall, E. T. (1964). Adumbration as a feature of intercultural communication. *American Anthropologist, 66*(6), 154–163. https://doi.org/10.1525/aa.1964.66.suppl_3.02a00110

Hild, A. (2015). Discourse comprehension in simultaneous interpreting: The role of expertise and information redundancy. In A. Ferreira & J. Schwieter (Eds.), *Psycholinguistics and cognitive inquiries into translation and interpreting* (pp. 67–100). Amsterdam: John Benjamins.

Hofstede, G. (1994). *Uncommon sense about organizations: Cases, studies, and field observations.* Thousand Oaks, CA: Sage Publications.

Hymes, D. H. (1972). On communicative competence. In J. B. Pride & J. Holmes (Eds.), *Sociolinguistics: Selected readings* (pp. 269–293). Harmondsworth: Penguin.

Imahori, T. T., & Lanigan, M. L. (1989). Relational model of intercultural communication competence. *International Journal of Intercultural Relations, 13*(3), 269–286. https://doi.org/10.1016/0147-1767(89)90013-8

Jackson, J. (2014). *Introducing language and intercultural communication.* London and New York: Routledge.

Kaur, J. (2010). Achieving mutual understanding in world Englishes. *World Englishes, 29*(2), 192–208.

Kaur, J. (2011). Intercultural communication in English as a lingua franca: Some source of misunderstanding. *Intercultural Pragmatics, 8*(1), 93–116.

Kecskes, I. (2013). Intercultures, encyclopedic knowledge, and cultural models. In F. Sharifian & M. Jamarani (Eds.), *Language and intercultural communication in the new era* (pp. 39–59). New York and London: Routledge.

Kiesling, S. F., & Paulston, C. B. (Eds.). (2005). *Intercultural discourse and communication: The essential readings*. Malden, Oxford and Carlton: Blackwell Publishing.

Koole, T., & ten Thijie, J. D. (2001). The reconstruction of intercultural discourse: Methodological considerations. *Journal of Pragmatics*, *33*(4), 571–587. https://doi.org/10.1016/s0378-2166(00)00035-7

Kramsch, C. (1998). *Language and culture*. Oxford and New York: Oxford University Press.

Kramsch, C. (2008). Ecological perspectives on foreign language education. *Language Teaching*, *41*(3), 389–408. https://doi.org/10.1017/s0261444808005065

Kramsch, C. (2013). History and memory in the development of intercultural competence. In F. Sharifian & M. Jamarani (Eds.), *Language and intercultural communication in the new era* (pp. 23–38). New York and London: Routledge.

Leclercq, J. (2003). *Facets of interculturality in education*. Strasbourg: Council of Europe Publishing.

Li, W. (2011). Moment analysis and translanguaging space: Discursive construction of identities by multilingual Chinese youth in Britain. *Journal of Pragmatics*, *43*(5), 1222–1235. https://doi.org/10.1016/j.pragma.2010.07.035

Li, W. (2018). Translanguaging as a practical theory of language. *Applied Linguistics*, *39*(1), 9–30. https://doi.org/10.1093/applin/amx039

Malcolm, I. G., & Sharifian, F. (2002). Aspects of aboriginal English oral discourse: An application of cultural schema theory. *Discourse Studies*, *4*(2), 169–181. https://doi.org/10.1177/14614456020040020301

Mason, I. (2009). Role, positioning and discourse in face-to-face interpreting. In R. de Pedro Ricoy, I. Perez, & C. Wilson (Eds.), *Interpreting and translating in public service settings: Policy, practice, pedagogy* (pp. 52–73). Manchester: St. Jerome Press.

Mauranen, A. (2007). Hybrid voices: English as the lingua franca of academics. In K. Fløttum (Ed.), *Language and discipline perspectives on academic discourse* (pp. 243–259). Newcastle, UK: Cambridge Scholars Publishing.

Neil, D. M. (1997). Joint production of intercultural discourse. *Monash University Linguistics Papers*, *1*(1), 3–10.

Nishida, H. (1999). A cognitive approach to intercultural communication based on schema theory. *International Journal of Intercultural Relations*, *23*(5), 753–777. https://doi.org/10.1016/s0147-1767(99)00019-x

Pöchhacker, F. (2006). Going social? On pathways and paradigms in interpreting studies. In A. Pym, M. Shlesinger, & Z. Jettmarová (Eds.), *Sociocultural aspects of translating and interpreting* (pp. 215–232). Amsterdam and Philadelphia: John Benjamins. https://doi.org/10.1075/btl.67.27poc

Pöchhacker, F. (2012). Interpreting participation: Conceptual analysis and illustration of the interpreter's role in interaction. In C. Baraldi & L. Gavioli (Eds.), *Coordinating participation in dialogue interpreting* (pp. 45–69). Amsterdam and Philadelphia: John Benjamins. https://doi.org/10.1075/btl.102.03poch

Pöchhacker, F. (2016). *Introducing interpreting studies* (2nd ed.). London and New York: Routledge.

Rennert, S. (2010). The impact of fluency on subjective assessment of interpreting quality. *The Interpreters' Newsletter*, *15*, 101–115.

Rudvin, M. (2004). Cross-cultural dynamics in community interpreting: Troubleshooting. In G. Hansen, K. Malmkjær, & D. Gile (Eds.), *Claims, changes and challenges in translation studies: Selected contributions from the EST Congress, Copenhagen 2001* (pp. 271–283). Amsterdam: John Benjamins. https://doi.org/10.1075/btl.50.23rud

Rudvin, M., & Tomassini, E. (2011). *Interpreting in the community and workplace*. Houndmills, UK: Palgrave Macmillan.

Ruiz, R. L., & Diur, M. (2017). Admission exams in international examinations: The United Nations' language competitive examination (LCE). *CLINA*, *3*(2), 33–52.

Rumelhart, D. E. (1975). Notes on a schema for stories. In D. G. Bobrow & A. Collins (Eds.), *Representation and understanding: Studies in cognitive science* (pp. 211–236). New York, San Francisco and London: Academic Press, Inc.

Russo, M. (2014). Testing aptitude for interpreting: The predictive value of oral paraphrasing, with synonyms and coherence as assessment parameters. *Interpreting*, *16*(1), 1–18. https://doi.org/10.1075/bct.68.07rus

Scollon, R., Scollon, S. W., & Jones, R. H. (2012). *Intercultural communication: A discourse approach*. West Sussex: Wiley-Blackwell.

Seleskovitch, D. (1978). *Interpreting for international conferences* (S. Dailey & E. McMillan, Trans.). Leesburg, VA: Pen & Booth.

Sharifian, F. (2011). *Cultural conceptualizations and language: Chapter 1: On cultural conceptualizations*. Amsterdam and Philadelphia: John Benjamins Publishing Company.

Sharifian, F. (2013). Globalisation and developing metacultural competence in learning English as an international language. *Multilingual Education*, *3*(7), 1–11. https://doi.org/10.1186/2191-5059-3-7

Sharifian, F., & Jamarani, M. (2013). Language and intercultural communication: From the old era to the new one. In F. Sharifian & M. Jamarani (Eds.), *Language and intercultural communication in the new era* (pp. 1–19). New York and London: Routledge.

Spencer-Oatey, H. (2008). *Culturally speaking: Culture, communication and politeness theory*. London and New York: Continuum.

Szalay, L. B. (1981). Intercultural communication: A process model. *International Journal of Intercultural Relations*, *5*(2), 133–146. https://doi.org/10.1016/0147-1767(81)90004-3

Tzou, Y.-Z., Eslami, Z., & Chen, H.-C. (2011). Effect of language proficiency and degree of formal training in simultaneous interpreting on working memory and interpreting performance: Evidence from Mandarin-English speakers. *International Journal of Bilingualism*, *16*(2), 213–227. https://doi.org/10.1177/1367006911403197

van Dijk, T. A. (1977). *Text and context: Explorations in the semantics and pragmatics of discourse*. London: Longman.

van Ek, J. A. (1986). *Objectives for foreign language learning* (Vol. 2). Strasbourg: Council of Europe, Council for Cultural Co-operation.

Van Lier, L. (2004). *The ecology and semiotics of language learning: A sociocultural perspective*. Boston and Dordrecht: Kluwer Academic.

Wadensjö, C. (1998). *Interpreting as interaction*. London, NY: Longman.

Xu, Z. (2013). Globalization, culture and ELT materials: A focus on China. *Multilingual Education*, *3*(1), 1–19. https://doi.org/10.1186/2191-5059-3-6

Xu, Z. (2017). Developing meta-cultural competence in teaching English as an international language. In F. Sharifian (Ed.), *Advances in cultural linguistics* (pp. 703–720). Switzerland: Springer.

Xu, Z., Leung, J., Hall, M., Jafari, J., & Pour, M. S. (2019). Linguistic diversity on an Australian university campus: An ethnographic case study. In J. Jenkins & A. Mauranen (Eds.), *Linguistic diversity on the EMI campus: Insider accounts of the use of English and other languages in universities within Asia, Australasia, and Europe* (pp. 197–225). London and New York: Routledge.

Zhu, H. (2014). *Exploring intercultural communication: Language in action.* London and New York: Routledge.

Zhu, H., Li, W., & Jankowicz-Pytel, D. (2019). Translanguaging and embodied teaching and learning: Lessons from a multilingual karate club in London. *International Journal of Bilingual Education and Bilingualism*, 1–16. https://doi.org/10.1080/13670050.2019. 1599811

2 Mediated intercultural communication involving Chinese speakers and English speakers

This chapter introduces intercultural communication involving Chinese speakers and English speakers, with a focus on intercultural pragmatics and mediated intercultural communication practices through Chinese–English interpreters. Drawing on established research paradigms for intercultural communication and more recently developed research frameworks, this chapter explores the extent to which intercultural communication among Chinese and English speakers can be effectively mediated through Chinese–English interpreters in domain-specific interactions.

2.1 Profiling Chinese and English speakers

Intercultural communication involving Chinese and English speakers has been increasing as the world becomes more globalized. The profiles of Chinese and English speakers have also been 'globalized' in the sense that Chinese and English speakers are no longer identified exclusively as monolingual 'native' speakers of Chinese and English respectively, nor necessarily coming either from China or Chinese-speaking diasporas, and English-speaking countries such as the United Kingdom and the United States. Chinese and English speakers may also involve a growing international community of bilingual and multilingual learners and users of Chinese and English as their 'non-native' language. In other words, they use Chinese or English as a second or subsequently acquired language for international or intercultural communication. We revisit the notions of 'Chinese speakers' and 'English speakers' in relation to the sociolinguistic developments of Chinese and English. Chinese and English are two of the world's most spoken languages, i.e. among the estimated 7.5 billion people that make up the world's current population, approximately one in five to six speak Chinese and another one in five to six speak English. In this section, we review Chinese language(s) and Chinese speakers, as well as world Englishes and English speakers.

2.1.1 Chinese language(s) and Chinese speakers

The People's Republic of China (PRC) and Chinese diasporas across the globe constitute, as predicted, the largest numbers of 'Chinese speakers'. The population of the PRC passed the 1.4 billion mark in 2015. In addition, the vast majority of residents in Hong Kong, Macau, and Taiwan with a total population of 31.2 million, are speakers of Chinese. Going beyond the PRC, there is also a large Chinese diaspora with a considerable population. The term 'overseas Chinese' refers to Chinese migrants and their descendants who emigrated from China in large numbers from the beginning of the nineteenth century onwards across many parts of south-east Asia. The vast majority of overseas Chinese are of *Han* ethnicity. They currently live across East Asia including South Korea and Japan, Southeast Asia, including Singapore, Malaysia, Thailand, the Philippines, Indonesia, Cambodia, Laos, and Vietnam, and in 'New World' countries, such as the US, Canada and Australia, and now they also live in Europe, South America, and Africa. An estimated number of overseas Chinese speakers across the diasporas, whether Chinese being their first language (L1), second language (L2) or an additional language, is approximately 50 million.

'Chinese speakers' are not a linguistically and culturally homogeneous community across the globe. They may speak a whole spectrum of Chinese language(s), dialects and Chinese varieties with considerable variation and varying proficiency.

> The word *Mandarin* denoting the major dialect family of China is an established linguistic term in the West. In popular as well as linguistic usage, the term also represents the speech of Beijing, which for centuries has been recognized as the standard language of China because of the political and cultural significance of that city.
>
> (Li & Thompson, 1981, p. 1)

An alternative term for *Mandarin* is *Pǔtōnghuà*, and it is commonly used by Chinese people from the PRC. It is worth pointing out that *Pǔtōnghuà* (literally a 'common language' used in the PRC) is far from being 'uniform' or homogeneous, for China has a large population spread over a vast geographical area, and consequently numerous other dialects inevitably influence and affect the versions of *Pǔtōnghuà* spoken by people from different regions. In this respect

> a truly uniform language in a country such as China can exist only in theory, not in reality. . . . when one speaks of 'the language' of China, one refers merely to an ideal, and that there will always be some variation between 'the *Mandarin* language' of one person and 'the *Mandarin* language' of another person
>
> (Li & Thomson, 1981, pp. 1–2. Original italics and punctuation)

The term 'dialects' is used here, although a more suitable term might be 'languages', as the differences between regionally based linguistic varieties in China can be so great that speakers of them may be unintelligible to monolingual speakers of *Pǔtōnghuà*. The sound structure and phonological inventory of each variety are the main features for classification of different Chinese 'dialects' (Li & Thompson, 1981, p. 2). We give here the Chinese names of the main Chinese languages with the English designations of the more widely known ones given in brackets: *Běifānghuà* (Mandarin), *Wú* (Shanghainese/Jiangsu/Zhejiang), *Yuè* (Cantonese), *Mǐn* (Fujianese/Taiwanese), *Kèjiā* (Hakka), *Xiāng* (Hunan), *and*

Gàn (Jiangxi). In addition, various other terms are used to refer to varieties of Chinese languages, such as *Hokkien*, *Teochew* and *Fujianese*, and urban varieties, such as *Shanghainese*. These terms and the varieties they refer to overlap to a large extent with the major Chinese dialect categories listed. As stated, *Mandarin* is by far the most widely spoken language, and the majority of the people of the People's Republic of China are native-speakers of Mandarin. Alongside the term *Pǔtōnghuà* which is used in mainland China, the synonymous terms *Guóyǔ* (national language) and *Huáyǔ* (Chinese language) are used in Taiwan and Singapore respectively to refer to the same language (Chen, 1999, pp. 2–3).

The distribution of dialect groups across mainland China is uneven. The latest statistics from online sources (e.g. "Baidu Zhidao: The population and percentages of Chinese dialects," 2019; Chinese Language Website: Eight Major Chinese Dialects, 2019) show that approximately 73% of Chinese speakers speak *Mandarin*, or *Pǔtōnghuà*. The other most spoken dialects include *Wú* (8.4%), *Xiāng* (5%), *Yuè* (5%), *Mǐn* (4.2%), *Kèjiā* (Hakka) (4%), and *Gàn* (2.4%).

Not unlike other languages, "the Chinese language has undergone drastic changes over the past 150 years in a way unparalleled in Chinese history" (Chen, 1999, p. xi). The standardization and use of *Pǔtōnghuà* has been greatly promoted in relation to dialects since the founding of the People's Republic of China in 1949. In 1986 at the landmark National Conference on Language and Script, a formal proposal was passed which would make *Pǔtōnghuà* "the language of instruction in all schools, the working language of government, the language of broadcasting and the national lingua franca" by the end of the twentieth century (Kirkpatrick & Xu, 2001, p. 14). At the start of the twenty-first century, in October 2000, *The Language Law of the People's Republic of China* (hereafter as the 'Law') was passed at the 18th session of the Standing Committee of the 9th National People's Congress. According to the law, the term 'Modern Standard Chinese' comprises both the spoken form of the language, known as *Pǔtōnghuà*, and the written form of standard Chinese characters. Various articles state that Modern Standard Chinese is to be used as the language of instruction in schools, that all citizens have the right to learn and use Modern Standard Chinese, and that its use is to be popularized at all levels of the government.

The status and use of languages other than *Pǔtōnghuà* is regulated in article 8 of the same law, with reference to regulations in areas with regional or other autonomy.

> Article 8: All the nationalities shall have the freedom to use and develop their own spoken and written languages. The spoken and written languages of the ethnic peoples shall be used in accordance with the relevant provisions of the Constitution, the Law on Regional National Autonomy and other laws.

Article 16 contains a description of when languages other than *Pǔtōnghuà* may be used.

> Article 16: Where the relevant provisions of this Chapter are concerned, local dialects may be used under the following circumstances: (1) when State

functionaries really need to use them in the performance of official duties; (2) where they are used in broadcasting with the approval of the broadcasting and television administration under the State Council or of the broadcasting and television department as the provincial level; (3) where they are needed in traditional operas, films and TV programs and other forms of art; and (4) where their use is really required in the publishing, teaching and research.

(Law of the People's Repblic of China on the Standard Spoken and Written Chinese Language, 2019)

As far as the Chinese mainland is concerned, internal migration and greater social and geographical mobility is leading to an increased use of *Pŭtōnghuà* as a lingua franca in interactions involving speakers of otherwise mutually unintelligible dialects. Although there is a specific law stipulating the use of 'standard spoken and written Chinese language' in China, there are no similarly clear directives about the provision of translation and interpreting services at a national level. The provision of translation and interpreting services appears to be determined by regional, local and very often situational or procedural features.

2.1.2 World Englishes and English speakers

Section 2.1.1 has shown that the term 'Chinese speakers' encompasses a vast number of Mandarin Chinese and Chinese dialect speakers from China and the Chinese diaspora. Likewise, the hypernym 'English speakers' also encompasses a vast number of speakers of heterogeneous varieties of English. The geographical area and the communicative functions within which English is used have expanded greatly over the last 50 years. English has also been characterized by changes over time and variation according to geographical or regional area. This has resulted in a heterogeneity in varieties that bear the designation of English, and in contemporary linguistics, it has now become common practice to refer to these different varieties of English spoken or used all over the globe as 'world Englishes' (Kachru, 1982). We mentioned before that one in every five or six people across the world is a user of English, i.e. some 1.12 billion people (Ethnologue, 2019). The same source reports that approximately, 378 million people are L1 speakers of English and 744 million are L2 speakers of English.

English is a language with many different names, including varieties based on nation-states, such as British English, American English, Australian English, Canadian English and New Zealand English, and a considerable number of other varieties such as Indian English, Singapore English and Malaysian English. In addition, the designation 'English' is used as part of various acronyms that describe a variety of English that is acquired or used, usually according to learners' acquisition of it as a second or subsequent language, or according to a particular function for which it will be used: EFL (English as a foreign language); ESL (English as a second language); ENL (English as a native language); EAL (English as an additional language); ESP (English for specific purposes); EAP (English for academic purposes); EIL (English as an international language); ELF

(English as a lingual franca); and WE (world Englishes). Indeed, over the past half a century English has been conceptualized as a pluricentric language with the designation 'Englishes'. Kachru and Smith (1985, p. 210) point out that "'Englishes' symbolizes the functional and formal variation in the language, and its international acculturation". They make the point that English is a language that is claimed not only by L1 users of it, but by those who use it as additional language, whether in its (national) standard form or regional, local, other non-standard form.

Since the 1980s, the term "world Englishes" (WE) has been debated and interpreted in various ways. Bolton and Davis (2006, p. 6) point out that the study of world Englishes

> [c]onsistently sought to ground its work in the "sociolinguistic realities" of all English-using societies worldwide. Its approach has had particular relevance for the English-using societies of the postcolonial Outer Circle (and Expanding Circle), including many African, Caribbean and Asian locations, but the resonances of WE are now felt in many Inner Circle societies.
>
> (Bolton & Davis, 2006, p. 6)

What has been pointed out as being the remarkable aspect about the increasing use of English among speakers of world Englishes is that "the majority of English speakers are now multilingual people who have learned English and who use English to communicate with fellow multilinguals" (Kirkpatrick, 2007, p. 1). Kirkpatrick also points out two common trends regarding the current development of world Englishes and what the future holds regarding world Englishes.

> One common trend that can be discerned across all these Englishes is that they are created via some form of mixing. They are all the result of some form of linguistic and cultural contact.
>
> (Kirkpatrick, 2010, p. 13)

Within a country which is claimed to be an English-speaking one, such as Australia, there are different languages and different varieties of a language co-existing. For example, Lo Bianco (1987, p. 7) points out that

> although English is the *de facto* national language of Australia its status as such has never been declared explicitly. It is the first and usually the only language of about 83% of the population as well as being the language of the major and powerful institutions of the society.

To this we add that other languages as well as varieties of English and indigenous Aboriginal languages permeate the linguistic landscape of Australia. Australia's National Policy on Languages, which was endorsed by the Australian Government in 1987, acknowledges the status of particular languages through three 'recognitions', namely,

1) recognition of the status of Australian English as the national, convenient and shared language of Australia and its major official institutions;

2) recognition of the rights of use and continued use of community languages other than English, including the languages and language systems of the deaf;
3) recognition of the rights of use, indigenous and unique nature of Aboriginal languages, Torres Strait Islander languages and Australian Creoles. (Lo Bianco, 1988, p. 33).

The guiding principles of Australia's National Policy on Languages reinforce the status of English for social and national cohesion in Australia, "whilst simultaneously recognising the diversity of the society and the inherent benefits of this diversity" (Lo Bianco, 1987, p. 4). Such a diversity encompasses maintenance and development of languages other than English (LOTEs), and provision of services in LOTEs (Lo Bianco, 1987, p. 5).

The National Policy on Languages (NPL) not only recognized LOTEs or community languages, but also different varieties of English, e.g. ethnolects such as Greek ethnolect, Indian ethnolect and Italian ethnolect of English in Australia (Xu, Leung, Hall, Jafari, & Pour, 2019, pp. 201, 211). The NPL also states that

> the English used in Australia has been modified by its speakers/writers to adapt it to the new demands and needs of its environment. These Australian contexts of use for the English language as well as the other language backgrounds of the users of English in Australia have led to the evolution of uniquely Australian varieties of English.
>
> (Lo Bianco, 1987, p. 7)

In regard to translation and interpreting the NPL has the following about the need for translation and interpreting services in Australia:

> A multilingual society needs to guarantee that language does not become a barrier to access to information and services. Consequently, the profession of interpreting/ translating is a necessary component in providing access and equity in relation to the provision of services paid for by the whole community, regardless of their linguistic backgrounds.
>
> (Lo Bianco, 1987, p. 164)

To the domestic needs of Australia's population, the NPL also mentions the importance of Mandarin Chinese as one of the languages in which translation and interpreting services are provided. Written in 1987 when there was still a comparatively small number of Chinese speakers in Australia, the NPL also drew attention to the importance of trade, scientific and tourist contact between Australia and neighbouring Southeast and East Asian countries, meaning that there would be a commensurate need for qualified and certified translators and interpreters for Mandarin Chinese, along with Indonesian/Malay and Japanese.

One of the central issues regarding intercultural communication in world Englishes involves "intelligibility of form, comprehensibility of meaning, and interpretability of sense" among speakers of different varieties of English (Proshina, 2014, p. 4). Although English is commonly adopted as a lingua franca across cultures globally as well as locally in English-speaking communities, regions and countries, it has been nativized in multilingual and multicultural societies to the extent that nativized varieties, e.g., Singapore English, Malaysian English and Indian English, as well as 'ethnolects' (Clyne, 1994), e.g. Greek, Italian and Indian ethnolects in multicultural Australia, develop local or regional forms and norms that are characteristic of the local needs and cultures, a process known as acculturation of English. Such issues of intelligibility, interpretability and comprehensibility at various linguistic and sociolinguistic levels including pragmatics are closely related to intercultural communication practice mediated through interpreting services. A wide range of examples and analysis of relevant issues will be explored in Chapters 3 and 4.

As far as 'speakers of English', more specifically, speakers of world Englishes, are concerned, it is important to know how they reflect on the way they have learnt and currently use English in terms of their metalinguistic awareness of their idiosyncratic variety and repertoire, and those of others with whom they communicate. In this day and age of globalization, those who identify as 'speakers of English' do not restrict themselves only to this designation of their linguistic repertoires. As stated, the majority of them are bilingual or multilingual users of English from multicultural speech communities and societies. The following are descriptions by 'speakers of English' in terms of what 'English' they think they speak. These speakers of English are international and domestic students from a university in Australia. We code the speakers as S1, S2, S3 and S4.

> S1:   *I think I speak a fairly neutral, native Australian form of English, however I do not really use that many specifically Australian expressions or phrases, nor do I believe I have a very strong Australian accent. I think the form of English I speak, while certainly Australian, would also be a sort of hybridized form that included influence from the UK and the USA.*

It can be seen from S1's reflection on her English that she speaks a 'hybridized form' of English, a 'neutral' variety as she claims, but a 'native Australian form of English'.

> S2:   *Regarding my variety of English, it is rather complicated. I'm from Indonesia and logically I would be speaking in Indonesian English. However, that would be oversimplifying the case. I used to learn English from British, American and Australian teachers and as a result, I have a mix of those Englishes plus Indonesian English. In addition, I'm developing a Singaporean/Malaysian accent ever since I've been in Melbourne due to over exposure to it, since most of my friends are Malaysian and Singaporean (even my housemate).*

S2's self-perception of his English is 'rather complicated' in that he thinks he speaks a 'mix' of the English varieties his British, American and Australian teachers have taught him 'plus Indonesian English'. He is aware that English is not a homogeneous entity, but a dynamic and developing means of communication.

> S3: *I was born in Poland, so I studied English there. But then I moved to France, where I continued to be taught by French teachers. I also took some classes of Italian language in Rome, where Italian teachers taught them in English . . . I have an accent, but it's not really French, it is not typically Polish either . . . I think I mixed all those influences and I simply speak my own variety of English. I speak many Englishes, which differ depending on context. When I was living in India, I spoke English with a typical accent. Having migrated to Australia two years ago, the varieties I speak here vary. I find that my Australian English blends with Indian English, and is interspersed with Spanglish now that I learn Spanish. Hence, I engage in a lot of code mixing among Spanish, Indian & Australian English.*

S3's reflection shows that a multilingual speaker of English has the capacity to speak his or her 'own variety of English' which differs 'depending on context', and S3 is well aware of the influences she's mixed in her own variety of English, and she's consciously engaging in 'a lot of code mixing among Spanish, Indian & Australian English'.

> S4: *I would be tempted to say more Australian English than any other Englishes having been here for so long. However, I am aware that I do use expressions that come from my L1 that I need to translate to others sometimes. I guess my cultural conceptualizations/world views are innate and cannot but influence my current English . . . Another situation that I speak different English is when I speak to people who have the same L1 as I. We code mix a lot without apologizing; we are at ease doing so.* [A speaker of a mixture of Mauritian Creole, Australian English and French]

S4 is a Mauritian migrant in Australia, speaking a mixture of Mauritian Creole, Australian English and French. Her self-reflection shows that multilingual migrant speakers of English communicate who they are through their 'current English' which embodies their 'cultural conceptualizations/world views' that are 'innate' and they code-mix unapologetically among people of their communities who share similar linguistic and cultural backgrounds.

This section shows that the world of English has been undergoing a paradigm shift from English to Englishes, alongside unprecedented globalization over the last decades.

> The paradigm shift not only embodies variations in lexis, syntax, discourse, pragmatics and cultural conceptualizations of English varieties in local contexts, but the shift has come to challenge the uneven ground underlying the traditional categorization of EFL, ESL and ENL.
>
> (Moody, Robinson, Xu, & Meierkord, 2018, p. 1)

The self-reflections of the 'speakers of English' regarding what 'English' they speak testify the mixed or hybridized nature of contemporary world Englishes, and the heterogeneity of cultural conceptulizations and world views embedded in the English they speak.

2.2   Intercultural pragmatics and communication practices of Chinese and English speakers

In this section we re-frame intercultural communication in light of traditional frameworks and models, as well as new developments in intercultural communication. In particular, we look at intercultural pragmatics in relation to speech acts and communicative events, such as: greetings, openers, 'ice-breakers', small talk, narrative structure, paralinguistic features, proxemics, different speech acts (explanations, responses, requests, bringing up problems, complaints/criticisms, compliments, leave taking). We also look at practices of intercultural communication and issues in relation to intercultural pragmatics, e.g., face and politeness, with reference to Chinese and English speakers.

2.2.1   *Intercultural pragmatics of Chinese and English speakers*

To quote the linguist, Chinese–English bilingual and intercultural communication researcher Li Wei, "[h]uman communication has always been multimodal: people use textual, aural, linguistic, spatial, and visual resources, or modes, to construct and interpret messages" (Li, 2018, p. 21). Aural messages are conveyed through human speech. As a practising public service interpreter and researcher remarked "[h]uman speech is made up of things we say (*language*), the way in which we say things (*paralanguage*), and the movement(s) we make when we say or communicate things (*kinesics*)" (Miletich, 2015, p. 165). These three aspects of human speech cannot be separated and they work holistically to achieve human communication, particularly across cultures through mediation involving interpreters. In such circumstances, intercultural pragmatics becomes more of a salient factor for effective communication, because human communication may go beyond words and grammar, or rule-governed constructions of utterances.

> The idea that language is systematic and rule-governed can get us a long way in describing how language works with regards to form and grammar, but clearly there are many aspects of the human experience of using language that remain to be explored.
>
> (Burridge & Stebbins, 2016, p. 16)

Therefore we need to adopt a 'much more open and socially oriented approach' to language and communication, as "there is so much to communication and social contact that falls outside of the concepts of signs and rules, competence and performance" (Burridge & Stebbins, 2016, p. 17).

What is unsaid during intercultural communication warrants exploration and analysis. According to Kecskes (2004, p. 2),

> in intercultural communication involving people from different linguistic and cultural backgrounds with different values, beliefs, schemas, and traditions, the exploration of what is unsaid but communicated in intercultural interactions is of critical importance, because, essentially, intercultural communication is about how people understand one another when they do not share a common cultural experience.

To explore what is 'unsaid but communicated' requires broader cultural and contextual knowledge. In this respect, traditional theories and models remain relevant and can be applied to interpreter-mediated situations of intercultural communication. One of these is Hymes' SPEAKING model, which elaborates on how components of socio-cultural contexts play a role in communicative speech acts and events. Hymes (1974) developed the model to assist the identification of components of linguistic interaction that was driven by his view that, in order to speak a language appropriately, one needs not only to learn its vocabulary and grammar, but also the context in which words are used and interactions take place. The model consists of components wittingly expressed through an acronym, i.e. SPEAKING. These include 'setting and scene', referring to the time and place of a speech act or event; 'participants', referring to interlocutors and audience; 'ends' for purposes, goals, and outcomes; 'act sequence', referring to form and order of an event; 'key', meaning clues that establish the tone, manner, or spirit of a speech act or event; 'instrumentalities', referring to forms and styles of speech; 'norms', referring to social rules governing the event and the participants' actions and reactions; and 'genre', meaning the kind of speech act or event (Hymes, 1972). In Xu's sociolinguistics research in relation to the norms that operate in varying socio-cultural contexts he finds out that

> different linguistic and cultural norms apply when using English in different settings. Norms of language(s) play a significant role in (inter-)cultural communication. As English becomes the *de facto* language for world-wide communication, the issues of who speaks what English to whom, when and where, are of increasing importance to language learners, teachers and researchers.
>
> (Xu, 2004, p. 287)

This has implications for interpreter-mediated intercultural communication involving English, currently used and practiced as a multicultural lingua franca.

Another model that has been commonly conceptualized and practiced regarding intercultural communication is Edward T. Hall's high-context and low-context culture distinction. This distinction offers explanatory power as an 'over-arching' feature in relation to the reported behaviour of interlocutors when they engage with speakers with different cultural affiliations. Following is a figure illustrating different aspects of the high-context and low-context cultures adapted from Hall's (1976) *Beyond Culture*.

High-context culture	*Low-context culture*
Relational, collectivist, and intuitive.	Linear, individualistic, and action-oriented.
Emphasis on interpersonal relations (group harmony), tradition and history.	Orientation towards facts, here and now.
Implicit and indirect communication (Things can be left unsaid, letting the culture explain).	Explicit and direct communication. (Being concise and efficient in telling what action is expected).
Much of the Middle East, Asia, Africa, and South America, e.g., African, Arab, Brazilian Chinese, French, Greek, Indian, Indonesian, Japanese, Korean, Persian, Russian, Thai, Vietnamese cultures.	North America, much of Western Europe, and Australia, e.g., American, British, Finnish, German, Australian cultures.

Figure 2.1 Different aspects of high-context and low-context cultures adapted from Hall (1976).

While Hall is credited for the 'high-context' and 'low-context' distinction with these as end-points along a continuum, and with the conventions of various cultural groups' being situated along this continuum, a framework with a greater degree of inter-group comparison was developed by Hofstede (1991, 2011). His model, commonly entitled 'dimensions of culture', uses five notions that represent core cultural values. On the basis of elicited and observed data from members of different groups, Hofstede makes claims about the presence of such dimensions in the behaviour of members of different groups. Although Hofstede's 'dimensions of culture' model has been critiqued in the past few decades, it remains insightful when looking at intercultural pragmatic practices among Chinese speakers, English speakers and Chinese–English interpreters.

Hofstede and his colleagues initially identified four primary dimensions of culture, including "power distance" regarding acceptability and expectation of power inequality in societies; "individualism" favouring personal achievement and individual rights versus "collectivism" fostering group harmony, lifelong group membership and unquestioning loyalty; "uncertainty avoidance" in terms of how rule-governed and reliant on laws and regulations societies are; and the level of pragmatics and tolerance of unstructured social situations and changeable environments; and "masculinity", valuing competitiveness, assertiveness, materialism and ambition, versus "femininity", valuing relationships (modesty and caring) and quality of life. Hofstede and his colleagues later expanded their model, and identified two more dimensions, including "long-term orientation" referring to people and societies that attach importance to future, persistence and saving; whereas "short-term orientation" attaching importance to the past and the present; and the "indulgence versus restraint" dimension, with indulgence being self-explanatory as enjoying life and having fun, whereas restraint means controlling desires and impulses. (Hofstede, 1991, 2011)

Unlike other pragmatic theories, intercultural pragmatics supports "a less idealized, more down-to-earth approach to communication than current pragmatic theories usually do" (Kecskes, 2011, p. 372), and this is precisely the challenge that interpreter-mediated intercultural communication needs to cope with. At this juncture we introduce a cultural linguistics approach to mediated intercultural communication with an aim to understand the heterogeneously distributed nature of cultural conceptualizations of Chinese speakers and English speakers.

Cultural linguistics (Sharifian, 2011, 2017a, 2017b) refers to a branch of linguistics that explores the relationship between language, culture, and conceptualization, and it examines how various features of language encode cultural conceptualizations. The concept of 'cultural conceptualization' is introduced as an analytical framework to decode cultural and intercultural communication phenomena. 'Cultural conceptualization' is a cover term that refers to fundamental cultural cognitive processes, involving cultural schema, cultural category and cultural metaphor (Sharifian, 2011). This concept of 'cultural conceptualization' is closely related to the Inter-Culturality Framework (ICF) put forward in Chapter 1 in the sense that cultural schemas, categories and metaphors are instantiations of intercultural discourse, and they are manifested by interlocutors through their intercultural agency. In terms of cultural schemas, there are different types, and those that are relevant to interpreter-mediated intercultural communication include: event schema (e.g., in settings or events where interpreters are involved for intercultural interaction); role schema (e.g., culturally expected behaviours from doctors, nurses, patients, judges, plaintiffs, defendants, prosecutors and lawyers, as well as the changing roles of interpreters); and emotion schema (e.g., when, where and why people feel shame, pride, and fear may vary from culture to culture).

In terms of 'cultural categories', people from different language backgrounds may or may not conceptually categorize aspects of their lives in the same way. From the perspective of interpreters in terms of 'inter-lingual transfer', such specifically cultural forms as cultural categories are likely to pose challenges to interpreters in a one-to-one way in terms of conveying messages in mediated intercultural communication. For example, Chinese may label many occasions as *festivals*, including the *Spring Festival*, the *Mid-Autumn Festival*, the *Lantern Festival*, the *Dragon-Boat Festival*, the *Qingming Festival* (which is actually a specific *day* dedicated to honouring ancestors and the deceased), and even the *National Day, Labour Day, Women's Day, Children's Day, Father's Day, Mother's Day*, and *Teachers' Day* are all literally called '*festivals*'. However, in most varieties of English, a 'festival' and a 'day', e.g., Labour Day, ANZAC Day, and Australia Day, may have different denotative and connotative meanings as opposed to a 'festival'. Such differences in cultural conceptual categories may require meta-cultural competence of interpreters involved in mediated intercultural communication between Chinese speakers and English speakers.

Cultural metaphors are cognitive structures that map onto two or more domains and enable people to understand certain abstract, culturally constructed experiences in terms of more concrete domains. Cultural metaphors, as the modifying adjective 'cultural' implies, can be culturally specific. For example, the following is an excerpt from a short story written by a Chinese migrant writer in English:

> *Unfortunately, his wife had died two years ago; people used to call them 'a pair of mandarin ducks,' meaning an affectionate couple. True, the two of them had spent some peaceful, loving years together and had never fought or quarrelled.*

The 'mandarin ducks' as a happy couple metaphor is widely conceptualized as a Chinese cultural metaphor, because the Chinese believe that mandarin ducks are lifelong couples, and these ducks symbolize fidelity and affection. In addition, Chinese people have a deep-rooted cultural category of Chinese zodiac animals, and they tend to associate people with certain characteristics of the zodiac animals; therefore they develop cultural metaphors accordingly, e.g. a clever monkey, a hardworking horse, and an ambitious and powerful dragon (Xu & Sharifian, 2018, p. 591).

As elaborated previously, Chinese cultural conceptualizations may help enrich English language in the sense that there is a co-presence or co-construction and (re)negotiation of existing and emergent schemas, categories and metaphors among speakers of varieties of English. However, such specific cultural knowledge and practice pose new challenges for interpreters during mediated intercultural communication.

2.2.2   Communication practices of Chinese and English speakers

Apart from different cultural conceptualizations between Chinese speakers and English speakers, there are also areas where speakers of Chinese and English have different social pragmatic practices, and these different practices are encountered and negotiated on a daily basis for those engaged in Chinese and English intercultural communication, particularly Chinese–English interpreters. These areas include naming practices, terms of address, e.g., kinship terms, honorifics, occupational terms of address, issues of face and maxims of politeness.

Naming and addressing practices vary across languages and cultures. Forms used in naming and addressing others index a number of features such as level of familiarity, status, context, role-relationship etc. The effects of not addressing a fellow interlocutor in an appropriate way are described by Bowe, Martin and Manns (2014, p. 146) in the following way: "[t]he incorrect usage of a particular name or not being aware of differing naming systems could lead to miscommunication and ultimately insult and hurt". Historically, Chinese culture is known to have had an elaborate naming system which has been somewhat simplified in recent years. Even so, an educated male adult in contemporary China typically has a number of names, e.g. a surname (姓), a given name (名), a style name (字) when a man reaches 20 and an alternative name (号), which is usually self-chosen. The most common convention in the Chinese naming system is for a person to have a surname and a given name, with the former preceding the latter.

In Chinese, kinship terms are used as forms of address for blood relatives and, by analogy according to age and level of closeness, also for non-family members. In Chinese, these terms of kinship relationships reflect the hierarchical social structure, irrespective of blood ties, and include forms such as e.g., *uncle* (叔叔), *auntie* (阿姨), *brother* (兄弟), *sister* (姊妹), *cousin brother* (堂兄弟，表兄弟), *cousin sister* (堂姊妹，表姊妹). For terms including *uncle, auntie, cousin brother* and *cousin sister*, there are also different derivative forms used to differentiate the paternal or maternal relatives. For example, one's mother's brothers are called *jiù* (舅), whereas one's father's brothers are called *shū* (叔) or *bó* (伯), making a further distinction between the father's younger brothers and older brothers. However, such terms do not exist as distinct semantic categories in English. This presents a challenge to Chinese–English interpreters interpreting from English where no specification is made in relation to 'uncle' or 'aunt' as to whether it is the brother or sister of which parent, and where in Chinese, the interpreter is compelled to make a distinction, or to concurrently use two or more equivalent forms.

In English, the opposite ordering of names pertains, with the first name preceding the surname, with many speakers having a middle name which is usually rarely used or mentioned. Further, for many speakers of English, and reflecting the 'horizontal' structure that Hall (1976) described as being characteristic of 'low-context' cultures such as that of American or British English, informality is normally practiced, even for communication with strangers. In order to indicate informality, speakers commonly use first names with each other. Bowe et al. (2014, p. 146) state that "[t]he general rule in English speaking cultures is that you move to first name terms as soon as possible" (Bowe et al., 2014, p. 146). However, in Chinese-speaking communities, informality can be carried out through other naming practices other than the use of the first name. These include the use of nicknames or by use of address terms commencing with *lǎo* or *xiǎo* ('old' or 'little') plus the addressee's surname, depending on how senior or junior the addressee is. Using first names in a Chinese cultural context is seen as being "overfamiliar and thus impolite, and instead distancing strategies in naming and addressing are employed to show politeness" (Bowe et al., 2014, p. 146). Chinese–English interpreters need to apply their knowledge of naming practices in both Chinese and English in considering which forms, and the order of these forms, should be used when interpreting a Chinese speaker's self-introduction to an English speaker, and an English speaker's self-introduction to a Chinese speaker (see 4.2.1).

Another issue with naming practices as far as intercultural communication is concerned involving Chinese speakers is the use of English (or Anglicised) names. The English names that Chinese speakers adopt for various reasons and in different circumstances may not be 'official' in the sense that they do not generally appear in their ID documents, e.g., passport, or driver's license. Following are responses from three Chinese–English bilingual participants in a survey conducted by the second author of the book for a project that he has been working on regarding naming practices and norms of Chinese speakers of English.

a. Female, 46, Beijing

My English name is Elizabeth. It was given by my English teacher in the first year of my college study. She named all the girls in her class with the queens' names in England history. I was the first one on her name list, so I was named Elizabeth, the name of two England queens. Unlike some girls who later changed to their own favourite names, thinking these names are too old-fashioned, I have kept this name till now and it has become a real part of my identity.

b. Male, 43, Hong Kong

I don't think Chinese people should have English names. I think originally Chinese people created English names so that foreigners can call them more easily. However, why should we do that? If they want to know us, they better remember our Chinese names. We would never call an English person by their Chinese names (I know some English people do create a Chinese name, but normally they are for fun, or for political reasons. They are seldom used in daily life.) If Chinese people use English names, we are losing our national identity. Once I heard an American journalist talking about a young Chinese golfer. He said, 'His name is Zhang Huachuang, but he preferred others to call him 'Andy'!' He said it in such a sarcastic way, it really made me feel uncomfortable.

c. Male, 48, Melbourne

One of the ways in which I am 'flexible' is that I choose to have an English name for contact with people who are not of Chinese background. I know that many people think about this very differently, and I sometimes also question myself, why should I have an English name? who am really I? etc. Well, if my English name helps the way I am able to communicate with others, and how they communicate with me, it may not be a bad move . . .

It can be seen from the responses that these Chinese–English bilinguals have different views and attitudes regarding using or not using English names. Some use their English names of convenience in intercultural communication and regard English names as an integral part of their identities; while others may insist on their Chinese 'official' names without considering an English name. There are also speakers who take a more flexible view towards this issue and think that it depends on the circumstances and contexts.

The practice of terms of address across Chinese and English can also be an issue in intercultural communication as Chinese and English speakers may follow different practices. In terms of pronouns of address, for example, the second person singular 'you' or *nǐ* (你), Chinese speakers use two forms, including *nǐ* (你) and *nín* (您). The distinction here implies power or status, and solidarity or intimacy. This distinction is similar to that between French *tu* and *vous*, or German *du* and *Sie*. When interpreters are working from English into Chinese and interpreting second person singular pronouns into Chinese, the appropriate choice would be *nín*, as this pronoun form indexes formality, unfamiliarity, respect and distance.

In Chinese, there is variation in the use of honorifics to address others. The equivalent term in Chinese to the English salutation *Ladies and Gentlemen*, is *nǚshìmen* (女士们) *xiānshengmen* (先生们). However, these salutations are derived from or based on Western forms, and their use in Chinese has occurred as a result of the adoption of naming practices from Western languages such as English. Before the popularization of *nǚshìmen* (女士们) and *xiānshengmen* (先生们), Chinese people would use *tóngzhìmen* (同志们) 'comrades' and *péngyǒumen* (朋友们) 'friends' as forms or address or as salutations. Xu's (2009, p. 134) research on the Englishization of Pǔtōnghuà in China shows a number of trends in the use of honorifics, particularly in the way how Chinese senior leaders address the general public. One trend is that the use of *tóngzhìmen* 'comrades' is gradually being replaced by *nǚshìmen xiānshengmen* 'ladies and gentlemen' and with *tóngshìmen* 'colleagues' emerging as another new address term. The terms *tóngzhìmen* 'comrades' and *péngyǒumen* 'friends' are more likely to be used by Chinese senior leaders when they address the domestic public in China. These same Chinese senior leaders will, however, use *nǚshìmen xiānshengmen* 'ladies and gentlemen' when addressing an international audience. An interesting use of address terms can be found is the 1st January "New Year" public addresses made by Chinese senior leaders, with an intended audience of both domestic and overseas Chinese. In their New Year greetings, four address terms are used in the following order: *nǚshìmen, xiānshengmen, tóngzhìmen* and *péngyǒumen* (ladies, gentlemen, comrades and friends).

Another area of the use of addressing terms is honorifics, such as titles, e.g. Mr. Mrs. Ms. Dr. and Prof., and 'honorific abstract nouns', e.g. *Your Honour, Your Grace, Your Majesty, Your Highness* and *Your Excellency*. Honorific abstract nouns are employed to convey honour or respect to the addressee.

In both Chinese and English, there are situations in which occupational terms, such as 'doctor', can be used as a term of address. However, in Chinese, there is a more extensive use of occupational terms as address terms, such as *lǎoshī* (老师) 'teacher', *hùshì* (护士) 'nurse', *lǜshī* (律师) 'lawyer', *jǐngchá* (警察) 'police', *biānjí* (编辑) 'editor', *jìzhě* (记者) 'journalist' and *shìzhǎng* (市长) 'mayor'. Occupation terms can be used as terms of address for quite specialized occupational designations as well, e.g. 'director', 'section head', 'dean', 'president', 'general', 'commander', 'manager', 'general manager' as well as 'boss' (Xu, 2009). It is important to be aware of the use of honorifics in discourse and how this operates across languages and cultures, particularly in intercultural communication mediated through interpreters.

> Honorific discourse is part of a complex interactional system that uses both linguistic and non-linguistic elements to convey respect, deference and solidarity . . . all languages and cultures use honorific forms whether they be honorific titles or a more complex system of pronouns, nouns, verbs and adverbs.
>
> (Bowe et al., 2014, p. 155)

Issues of face and politeness also play a crucial role in mediated intercultural communication between Chinese speakers and English speakers. Research up to now has indicated that there is a lack of clarity about politeness, in terms of defining politeness, and seeking politeness universals across cultures. Meier (1995, p. 350) points out that "claims for universality [of politeness] are clearly fraught with problems of interpretation, i.e. with problems of establishing objective measures for application across cultures". Politeness has been perceived and defined differently across cultures. For example, Lakoff (1973, p. 3) proposes three politeness rules: 1) Don't impose; 2) Give options; 3) Maintain friendliness. However, Yu (2011, p. 389) argues that "imposition can be connected with politeness in some cultures such as Japanese and Korean". "Many people tend to think of politeness as the use of extremely formal language, but most linguists perceive politeness as a continuum of appropriate communication" (Bowe & Martin, 2007, p. 26). For example, in terms of preferred ways of speaking, including names and greetings, addressing someone as Prof. or Dr. Brown, and greeting someone with 'How do you do?' in certain contexts, albeit high levels of formality, may not be considered as being polite. What is socially and linguistically appropriate behaviour depends on 1) levels of familiarity (e.g. family, friends, acquaintances, strangers); 2) levels of formality (e.g. extremely formal to informal); 3) types of situations (e.g. professional, business, sport, private, public); 4) relative age, and 5) gender (Bowe et al., 2014, p. 48).

Xu's (2010, p. 114) research shows that the term 'politeness' varies in its denotative and connotative meanings across cultures. He understands Chinese cultural conceptualizations of *lǐmào* (礼貌) 'politeness' as involving sacrifice, gift-giving, ceremony, ritual, and face, public self-image or social perception of a person's prestige.

> The most approximate equivalent in Chinese to 'politeness' is 礼貌 (lǐmào). The Chinese character 礼(lǐ) originally had the religious meaning of 'sacrifice,' from which the present meaning of 'present/gift' or 'protocol/ceremony' derives. The modern interpretation of li has moved from the Confucian rites and rituals to propriety and politeness. The Chinese character 貌 (mào) literally means 'face' or 'appearance.' It is related to two separate but related concepts in Chinese social relations, namely, liǎn and miàn (or miànzi). Liǎn is commonly associated with a person's physical face or moral character, while miànzi represents social perceptions of a person's prestige.
>
> (Xu, 2010, p. 114)

An alternative translation of 'politeness' in Chinese is *kèqi* (客气), which is associated with being modest so as to cultivate harmonious and concordant interpersonal relationships. As far as Chinese speakers and English speakers are concerned, the notion of face also operates to a greater or lesser degree when they communicate with each other. Face is a public self-image that every adult generally protects. In social interactions, people have the desire to maintain their face, and they are generally afraid of losing face. There are many 'face'-related expressions in Chinese, including *losing face* (丢面子), *saving face* (留面...) *giving face* (给面子), *loving face* (爱面子), *paying attention to face* (讲面子), *struggling for face* (争面子), *needing face* (要面子), *protecting face* (护面子), *sweeping face away* (扫面子), and *rewarding face* (赏面子). Such expressions are used by Chinese speakers commonly and extensively in their social interactions. Therefore the notion of face and its associated politeness has implications for mediated intercultural communication between Chinese speakers and English speakers.

In relation to face and politeness across cultures, there has been various research; one of the most widely drawn-on models, based mainly on English-language data, is put forward by Leech (1983). Leech uses the term 'maxim' referring to the notion of a principle with some moral or functional basis to describe different notions of politeness. His six politeness maxims are: 1) tact maxim, i.e., minimize cost to others, maximize benefits to others; 2) generosity maxim, i.e., minimize benefits to self and maximize cost to self; 3) approbation maxim, i.e., minimize dispraise of other; maximize praise of other; 4) modesty maxim, i.e., minimize praise of self, maximize dispraise of self; 5) agreement maxim, i.e., minimize disagreement between self and other; maximize agreement between self and other; and 6) sympathy maxim, i.e., minimize antipathy between self and other, maximize sympathy between self and other (Leech, 1983).

It is thought that Chinese speakers, particularly Chinese–English bilingual speakers, also observe these maxims of politeness to a large extent. However, Chinese speakers also perceive politeness or its near equivalent in Chinese, which is *lǐmào*, in a somewhat different way. According to Gu (1990, p. 239), "there are basically four notions underlying the Chinese conception of *lǐmào*: respectfulness, modesty, attitudinal warmth, and refinement". Further, Gu (1990) states:

> 'Respectfulness' is self's positive appreciation or admiration of other concerning the latter's face, social status, and so on. 'Modesty' can be seen as another way of saying 'self-denigration'. 'Attitudinal warmth' is self's demonstration of kindness, consideration, and hospitality to other. Finally, 'refinement' refers to self's behaviour to other which meets certain standards.
>
> (Gu, 1990, p. 239)

Gu (1990, p. 239) argues that "denigrating the self and respecting the other remain at the core of the modern conception of *lǐmào*", and he suggests four politeness maxims regarding Chinese speakers, including 1) the self-denigration maxim, i.e. denigrate the self and elevate the other; 2) the address maxim, i.e. address your interlocutor with an appropriate address term; 3) the tact maxim (in impositives), i.e., minimize cost to the other and maximize the benefit received; and 4) the generosity maxim (in commissives), i.e., maximizing the benefit to the other and minimize the cost to the self (Gu, 1990, pp. 245–249). What remains essential in the notion of *lǐmào* or 'politeness' and the four politeness maxims in Chinese society is the role of hierarchy, that is, to assign everyone their defined place in society and the behaviours appropriate to their position. In other words, to behave cordance with one's social positions is also considered as being ~~~ractice of 'politeness' applies to Chinese speakers generally in communication (Xu, 2010, p. 115).

~~~nicative events and non-verbal communication

~~~understanding of mediated intercultural communication through ~~~sh interpreters are areas that remain underrepresented in interactions featuring both Chinese and English speakers. Interpreters are a group who are required to recognize and understand the discourse-pragmatic features in intercultural interactions and to transfer these cross-linguistically via linguistic (and sometimes with accompanying paralinguistic) means. As such, their perspectives and views on Chinese–English encounters are multi-faceted: as Chinese speakers; as English speakers; and as linguistic mediators. At a fundamental level, interpreters express in one language content that has been expressed in another, retaining the intent of the source speech in the target speech. Nonverbal communication also plays an important role in speech events where interpreters are involved, as discourse and agency of interculturality are explicitly at play. In this section we explore the extent to which various forms of nonverbal communication in the process of mediated communication involving interpreters may also form an integral part of interactive 'acts' involving speech among interlocutors and interpreters in communicative events.

Nonverbal communication is important in interpreter-mediated encounters (as it is in non-mediated encounters) since "nonverbal behaviours are often more subtle and abstruse than verbal behaviors, hence they tend to be poorly understood. Becoming familiar with these behaviors is an important part of the interpreter's work" (Miletich, 2015, p. 169). Non-verbal communication and non-verbal behaviours involve what is commonly known as 'paralanguage', described in the following way:

> Paralanguage includes primary qualities such as timbre (which allows us to recognize someone's voice), resonance and loudness; *qualifiers* such as respiratory control and harshness; *differentiators* such as laughter and shouting; and *alternants* such as sighs, hisses, and moans.
>
> (Miletich, 2015, p. 166)

As mediated intercultural communication through interpreters concerns primarily 'interlingual transfer', interpreters are expected to provide renditions that are optimal and complete, without distortion or omission and that preserve the content and intent of the source message. "Perceptions of meaning and intent from source messages are conveyed not only in the semantic content of them, but also through context, role, situation, and other paralinguistic features enacted by interlocutors" (Hlavac, Xu, & Xiong, 2015, p. 98).

The role of understanding 'context' in mediated intercultural communication cannot be underestimated. Being aware of the intercultural dynamics and treating contextual clues as resources, hence drawing upon relevant cultural schemas and intercultural strategies, are vital for effective communication. Baker (2006, p. 332) suggests that it would be productive for interlocutors and interpreters to treat context as a resource, "something that we selectively and strategically construct as we engage in any act of communication, including the act of translation". According to Baker (2006, p. 332), this suggests "both an emphasis on the dynamic and ever-changing nature of context *and* directing our attention to the strategic process of contextualization in which translators and interpreters engage".

Interpreters are expected to show alignment with interlocutors for some types of interactional competence, e.g. the awareness of physical proximity, some types of formulaic competence, such as greeting and small talk, and some types of sociocultural competence, e.g., engaging in conversations with appropriate topics, and leave taking. It is incumbent on interpreters that they have a knowledge of the most of the cultural-pragmatic features of the speech communities that they work with, and are able to recognize and understand their linguistic behaviour patterns.

To understand paralanguage and how it operates in intercultural communicative events, it is important to know some major types of non-verbal acts, for example 'kinesic acts' (Miletich, 2015, p. 167), that commonly occur in mediated intercultural communicative events. Kinesics consists of "gestures, manners and postures that occur in isolation or in combination with words and/or paralanguage" (Miletich, 2015, p. 166). Kinesics also involves proxemics, i.e., the use of space and how various differences in that use can make someone feel more relaxed or anxious. People from different cultures may have different views regarding public, social and personal space. As far as Chinese speakers and English speakers are concerned, the notion of public and social space can be negotiated and it does not seem to give rise to much intercultural misunderstanding. However, as far as personal space is concerned, there can be variations due to commonly perceived characteristics of high context versus low context cultures and positive versus negative face and politeness. Chinese–English interpreters are mindful of the meanings of kinesic acts and where there are differences in the way that such 'acts' are perceived, it is incumbent on Chinese–English interpreters to relate to the other person what the intended meaning is. This is an intercultural strategy to avoid a situation in which misunderstanding or even conflict could arise.

In the following section, we explore interculturality through mediated intercultural communication, in particular the changing roles of Chinese–English interpreters involved in communicative events among Chinese speakers and English speakers.

2.3 Mediated intercultural communication practices through Chinese–English interpreters

Mediated intercultural communication through interpreters is multifaceted, multimodal, and it is also co-constructed among interlocutors and interpreters as intercultural agencies. Framed and modelled in a particular intercultural space when speech acts are performed and speech events take place, interlocutors and interpreters act as 'agencies' linguistically and culturally, and they act in accordance with their intercultural schemas and strategies in professional contexts. The interpreted interaction is one in which all interlocutors bring prior experiences, knowledge of their own societal traits, and beliefs about other groups' traits. In the interpreted interaction, communication is not only co-constructed on the spot, but also 'relayed', 're-constructed' and 're-presented'. Such a co-constructive process requires interlocutors as well as interpreters to acquire knowledge of intercultural pragmatics enacted in the zone of interculturality. Hlavac et al. (2015) describe this in the following way, "[i]nterpreters are expected to have an advanced command of not only the vocabulary and grammar of their working languages, but also the pragmatic norms that speakers of their working languages employ in communicative interactions" (Hlavac et al., 2015, p. 91).

As far as our research on interpreter-mediated intercultural communication is concerned, we argue that it is essential for all parties, including interlocutors and interpreters, to develop awareness of the zone of interculturality and its interlingual and intercultural ramifications at work. Alongside the role of intercultural expert, the interpreter also plays the role of 'interactional manager' in interpreter-mediated encounters. Baraldi and Gavioli (2007) employ the term 'coordination' to refer to the moves or conversational footings that interpreters adopt:

> There can be 'implicit' and 'explicit' coordination: e.g., interpreters coordinate the talk simply by translating and taking turns in the one or the other language ('implicit coordination'). More explicit actions/acts of coordination include: 'requests for clarification, requests for time to translate, comments on translations, requests to observe the turn-taking order, invitations to start or continue talking . . . Such coordination activity is aimed at making the interaction between the participants of different languages possible and successful and it is concerned with the promotion of their participation and understanding.
>
> (Baraldi & Gavioli, 2007, pp. 155–156)

Lü and Li (2012, p. 145) contend that "interpreter-mediated communication is always an instance of intercultural communication, and that cultural mediation is an essential part of the interpreter's responsibility". Baraldi (2018, p. 15) also suggests that interpreting should be "seen as a way of negotiating cultural and/ or linguistic differences in interaction and interpreter-mediated interaction as a specific case of intercultural communication, in which cultural and linguistic differences are constructed and negotiated". In addition, Bourne (2016, p. 15) who studies the pragmatic features of both Chinese and English speakers argues that

> [i]nterpreters should also possess intercultural competence to mediate cultural differences. Indeed, the work of interpreters goes beyond decoding and encoding verbal messages between languages. It involves 'cognitive competence', 'affective competence' and 'operational competence'. Cognitive competence refers to knowledge of the host language and culture; affective

competence refers to emotional and motivational capacity to deal with the challenges and to establish a meaningful psychological connection with the host environment; and operational competence refers to the capacity to take verbal and nonverbal actions that are appropriate for the host culture.

(Bourne, 2016, p. 17)

Elsewhere, Bourne remarks that,

[a] cognitively and operationally competent interpreter needs to have a good mastery of both the source culture and the target culture and be able to choose words and expressions that are appropriate for the target audience from a different cultural background. A professional interpreter should develop affective competence to establish connection with the audience and gain their confidence. Culturally competent interpreters should take the environment into consideration to evaluate the receptivity and the pressure of conformity in the target culture.

(Bourne, 2016, p. 22)

Like translators, interpreters are not "all-purpose code-switching machines with built-in dictionaries" either (Jääskeläinen, 2007, p. 7). Professional interpreters are expert language users and linguistic professionals, and at the same time, they are cognizant of the local features in which they work, so that those that are specific to the healthcare situation co-determine both English and Chinese speakers' responses to questions about their use of pragmatics. In this way "interpreters attend to each group's enactment of pragmatic features and, as expert language users, are able to recognize features and components of interactions and their functions to a greater degree than the Chinese and English speakers" (Hlavac et al., 2015, pp. 91–92).

Gavioli and Baraldi's (2011, p. 205) analysis of the linguistic and communicative functions of interpreter-mediated public service encounters has shown that "the interpreter's discourse roles, including those of language facilitator and of cultural and social mediator, are highly complex". The complex nature of interpreter-mediated public service encounters can be partly attributed to the nature of its intercultural discourse which consists of co-constructed speech events, as set out in Chapter 1 regarding the ICF framework, consisting of intercultural frame and intercultural model. In Gavioli and Baraldi's words,

Through co-construction of the conversation, the interpreter as well as the other participants orient themselves to both the 'local context' (what is actually said in the interaction) and the broader 'frame', provided by the setting (hospital, court) in which the interaction takes place and by the respective participants' roles as patients, defendants, doctors or judges.

(Gavioli & Baraldi, 2011, p. 206)

The role of the interpreter is central, as argued by Gavioli and Baraldi (2011, p. 227) who state that "the interpreter's function in dialogue organization and the effects of his/her interpreting on the process of intercultural mediation 'concerns the dynamics of interpreting as a *pas de trois*, a triadic interaction in which the interpreter is quite central". In the following sections, we elaborate on the positioning, agency and the changing roles of an interpreter with regards to the Inter-Culturality Framework for mediated intercultural communication

Translation Studies scholar, Anthony Pym (2006, p. 4) sums up some of the current trends in terms of the ways in which the social and the cultural manifest themselves in translation and interpreting studies. He makes the remark that

> we might thus posit that, for some scholars and more particularly in some fields of research, the focus has shifted from texts to mediators (i.e., translators and interpreters). Many of us are no longer stopping at the sociocultural dimensions of source and target texts. We would like to know more about who is doing the mediating, for whom, within what networks, and with what social effects.
>
> (Pym, 2006, p. 4)

2.3.1   *Positioning and agency of an interpreter*

Linking Pym's call to study those providing mediation, we are reminded of the cultural and situational context in which *all* languages and *all* forms of language exist (Halliday, 1978), and that the interpreter has a position in this context. We conceive of the interpreter's position as a process more than as a static state, and use the gerund form 'positioning' to reflect this.

Positioning can be defined as a discursive construction that makes a participant's actions intelligible in the interaction. It is important to analyse the intercultural interactive moves and discursive practices that display the interpreter's contingent positioning. "Positioning is both mutual, in that participants' actions position themselves (self-positioning) and their interlocutors (other-positioning), and reflexive, in that each participant's positioning is based on other participants' positioning" (Baraldi, 2018, p. 15). The position is a relative construct that operates in a certain intercultural discourse that involves the Inter-Culturality Framework. In this sense Hymes' SPEAKING acronym consisting of setting or scene, participants, ends, act sequence, key, instrumentalities, norms and genre, still plays a key role for mediated intercultural communication. In addition, aspects of high-context versus low-context cultures, as well as varying dimensions of culture also affect the nuances and moment-by-moment positioning of the interpreter, because, as pointed out by Zhu (2014, pp. 127–128) participants in an intercultural communication event use "interactional devices" relative to their positioning, to "define the boundary of an event and foreground the contextual information in interactions. Shared frames are central to creating the conditions for shared interpretations".

The positioning of an interpreter is contingent on intercultural models, as part of the Inter-Culturality Framework, that are in operation during the interactive events, and the intercultural models are jointly established among participants of intercultural communication, including interlocutors and the interpreter, on the basis of intercultural knowledge, goals, values, perceptions, emotional states and actions in different intercultural contexts. It is important to revisit Kecskes' (2013, p. 48) definition of an intercultural model, which consists of "a set of context-based action plans, including judgements of the formality of the situation, what is the most appropriate thing to do". When interlocutors and the interpreter set up certain routines and they repeatedly do things in a mutually acceptable way relative to their respective intercultural positioning, then their shared action plans emerge as an intercultural model.

Interpreters are not decoding and encoding devices, and neither are they all-purpose interlingual transfer machines, but active agents with an increasingly salient mediating role. Baraldi (2018) states that

> Interpreters' agency is displayed as both implicit and explicit coordination of interactions. Implicit coordination is achieved through interpreters' renditions (recapitulating), which may modify, i.e., expand, reduce, substitute, or summarise, the content of previous utterances. Explicit coordination is carried out through actions focusing on the organization of the interaction, i.e., mainly 'non-rendition', such as requests for clarification, comments on translations, invitations to start or continue talking. Both implicit and explicit coordination show that interpreters are active agents, but while implicit coordination provides opportunities of transforming original utterances through renditions, explicit coordination is performed in dyadic sequences of the interaction in which interpreters negotiate the meanings of information and the relationships with other participants.
>
> (Baraldi, 2018, p. 15)

Interpreters have agency and need to know how to wield it, because they are the participants who are in the position to understand what other interlocutors say, and therefore, they are responsible for the flow of information. Interpreters are also central participants, according to Müller (2001, p. 248), as they have full linguistic access to everything that is uttered in conversation, rather than to only one 'half' of it, as is often the case with primary parties. In the context of public services such as health care interpreting, interpreters play an even more crucial role in relation to their agency in that "they coordinate talk activity by selecting information to translate, asking and providing clarification, and giving support to the interlocutors" (Farini, 2016, p. 28).

To further elaborate on the positioning of a dialogue interpreter, Müller (2001, pp. 247–248) argues that interpreters can be perceived and recognized in an intermediary position as a verbal and cultural cognate, or 'co-members' to be trusted sufficiently. Interpreters are not only visible but also prominent participants and have a status which is different from translators, who tend to remain invisible.

2.3.2 *The changing roles of an interpreter*

In formal settings where simultaneous or consecutive interpreting occurs, such as at major international conferences and diplomatic visits, the interpreter's function and role can be certainly constrained by the event, and the impact that the interpreter can have on the primary interlocutors (although not on the message conveyed) is limited. Interpreter-mediated intercultural communication involves speech-act based forms and (para-)linguistic behaviours, e.g., (self-)introductions, physical proximity, small talk, elicitation of specific information, and leave taking. It also involves intercultural pragmatics approach to behaviour analysis through the inclusion of data relating to actual situational experiences and the reported enactment of socio-cultural norms of not only oneself, but of oneself through another (as 'relayed constructions'). In public services settings, such as healthcare and legal services, 'dialogue' interpreting is the norm, and as an integral part of the ongoing or sustainable 'dialogue' among interlocutors, the interpreter needs to manage his or her changing roles, not only as a message converter, or clarifier, but as a co-participant, co-ordinator, cultural broker, active agent, facilitator and mediator. In certain circumstances, the interpreter may also act as an 'author', or speaker who initiates his or her own utterances, a 'principal' in relation to other interlocutors, a 'responder' when interlocutors become vulnerable emotionally or culturally, and an 'advocate' when issues of (in)justice may be involved in the mediated intercultural communication. "The idea of the interpreter as mere *conduit* has now been put into question, and with reason" (Miletich, 2015, p. 162).

This brings us also to the question of the interpreter's visibility. Angelelli (2004, pp. 9–10) argues that "interpreters are opaque rather than transparent, or visible rather than invisible", and she proposes a 'model of visibility', which "portrays interpreters who are not only linguistically visible, but who are also visible with all the social and cultural factors that allow them to co-construct a definition of reality with the other co-participants of the interaction". Interpreters perceive and self-describe themselves as "communication facilitators", and their primary role is "interlingual transfer but with greater visibility to other parties" (Hlavac et al., 2015, p. 97).

One of the aspects of the 'visibility' of interpreters (Ozolins, 2016) lies in the opportunity for them to 'intervene', as pointed out by Miletich (2015), particularly in healthcare settings. "These interventions occur in order to stop the flow of the conversation and clarify terms, expressions or ideas; point to a misunderstanding; signal a cultural reference; and/or relay the meaning of specific nonverbal behavior" (Miletich, 2015, p. 162). The interpreter is "regarded as a visible co-participant in a verbal and nonverbal interaction that allows two people from different languages and cultures to communicate with each other" (Miletich, 2015, p. 162). In this sense healthcare interpreters are considered "active interlingual communication facilitators" (Miletich, 2015, p. 178). Interpreters are active participants and facilitators mediating intercultural communication in the sense that "they select information to translate, ask and provide clarification, give support to the interlocutors", and that they "play a double role in the conversation, they translate and they also coordinate the talk activity" (Baraldi & Gavioli, 2007, p. 155). Another aspect of the 'visibility' of interpreters lies in the understanding that interpreters may assume a "coordinating role" for particular types of interventions such as "clarification, accommodation of the parties involved, someone not understanding an interpretation or cultural differences' (Miletich, 2015, p. 164).

It is commonly understood that interpreters play an important role in mediated intercultural communication, because the nature of their work involves the in-between-ness of multiple languages, varieties of a language, and hetereogeneous cultures. Both linguistic and cultural factors have a pivotal impact on the active professional involvement of the interpreters as effective mediators of intercultural communication.

Although there are commonly acknowledged roles of interpreters, e.g. "message converter, message clarifier, cultural clarifier, and patient advocate" as identified by the California Healthcare Interpreters Association (Spencer-Oatey & Xing, 2009, p. 220), in reality, the act of interpreting is "deeply embedded in wider social and cultural practices" (Baker, 2006, p. 321) (see Section 3.2). What may add to the complexity of the "wider social and cultural practices" is the fact that both Chinese and English have the largest numbers of speakers in the world, and the heterogeneity of their speech interactions, communities and cultures is enormous. Therefore, it is not surprising that the role enactments of Chinese–English interpreters are varied and diverse.

2.4   Conclusion

This chapter has built on Chapter 1, where we outlined fundamental concepts that are relevant to 'intercultural communication', including language, culture, interculture and interculturality, communication, intercultural communication, and competence for intercultural communication, and where we proposed an adapted framework for intercultural communication research, the Inter-Culturality Framework (ICF). The ICF involves intercultural discourse, including intercultural frames and models, and intercultural agency, involving intercultural schemas and strategies. In this chapter, we have explored intercultural communication that primarily involves Chinese and English speakers. Our focus has been on intercultural pragmatics of Chinese and English speakers, and mediated intercultural communication practices through Chinese–English interpreters in the current globalized world. Drawing critically upon traditional as well as current research on intercultural communication, we have elaborated on the changing roles of interpreters, in particular, Chinese–English interpreters, in mediated intercultural communication with a particular focus on public services settings in multilingual and multicultural societies.

In Chapter 3 we present key concepts and terms used in contemporary interpreting and provide a closer focus on the roles and footings that interpreters enact. We then move to examples of Chinese–English interpreting across eight of the most common settings that interpreters work in. Chapter 4 presents data from all parties to the mediated interaction: Chinese and English speakers and Chinese–English interpreters. Multiple perspectives on a number of key situational features that relate to intercultural communication are outlined in this chapter. Discourse-pragmatic conventions of Chinese and English speakers discussed in Chapter 2 are re-visited in Chapter 4 and applied to these key situational features.

References

Angelelli, C. (2004). *Medical interpreting and cross-cultural communication*. Cambridge: Cambridge University Press.

Baidu Zhidao: The Population and Percentages of Chinese Dialects. (2019). Retrieved August 19, 2019, from https://zhidao.baidu.com/question/208131234.html

Baker, M. (2006). Contextualization in translator- and interpreter-mediated events. *Journal of Pragmatics, 38*(3), 321–337. https://doi.org/10.1016/j.pragma.2005.04.010

Baraldi, C. (2018). Interpreting as mediation of migrants' agency and institutional support: A case analysis. *Journal of Pragmatics, 125*(2018), 13–27. https://doi.org/10.1016/j.pragma.2017.11.012

Baraldi, C., & Gavioli, L. (2007). Dialogue interpreting as intercultural mediation: An analysis in health care multicultural settings. In M. Grein & E. Weigand (Eds.), *Dialogue and culture* (pp. 155–175). Amsterdam and Philadelphia: John Benjamins Publishing.

Bolton, K., & Davis, D. R. (2006). A content analysis of world Englishes. *World Englishes, 25*(1), 5–6. https://doi.org/10.1111/j.0083-2919.2006.00442.x

Bourne, J. S. (2016). Exploring international communication challenges: A case study on Chinese–English interpreting. *China Media Research, 12*(1), 14–24.

Bowe, H., & Martin, K. (2007). *Communication across cultures: Mutual understanding in a global world*. Cambridge, New York and Melbourne: Cambridge University Press.

Bowe, H., Martin, K., & Manns, H. (2014). *Communication across cultures: Mutual understanding in a global world* (2nd ed.). Melbourne: Cambridge University Press.

Burridge, K., & Stebbins, T. N. (2016). *For the love of language: An introduction to linguistics*. Cambridge, New York, Melbourne, New Delhi, and Singapore: Cambridge University Press.

Chen, P. (1999). *Modern Chinese: History and sociolinguistics*. Cambridge and Melbourne: Cambridge University Press.

Chinese Language Website: Eight Major Chinese Dialects. (2019). Retrieved August 19, 2019, from www.cnlangs.com/news-342.html

Clyne, M. (1994). *Intercultural communication at work: Cultural values in discourse*. Cambridge and New York: Cambridge University Press.

Ethnologue: Languages of the World. (2019). Retrieved from www.ethnologue.com/language/eng

Farini, F. (2016). Meanings and forms of intercultural coordination: The pragmatics of interpreter-mediated healthcare communication. In F. Bianchi & S. Gesuato (Eds.), *Pragmatic issues in specialized communicative contexts*. Online Publication. Utrecht: Brill.

Gavioli, L., & Baraldi, C. (2011). Interpreter-mediated interaction in healthcare and legal settings: Talk organization, context and the achievement of intercultural communication. *Interpreting, 13*(2), 205–233. https://doi.org/10.1075/intp.13.2.03gav

Gu, Y. (1990). Politeness phenomena in modern Chinese. *Journal of Pragmatics, 14*(2), 237–257.

Hall, E. T. (1976). *Beyond culture*. New York: Random House, Inc.

Halliday, M. A. K. (1978). *Language as social semiotic: The social interpretation of language and meaning*. London. Arnold.

Hlavac, J., Xu, Z., & Xiong, D. Y. (2015). Intercultural pragmatics at work: (Self-)perceptions of intercultural behaviour of Chinese and English speakers and interpreters in healthcare interactions. *Intercultural Pragmatics, 12*(1), 91–118. https://doi.org/10.1515/ip-2015-0004

Hofstede, G. (1991). *Cultures and organizations: Software of the mind.* London: McGraw-Hill.

Hofstede, G. (2011). Dimensionalizing cultures: The Hofstede model in context. *Online Readings in Psychology and Culture, 2*(1), 1–26. https://doi.org/10.9707/2307-0919.1014

Hymes, D. H. (1972). On communicative competence. In J. B. Pride & J. Holmes (Eds.), *Sociolinguistics: Selected readings* (pp. 269–293). Harmondsworth: Penguin.

Hymes, D. H. (1974). *Foundations in sociolinguistics: An ethnographic approach.* Philadelphia: The University of Pennsylvania Press.

Jääskeläinen, R. (2007). The changing position of "the Translator" in research and in practice. *Journal of Translation Studies, 10*(1), 1–15.

Kachru, B. B. (Ed.). (1982). *The other tongue: English across cultures.* Urbana and Chicago: University of Illinois Press.

Kachru, B. B., & Smith, L. (1985). Editorial. *World Englishes, 4*(2), 209–212. https://doi.org/10.1111/j.1467-971x.1985.tb00408.x

Kecskes, I. (2004). Editorial: Lexical merging, conceptual blending, and cultural crossing. *Intercultural Pragmatics, 1*(1), 1–26. https://doi.org/10.1515/iprg.2004.005

Kecskes, I. (2011). Intercultural pragmatics. In D. Archer & P. Grundy (Eds.), *The pragmatics reader* (pp. 371–384). London and New York: Routledge.

Kecskes, I. (2013). Intercultures, encyclopedic knowledge, and cultural models. In F. Sharifian & M. Jamarani (Eds.), *Language and intercultural communication in the new era* (pp. 39–59). New York and London: Routledge.

Kirkpatrick, A. (2007). *World Englishes: Implications for intercultural communication and English language teaching.* Cambridge and New York: Cambridge University Press.

Kirkpatrick, A. (2010). Introduction. In A. Kirkpatrick (Ed.), *The Routledge handbook of world Englishes* (pp. 1–14). London and New York: Routledge.

Kirkpatrick, A., & Xu, Z. (2001, April/May/June). The new language law of the People's Republic of China. *Australian Language Matters*, 14–15.

Lakoff, R. T. (1973). *The logic of politeness: Or minding your p's and q's.* Paper presented at the Proceedings of the ninth regional meeting of the Chicago Linguistic Society, University of Chicago.

Law of the People's Republic of China on the Standard Spoken and Written Chinese Language. (2019). Retrieved February 13, 2019, from www.gov.cn/english/laws/2005-09/19/content_64906.htm

Leech, G. N. (1983). *Principles of pragmatics.* London: Longman.

Li, C. N., & Thompson, S. A. (1981). *Mandarin Chinese: A functional reference grammar.* Berkeley, Los Angeles and London: University of California Press.

Li, W. (2018). Translanguaging as a practical theory of language. *Applied Linguistics, 39*(1), 9–30. https://doi.org/10.1093/applin/amx039

Lo Bianco, J. (1987). *National policy on languages.* Canberra: Australian Government Publishing Service.

Lo Bianco, J. (1988). Multiculturalism and the national policy on languages. *Journal of Intercultural Studies, 9*(1), 25–38. https://doi.org/10.1080/07256868.1988.9963326

Lü, S., & Li, S. (2012). The role shift of the interpreter to a cultural mediator: From the perspective of cultural orientations and contexting. *Babel, 58*(2), 145–163. https://doi.org/10.1075/babel.58.2.02lu

Meier, A. J. (1995). Defining politeness: Universality in appropriateness. *Language Sciences, 17*(4), 345–356. https://doi.org/10.1016/0388-0001(95)00019-4

Miletich, M. (2015). Accounting for nonverbal communication in interpreter-mediated events in healthcare settings. *Translation and Translanguaging in Multilingual Contexts, 1*(2), 162–181. https://doi.org/10.1075/ttmc.1.2.02mil

Moody, A., Robinson, J., Xu, Z., & Meierkord, C. (2018). Editorial. *English Today*, *34*(4), 1–2. https://doi.org/10.1017/s026607841800041x

Müller, F. E. (2001). Inter- and intra-cultural aspects of dialogue-interpreting. In A. Di Luzio, S. Günthner, & F. Orletti (Eds.), *Culture in communication: Analyses of intercultural situations* (pp. 245–270). Amsterdam and Philadelphia: John Benjamins Publishing.

Ozolins, U. (2016). The myth of the myth of invisibility? *Interpreting*, *18*(2), 273–284. https://doi.org/10.1075/intp.18.2.06ozo

Proshina, Z. G. (2014). Language revolution behind the cultural curtain. *World Englishes*, *33*(1), 1–8. https://doi.org/10.1111/weng.12051

Pym, A. (2006). On the social and the cultural in translation studies. In A. Pym, M. Shlesinger, & Z. ZJettmarová (Eds.), *Sociocultural aspects of translating and interpreting*. Amsterdam and Philadelphia: John Benjamins.

Sharifian, F. (2011). *Cultural conceptualizations and language*. Amsterdam and Philadelphia: John Benjamins Publishing Company.

Sharifian, F. (2017a). Cultural linguistics: The state of the art. In F. Sharifian (Ed.), *Advances in cultural linguistics* (pp. 1–28). Singapore: Springer.

Sharifian, F. (Ed.). (2017b). *Advances in cultural linguistics*. Singapore: Springer.

Spencer-Oatey, H., & Xing, J. (2009). The impact of culture on interpreter behaviour. In H. Kotthoff & H. Spencer-Oatey (Eds.), *Handbook of intercultural communication* (pp. 219–236). Berlin and New York: De Gruyter Mouton.

Xu, Z. (2004). From "Recessive" to "Dominant" linguistic and cultural norms: Moving out of the comfort zone. In G. Pass & D. Woods (Eds.), *Alchemies: Community exchanges*. Perth: Black Swan Press.

Xu, Z. (2009). Linguistic, cultural and identity issues in Englishization of Pŭtōnghuà. In T. Kwok-kan (Ed.), *Englishization in Asia: Language and cultural issues* (pp. 119–139). Hong Kong: Open University of Hong Kong Press.

Xu, Z. (2010). *Chinese English: Features and implications*. Hong Kong: Open University of Hong Kong Press.

Xu, Z., Leung, J., Hall, M., Jafari, J., & Pour, M. S. (2019). Linguistic diversity on an Australian university campus: An ethnographic case study. In J. Jenkins & A. Mauranen (Eds.), *Linguistic diversity on the EMI campus: Insider accounts of the use of English and other languages in universities within Asia, Australasia, and Europe* (pp. 197–225). London and New York: Routledge.

Xu, Z., & Sharifian, F. (2018). Cultural conceptualizations of Chinese zodiac animals in Chinese English. *World Englishes*, *37*(4), 590–606. https://doi.org/10.1111/weng.12351

Yu, K. A. (2011). Culture-specific concepts of politeness: Indirectness and politeness in English, Hebrew, and Korean requests. *Intercultural Pragmatics*, *8*(3), 385–409. https://doi.org/10.1515/iprg.2011.018

Zhu, H. (2014). *Exploring intercultural communication: Language in action*. London and New York: Routledge.

3 The interpreted interaction

The interpreted interaction is a situation par excellence to examine how Chinese and English speakers bring their own discourse-pragmatic norms and notions of intercultural communication to an encounter with a speaker of the other language. In interactions in which there are at least two participants who do not share a common language, inter-lingual mediation is required for the participants to communicate with each other effectively. We commence with a brief discussion of some of the things that can and do happen in mediated encounters. The task of inter-lingual and inter-cultural transfer, in a stereotypical sense, is left up to the interpreter, and so the interpreter typically provides 'on-the-spot', relayed renditions of others' spoken (or signed) texts. In reality at least one of the participants present may sometimes have some proficiency in the language of the other party, and may seek to actively use this in the form of greetings, brief 'small talk', or through the occasional use of words or phrases. These may be attempts to 'tell something' to the other party in a direct sense, i.e. to convey referential content. More often the motivation is not content-focused; instead, it is inter-personally focused, and speakers index others' languages usually as a means to show their recognition of the other party's linguistic repertoire and/or background. This is a classic example of a person using their intercultural agency and employing an intercultural strategy. It is up to the interpreter, using their linguistic skills to evaluate if what was said was comprehensible and pragmatically appropriate, and for the interpreter, using their inter-cultural skills to evaluate whether an intervention (e.g. repetition or 'correction' of what was said) is warranted or not. Even where parties to an interpreted interaction have no knowledge of each other's languages, they may avail themselves of para- and extra-linguistic cues to signal acknowledgement and alignment to the shared goals of the interaction. This is another instance of parties to an interpreted interaction applying inter-cultural agency and employing an intercultural strategy. Thus, we find that linguistically mediated interactions offer a gamut of features in which the interpreter is the main protagonist enabling cross-linguistic communication and practising intercultural agency, but not necessarily the only protagonist doing this.

This chapter commences with an outline of contemporary interpreting: models, fields, modes, situational and positional aspects in section 3.1. This is followed by a discussion of the role(s) of the interpreter in section 3.2. The areas focused on most in this chapter are actual settings of interpreting and section 3.3 provides coverage of a selection of these: conference, diplomatic, media, business, police, legal and court, and healthcare interpreting. Section 3.4 concludes this chapter with a discussion on culture, cultural mediation and inter-lingual mediation provided by interpreters as well as non-interpreters. In each of the sections and subsections, we typically present data from Chinese settings, then English-speaking settings.

3.1   What is interpreting?

In a basic sense, interpreting is understood as the transfer of speech or signing from one language into another. Conceptualizations of interpreting needed to go beyond seeing it as 'oral translation' (which also needlessly excluded sign language interpreting) to include the feature of time pressure and the little or no chance for correction or revision (Kade, 1967). A definition that reflects this is from Pöchhacker (2016, p. 11): "Interpreting is a form of translation in which a first and final rendition in another language is produced on the basis of a one-time presentation of an utterance in a source language". In this book the focus will be on spoken-language interpreting and discussion and examples are from spoken-language interpreting only. But much of what is contained here may be relevant to sign language interpreting, either between spoken Mandarin and Signed Chinese, or between spoken English and a signed language such as American Sign Language (ASL), or even between spoken Mandarin and ASL, or between spoken English and Signed Chinese, where an interpreter has multiple working languages. However, there are features specific to Deaf people and people with limited hearing on the one hand, and features specific to the work of signed language interpreters working with them and hearing people that this book does not address. (See Napier, 2004; Xiao & Yu, 2009; Xiao & Li, 2013 for descriptions of signed language interpreting, including Chinese Sign Language interpreting.)

   Proficiency in two languages is certainly axiomatic to interpreting. This led some earlier translation researchers to coin the term 'natural translation', and to contend that "translating is coextensive with bilingualism" (Harris & Sherwood, 1978, p. 156), applying this also to the situation of language-learners where they engage in self-directed translation activities (cf. Müller, 1989). Implicit in Harris and Sherwood's (1978) descriptions of this was the notion of 'enablement', i.e. those with bilingual proficiency felt obliged or compelled to provide inter-lingual transfer. But the attribute of bi- or multi-lingualism alone does not automatically endow a person with the ability to interpret. To be sure inter-lingual transfer is something that many bi- and multi-linguals engage in, at the level of words, or phrases, but few are required to transfer whole stretches of speech or act as a mediator for others through lengthy communicative interactions. Those bi- or multi-linguals who do this on an impromptu or spontaneous basis, do not see themselves as interpreters, nor do others usually see them as interpreters. Where this happens we usually speak of this as ad-hoc interpreting (see section 3.4). Bilinguals may sometimes volunteer or be called on to mediate between others who do not have a common language. In either case the motivation for this was social responsibility and/or activism, whether this was felt by the bilingual protagonist him-/herself, or imposed on him/her by another.

While bilingualism is a pre-requisite for inter-lingual transfer, not all bilinguals, however, are amenable to providing inter-linguistic transfer for others, and a sense of duty or desire to assist the communication needs of others is no guarantee that a person can interpret for others. Valdés and Angelelli (2003) provide an overview of definitions of bilingualism and the relationship between bilingualism and inter-lingual transfer. They note that interpreting or 'natural translation' is *not* an automatic by-product of bilingualism. Some form of focused practice or training is typically required for formal instances of interpreting.

Historically, interpreters or those who have provided inter-lingual transfer for others were usually 'self-taught', and often viewed interpreting as but one role that they enacted alongside or as part of their role as, for example, public servants, diplomats or traders. Those practitioners who reflected on their interpreting practice and who described, generalised and analysed the skills that they employed when interpreting became the early founders of interpreting practice and pedagogy in the mid-twentieth century (Herbert, 1952; Seleskovitch, 1978).

The first formal training programs for interpreters were established in Europe in the 1940s and 1950s. Their approach to interpreting reflected the legacy of the first trainers and the emergent image at the time of the interpreter as a linguistic intermediary in political, diplomatic and business settings. In these 'early years' interpreter training focused on the transfer of speech in inter-social settings; that is, between interlocutors from different societies but with an equivalent status, e.g. diplomats, government officials, businesspeople. Technological advances in the second half of the twentieth century saw the development of simultaneous interpreting equipment. This mode of interpreting became the aspirational skill to be acquired by trainees in what was still a 'young profession'. Conference, business and diplomatic settings became the workplace of trained interpreters where ethical principles such as impartiality, neutrality, accuracy (fidelity to the source speech) and completeness (absence of additions, omissions or alterations) were the performance skills sought after.

The association with technology, together with the image of the interpreter as a highly skilled, autonomous and independent professional, 'seamlessly' transferring speech from one language into another led to the view that interpreting is a 'conduit-like' activity. Some were even more graphic in the 'mechanical' description that they awarded to interpreters: "the interpreter's function in general is comparable to that of a machine, giving a more or less literal translation of what is said in language A into language B" (Knapp-Potthoff & Knapp, 1986, p. 152). The conduit view suggests that interpreting is some form of "verbatim translation". However, this notion of cross-linguistic "literalism" is an unworkable standard, and it has now given way to perceptions and self-descriptions of interpreters as "communication facilitators", whose primary role is inter-lingual transfer but with greater visibility to other parties (Angelelli, 2000; Roy, 2000) (see 3.2).

3.1.1   *Theoretical conceptualizations of interpreting*

This section contains a brief overview of some of the main concepts and constructs and information on some of the theoretical models that have been developed to more closely describe the cognitive, interpersonal, and linguistic (language-transfer) features of interpreting. Consecutive and simultaneous interpreting have been the basis for models that describe the cognitive processes of interpreting. Such models initially focused on inter-lingual transfer only, with less focus on situational and interaction-specific features. The most prominent first model was Seleskovitch's (1962) *théorie du sens* ('theory of sense') that foregrounds the interpreter's understanding and perception of the 'sense' of the source speaker's speech, and that this is the key attribute of interpreting, not a focus on transcoding the source speech's form. Seleskovitch terms the 'capturing of sense from the form' as 'deverbalization'. The parallels between Seleskovitch's notion of form and the notion of locutionary act from Speech Act Theory on the one hand, and her notion of sense and illocutionary force on the other are clear. Within the *théorie du sens* tradition, Seleskovitch (1978) and Lederer (1978/2002) distinguish the following cognitive processes as 'continuous': listening, comprehension, conceptualization (matching input with prior knowledge) and expression (output based on retrieval from short-term memory). These, as well as other operations are accompanied by features such as self-monitoring and awareness of situation.

Seleskovitch and Lederer's model is the basis for Ginori and Scimone's (1995) definition of interpreting as an activity that consists of at least three processes: comprehension, conversion and delivery. While these descriptions, as well as that of Kirchhoff (1976/2002) locate the cognitive processes operating, they remain descriptive and do not offer an interpretive or even predictive picture of *how* optimal interpreting occurs (or does not occur) or *why* it occurs (or does not occur). The problem of multiple task performance, with the activation of many operations concurrently, is the basis of Gile's (1995a, 1995b, 2009) effort models. Gile (2009) contends that while capabilities can be increased and cognitive abilities augmented through systematic practice, there are finite limits to the enactment of skills contemporaneously. In other words, where the source speech is particularly rapid or incoherent, this will place increased demands on the interpreter's "listening and analysis" skills and possibly have negative effects on other areas of online skill activation, such as "memory" or "production" (Gile, 1999). The ability to co-ordinate these abilities at the same time is itself recognized as an ability, i.e. "coordination effort" which is added to the activities that an interpreter is engaging in online, while simultaneously interpreting: interpreting = listening and analysis + production + memory + coordination effort; or in other words "total available capacity must be at least equal to total requirements" (Gile, 1999, p. 165). The model can be applied pre-emptively where interpreters know that a rapid speaker or a complex speech awaits them, but more often retrospectively as an appraisal tool to account for why performance in certain segments may have been optimal while in others less than optimal. To be sure the notion of *finite* capacity is a useful one to remind us of the limits of 'multi-skilling' when an interpreter is working online.

Others who have provided cognitive-based descriptions that foreground the mental processes of interpreting have also been cognisant of features other than cognitive information processing skills. For example, cognitive processing researchers remarked that "linguistic, motivational, situational and a host of other factors cannot be ignored" (Gerver, 1976, p. 167), while Kirchhoff (1976/2002), although focusing mainly on encoding and transmission identifies not only 'verbal' but also 'non-verbal' signals and information that are present in interactions.

From universities and specialist schools that trained interpreters, what has emerged over the last 20 years in Interpreting Studies as a discipline is that it encompasses not only pedagogy but also research in interpreting practice and engagement with practitioners. Within the discipline there are numerous practitioner-researchers, which led to Gile's coining of the term "*practisearcher*" (Gile, 1995b, p. 16) to refer to those academics and practising interpreters who examine and analyse interpreter practice (their own and/or that of their colleagues). Interpreting is both an applied skill as well as a research area, and the experience of most interpreting trainers as practitioners, researchers *and* as trainers provides for an approach that Orlando (2016, p. 81) describes as a "three-way nexus" that is not commonly present in other disciplines.

In the last 20 years a broadening of interpreting practice, training and research has occurred beyond the conference, diplomatic or business settings, to settings such as education, the courtroom, general and mental health, emergency services, media and faith-based organizations. This has become known as the 'social turn' of Interpreting Studies (Garzone & Viezzi, 2002; Pöchhacker, 2006). Research within the discipline now encompasses all sorts of spoken and sign language mediation, and looks at instances of inter-lingual transfer with a view to the (micro-)sociology of the interaction and/or the (macro-)sociology of societal institutions. The disciplines of sociology of interaction and anthropology have influenced Interpreting Studies so that institutional contexts, in particular publicly funded social institutions such as healthcare, education, the legal system, are viewed themselves as the distinguishing features of public service interpreting (cf. Inghilleri, 2003).

Further to this, the 'social turn' has enabled investigations into macro- and micro-level social dynamics that pertain to interpreting (and how linguistic mediation and linguistically mediated situations re-shape social relations). It has also allowed a re-appraisal of phenomena that have never been absent from mediated situations: acknowledgement of social and power relations, advocacy and even activism. Social responsibility, often associated previously perhaps with volunteer or non-professional interpreting, is re-emerging as a notion that can be located in many forms of professional linguistic mediation (Drugan & Tipton, 2017). It can be examined as a macro-level feature structurally present across a variety of fields and situations, as well as a micro-level feature enacted through mediators' moves enabling all participants' participation in an interaction.

The social turn in Interpreting Studies also enabled a 'freer' and closer association with the discipline of intercultural communication. The conventional view within pedagogy of Interpreting Studies was that interpreting is typically performed between speakers who have little or no proficiency in each other's languages and whose linguistic profile is co-terminous with their ethnicity, place of residence, and cultural mores. A stereotypical example of this would be an interpreter interpreting for a monolingual Chinese businessperson living in China and an American, monolingual Anglophone businessperson from the United States who is visiting China. In this vein, studies in the discipline of cross-cultural communication are commonly premised on speakers displaying the pragmatic-discourse features characteristic of their ethno-cultural group only, with instances of miscommunication often attributed to the way speakers interpret others' pragmatic-discourse features.

In a similar way, the assumption that speakers who are allophones to each other (i.e. neither speaker speaks the language of the other) at the same time remain 'impervious' to the speech and other forms of behaviour displayed by the other party is also questionable. There are various degrees of engagement that allophone users of interpreting services show towards each other. These range at one extreme from complete non-engagement that includes avoidance of eye contact, disregard for prosodic and paralinguistic features of the other's speech and appearing 'not to hear', 'not to listen to' or 'not to see' what the other is saying or how they are say-ing it. At the other extreme, allophone interlocutors may actively engage with each other (usually via paralinguistic strategies) to achieve their own co-negotiation of the meaning of individual conversational sequences. Of course, allophone speakers may engage with each other in ways that are anywhere between these two extremes. In any case, the interpreter is rarely the sole negotiator of meaning in interpreted interactions and the role of co-negotiator and co-constructor of meaning is enacted by allophone speakers as well. In this way we see the interpreted interaction also as an intercultural communication setting in which interlocutors not only display their own and observe others' discourse-pragmatic features that may be culturally bound, but as a setting in which the meaning of the other interlocutor's discourse-pragmatic features *and* the interpreter's target speech are evaluated and negotiated. Allophone interlocutors may themselves apply their knowledge of intercultural communication towards each other and the interpreter in the interpreted interac-tion. The interpreter should not be presumed to be the only protagonist with inter-cultural communication competence.

3.1.2   *Fields and modes of interpreting*

The most conspicuous attribute of the 'social turn' in Interpreting Studies in the 1990s has been the study of emergence and establishment of public service inter-preting (or community interpreting) in predominantly Anglophone countries of the New World since the 1970s and 1980s, especially in Canada (Carr, Roberts, Dufour, & Steyn, 1997) and Australia (Gentile, Ozolins, & Vasilakakos, 1996). The establishment of public-service interpreting occurred as a result of egalitarian social policies that promoted access and equity for residents who faced linguistic barriers. The popular concept of what interpreting was has widened from confer-ence and diplomatic interpreting to include linguistic mediation in the following areas: public service (i.e. interactions with government-employed personnel and others in areas of public administration such as housing, welfare, counselling etc.); education; healthcare; legal (police, lawyer-client, courtroom, prison) and faith-based organizations. Public service interpreting has become a hypernym that encompasses all forms of interpreting other than conference, business, media and diplomatic interpreting (Corsellis, 2008; Valero-Garcés, 2014; Hlavac, 2015). The 'social turn' was a development that simply 'caught up' with what had started to become an otherwise very commonplace occurrence. Public service interpreting is now a variety of interpreting commonly practised across Europe, North America, Australia and New Zealand, and regions of Asia, the Middle East and Africa with allophone migrant populations or groups of people displaced by conflict or natural disaster. In China it is an emerging area of interpreting work (Lai, 2017).

The physical environment and the discourse features that public service interpreting takes place in determines the mode of interpreting used: typically this is dialogue interpreting (also known as liaison interpreting), sometimes with long consecutive interpreting. At the same time, sight translation, often with little or no preparation time, is also a characteristic of public service interpreting where written texts such as legal subpoena, an insurance policy, a school student's report or directions of use for medication are transferred verbally into the other language. Simultaneous interpreting occurs less often, but is common in court interpreting or at information sessions where verbal text is uni-directionally delivered to many groups concurrently. In these cases chuchotage is often employed. Simultaneous interpreting also occurs in mental health interpreting. In contrast to conference or diplomatic interpreting, public service interpreting takes place as an intra-social activity, i.e. in general, interlocutors belong to the same (local) society in terms of place of residence.

The face-to-face and dialogic nature of public service interpreting brings with it dynamics that are often less present in conference or government settings. These include procedural steps such as the interpreter's (self-)introduction, explication of his/her role to others and assurances of confidentiality as well requests on length of turns and direction of gaze. There are discourse management features such as explicit co-ordination of the interaction by the interpreter (Wadensjö, 1998) that is necessitated either due to possible translation problems or problems in the way that others sequence their turns. Translation problems may precipitate requests for repetition or clarification; problems in turn sequences may compel the interpreter to intervene in overlapping speech by employing facial or hand signals or to verbally interrupt. Minimal responses typical of dialogues, e.g. *okay, mhm* are employed by some interpreters as a management strategy, while other interpreting theorists such as Baraldi and Gavioli (2012) locate clarifications, expansions and repairs as features of some interpreters' management of the interaction.

3.1.3   Situational and positional aspects of interpreting

The physical positioning of the interpreter vis-à-vis other interlocutors or audience members is important as a logistical aspect of interpreting that has a direct bearing on interpreter performance. For conference interpreters the line of vision to speaker and audience members is vital. For business interpreters visual and aural contact with others is important, as well as features relating to protocol and role-explication. Diplomatic interpreters must remain inconspicuous while retaining clear access to source speakers' speech. Public service interpreting typically takes place in a triangular configuration where the interpreter occupies equal distance to the two other interlocutors; a similar principle applies in multi-party interactions (Wadensjö, 2001). In court the interpreter is typically seated next to the interlocutor/s who does not speak the language of the court, using chuchotage with him/her/them, and otherwise directing his/her voice to all others present when interpreting into the other direction. In some therapy interactions the interpreter may be seated away from a patient, or even behind him/her, or next to the therapist (e.g. Wiener & Rivera, 2004, p. 97; but cf. Bot, 2005; Pokorn, 2015). The physical constellation of the interaction brings with it the question of proxemics, i.e. at points throughout the interaction such as the initial coming together of all participants, greetings, invitations or signals to sit down, stand or physically move, body movement/animation of all interlocutors including the interpreter (kinesics), leave-taking norms and disengagement. Other features such as haptics (touch) and eye contact are features of interlocutors' displayed behaviour that interpreters may have to include in their management or co-ordination of the interaction.

3.2   The role(s) of the interpreter

Interpreters are endowed with not only linguistic skills but ideally also knowledge of the cultural practices and pragmatic norms of speakers with whom they work. This knowledge of pragmatics enables interpreters to understand not only the referential content of speech, but to relate their speech and other forms of behaviour to speakers' intended actions.

The role of the interpreter is often not well understood by others – that is, those who are unused to working with interpreters may not have clear expectations about the interpreter's impartiality, about their ability to maintain confidentiality or about certain ways that they work. They may request from the interpreter actions that are not associated with inter-lingual transfer, such as providing advice, giving an appraisal, or acting on their behalf. The AUSIT Code of Ethics in Australia has a principle that addresses this uncertainty – *clarity of role boundaries* – in which the following is recommended, particular in reference to acting on behalf of others:

> Interpreters and translators maintain clear boundaries between their task as facilitators of communication through message transfer and any tasks that may be undertaken by other parties involved in the assignment.
>
> (AUSIT, 2012, p. 5)

If an interpreter considers that they need to intervene in an interaction, the implication of the (Australian AUSIT) Code of Ethics warning is that they should signal to all other parties that they are doing so as a participant in the interaction who is stepping out of their usual or sanctioned role. The question of intervening in an interaction is one that interpreters may often pose to themselves. For example, there may be discourse-pragmatic or para-linguistic norms displayed by one speaker that strongly diverge from those of the other speaker, and which could be misunderstood by the other speaker in a way that is offensive to them or perilous to the interaction overall. If they decide to intervene, the interpreter is using his/her knowledge of pragmatics of both groups to 'step out' of their position as inter-lingual mediator and to alert interlocutors to pragmatic features (e.g. eye contact, proxemics, tone, rhetorical features) displayed by others whose illocutionary force is significantly different from those familiar to speakers of the other language, i.e. so different that it may inhibit their ability to comprehend the interpreter's interpretation that is otherwise fidelitous to the illocutionary force of source speech. This may occur pre-emptively where interpreters foresee significant differences in the anticipated forms used by speakers and in the intended and perceived illocutionary force of these. It can occur retrospectively as well.

This kind of 'stepping out' is an *intervention* that the interpreter can, but need not make. The decision to do so is based on the interpreter's on-the-spot assessment of the situation and belief that forms of behaviour displayed could impede or constrain reception of the interpreter's interpretations. The interpreter exercises his/her judgement in doing so, and there are inevitably differences amongst interpreters as to whether they would do this or not. Ethical codes (e.g. AUSIT Code of Ethics, 2012) advise the interpreter to signal to others that they are stepping out of their normative role of inter-lingual mediator when this occurs. A nuanced discussion of the interpreter's management of the interaction and their own 'presentation of self' as an attribute of their role is provided by Llewellyn-Jones and Lee (2014) (see 3.4.1). Instances of an interpreter stepping out are perhaps the most conspicuous examples of intercultural agency. It is likely though that intercultural agency is most often employed or exercised in an embedded way, i.e. the practice of intercultural strategies is evident within the delivery of the interpreter's target texts.

Accompanying the professionalization of interpreting in the twentieth century, the role of the interpreter became codified in specific terms that emphasized the "neutral" and "conduit" position of an interpreter as a provider of accurate, complete and faithful renditions into another language (Pöchhacker, 2016, p. 170). The role of interpreter, which bilinguals have assumed in various contexts throughout history, has been closely linked with intermediary functions such as those of a messenger, guide and negotiator, which are discussed further in the following section 3.2.1.

3.2.1   Contemporary role(s) of the interpreter

This section focuses on features related to the settings and situations that interpreters work in. In most fields of interpreting, but especially in the field of public service interpreting, the 'local' or 'enacted' role of the interlocutors using interpreting services in the interaction, in general terms, is likely to shape if not determine their behaviour, i.e. their role is strongly based on how they come to an interaction – as a customer service officer, mental health nurse, undertaker etc. The occupation or employment profile of a participant influences his/her behaviour and these also influence the behaviour of others towards them. Further, other macro-social features such as gender, age, ethnicity, class and physical ability, along with country/region of origin and educational level, are never completely disregarded, while other more micro-social ones such as experience level, personality, disposition, displayed work ethic or specialist knowledge may or may not be openly practised and recognized by others. In any case, all of these attributes can and usually influence participants' behaviour.

Within sociology and psychology, there are two 'views' or 'gazes' that can be made of human beings: the 'self-directed gaze' or ideographic dimension, i.e. 'How I see myself'; and the 'gaze from another' or nomothetic dimension, i.e. 'How others see me' (cf. Mead, 1965). These two dimensions represent two separate perspectives, but they need not be different from each other. There are often correlations between the evaluations made about the same person due to the influence that self-representation has on external perception. In other words how a person sees him-/herself influences how s/he interacts with others, and this subsequently influences how others view him/her. Within linguistics and discourse analysis, this dual dimension of perspective underpins the distinction between our understanding of the locutionary and illocutionary force of utterances (those aspects of speech that are authored and controlled by the speaker or 'self') and their perlocutionary force (those aspects of speech that are defined by reference to the effect it has on the hearer, that are controlled by the 'other').

Our discussion of roles is informed by Goffman's (1961) definitions of role on a continuum ranging from (macro-level) *normative role* to *typical role* (referring to variation from the *normative role* over time, including behaviours that are possibly expected but not considered obligatory) to *role performance* (the manifestation of how a person enacts a role that reflects the dynamics of the situation and specific characteristics such as aptitude, personality and so on). The concept of normative role is a top-down one, akin to the duty statement that may accompany an employment position or a code of general behaviour contained in a profession's code of ethics. The notion of role performance is a bottom-up one that is based on a dynamic examination of role. In relation to the category of *role performance*, in later work Goffman (1981) distinguished participants according to their role as *hearers* or *speakers*, with the latter group being further differentiated as *animator, author* and *principal*, depending on the alignment, by way of *footing*, shown towards the production of an utterance.

Goffman's categories have been adopted and adapted by others who have conducted discourse-based examinations in Interpreting Studies (e.g. Wadensjö, 1998; Mason, 2009; Takimoto & Koshiba, 2009). Further analytical models have been proposed in relation to speaker and hearer roles (e.g. Levinson, 1988), some addressing specifically the position of interpreters (e.g. Edmonson, 1986) with Pöchhacker (2012) providing a detailed description and comparison of these, with a selected application of these to his own examples of communicative events featuring interpreting. In an interactively oriented approach Wadensjö (1998, pp. 91–92) locates hearer roles congruent to those of the speaker, this time looking at the way interpreters as listeners align to the talk of others and to their own talk. The *reception format* proposed by Wadensjö ranges from *reporter* who takes on minimal responsibility for the content and the progression of the interaction, to roles where greater responsibility is taken on: *recapitulator* and *responder*. Wadensjö's (1998) description of the intercultural (Russian-Swedish) differences in responses to yes-no questions and how an interpreter may deal with these has become a 'textbook' example of intercultural communication in the interpreted interaction. Other descriptions of the interpreter's role are provided by Angelelli (2004) and Baraldi and Gavioli (2012).

Goffman's notion of footings has been further developed by interpreting researchers such as Merlini and Favaron (2005) who distinguish a fine-grained set of seven footings that are distinguished not only on the basis of the interpreter as speaker, but on the basis of the utterances of other interlocutors who include interpreters as addressees. These are *reporter* (as the "unmarked" alignment with the interpreting hearing and using the first person) to *narrator* (use of third person), *pseudo-co-principal* (use of first person plural), *recapitulator* (where the interpreter is the direct addressee), to *principal* (interpreter assuming role of initiator of the utterance) to *responder* (interpreter reacting to another's utterance which may or may not be addressed to him/her). We employ Merlini and Favaron's categories of footing in some of the examples of interpreting presented in the following sections – see Figure 3.1.

Primary Speaker	Interpreter		Footing
	Initiator	请问你可以去那边吗？ Will you move over there, please?	Principal
Who will take me there?	Interlocutor	医生会。 The doctor will.	Responder
(Tell her) I will ask her some questions now.	*Translator — unaddressed addressed*	现在我将问你一些问题。 Now I will ask you some questions.	Direct Recapitulator
		（她说）她将问你一些问题。 (She says) she will ask you some questions.	Indirect Recapitulator
Now I will ask you some questions		现在我将问你一些问题。 Now I will ask you some questions.	Reporter
		（她说）她将问你一些问题。 (She says) she will ask you some questions.	Narrator
		现在我们将问你一些问题。 Now we will ask you some questions.	Pseudo co-principal

Figure 3.1 Categories of footing

Source: (Adapted from: Merlini & Favaron, 2005, p. 280)

Features of speakers' intercultural agency are also revealed through their conceptualization of roles (in terms of 'footing') that they assume in interpreted interactions: as speakers they are likely to be animator, author and principal; as hearers they may feel that they are addressed (as 'responders' or 'understanders') or unaddressed (as 'attenders' or 'uptakers') while the allophone speaker is speaking.

3.3.   Settings of interpreting

Spoken interactions can be described in a variety of ways. In the presentation of different settings of interpreting, i.e. the contexts or domains in which interpreting occurs, we usually commence with a 'top-down' approach that lists macro-level features of speakers and of the context of the interaction which are based mainly on social categories. Where possible, we then look at how interactions can be described from a 'bottom-up' approach where analysis of the discourse of participants can often reveal how and why speakers behave in the way that they do. Our discussion here focuses on the following: speakers interacting with interpreters; speakers interacting with the allophone 'receivers' of their speech (via interlingual relay); interpreters interacting with the target language recipients of their target speech; both groups of speakers' interactions with each other, whether verbal or non-verbal; interpreters' interactional management of the mediated encounter.

In the sections that follow, we present data and excerpts from six different interpreting settings: conference interpreting (3.3.1); diplomatic interpreting (3.3.2); media interpreting (3.3.3), business interpreting (3.3.4) police, legal and court interpreting (3.3.5); and healthcare interpreting (3.3.6). These six fields are the most common and best-studied fields within which Chinese–English interpreters work. The last two sections, police, legal and court interpreting (3.3.5); and healthcare interpreting (3.3.6) are the two settings within the larger field of public service interpreting in which interpreters commonly work. This chapter does not present information on the following fields: social welfare interpreting; education interpreting; interpreting in faith-based organizations; sports interpreting; emergency services and humanitarian interpreting; or conflict zone interpreting, to name but a few. In some sections, there are excerpts presented from our sample of 33 Chinese–English interpreter informants. These excerpts are followed by the following details that identify the interpreter, i.e. '(Chi-Eng.inter.3)' relates to Chinese–English interpreter informant no. 3.

3.3.1   Conference interpreting

The term *conference interpreting* was probably first used in relation to large-scale bi- or multi-lateral meetings where consecutive interpreting was delivered contemporaneously from and into different languages for heads-of-state, senior government officials and/or diplomats. The term has become a hypernym that encompasses not only high-level conferences involving officials or diplomats, but specialists in particular areas of science, commerce or academia as well as other areas where the common feature is usually large-scale exchange across linguistic boundaries.

Conference interpreting has also become a synonym for *simultaneous* inter-preting, but it also encompasses 'long-consecutive interpreting' of monologues, particularly of welcome speeches, banquets, and other celebratory or group occa-sions. It is instructive to see how common it is cross-nationally. Quoting from statistics from the International Association of Conference Interpreters, the AIIC, Setton and Darwant (2016, p. 30) report that:

> inter-governmental organizations account for only about half of all AIIC con-ference interpreters' work in Europe . . ., and just 37% in North America, 30% in the Asia-Pacific and 20% in Latin America, with private sector meetings and other kinds of assignments making up the rest.

In contrast to public service interpreting, conference interpreting takes place in inter-social settings, i.e. international ones where participants are from different countries but congruent to each other in status, area of work, or shared knowledge. There is usually little scope (or allowance) for role explanation, while specific instructions or a briefing about the setting may be provided but is often not.

Two Chinese–English interpreters and AIIC members, Andrew Darwant and Hong Jiang, made the following comments about the settings and contexts that conference interpreters in mainland China work at the turn of the millennium:

> The government is by far the largest user of interpretation (and translation) at the start of the 21st century, and mostly meets its needs in-house. Almost every government entity, from the central government to the provinces and municipalities, and from ministries to agencies to state-owned enterprises, has a unit specifically in charge of dealing with the "non-Chinese" world.
>
> (Dawrant & Jiang, 2001)

According to China-based interpreters, nearly 20 years later it is reportedly still the case that government entities rely mostly on in-house interpreters for contacts with allophone speakers. Dawrant and Jiang (2001) follow the development of conference interpreting from before the 1990s where in-house or seconded inter-preters worked at the first international conferences, to a situation where by the 2000s, the bulk of conference work is being taken on by private, usually local but also some externally based interpreters:

> The most dynamic segment of the conference market, however, is the private market sector, as the international corporate community implements aggres-sive business plans in a growing and more open China, and becomes increas-ingly active in organising conferences, seminars, and workshops as part of its government and public relations campaigns.
>
> (Dawrant & Jiang, 2001)

While features relating to intercultural communication may appear more con-spicuous in the dyad or multi-party settings of public service interpreting,

Chinese–English conference interpreting offers an abundance of intercultural features. Setton (1993) mentioned a number of these: the use of honorifics, the status of the speaker, the linearity of discourse to name but a few. Setton (1993) also reminds us that these differences can almost be seen as paradigmatic, i.e. that the basis of many aspects of life and thought is underpinned by different conceptualizations:

> Chinese and European stocks of cultural referents, which form the backdrop of all thought and discourse, evolved separately over centuries from entirely different cosmogonies, generating parallel worlds of astronomy and mythology, different elemental, animal, plant, number, colour and anatomical symbolisms as well as different histories of art, science, and religion, all of which are alive and well in the Chinese and European languages today.
>
> (Setton, 1993, p. 243)

While Setton emphasizes the importance of culture, inter-cultural features appear to be afforded less attention in some China-based studies of Chinese–English conference interpreting. For example, Hu and Tao (2013, p. 628) present the Chinese–English Conference Interpreting Corpus that contains transcriptions of US and Chinese government press conferences between 1998 and 2008, with a total word count of 544,211 words. The functionality of the corpus is that it has segmentation of texts and narrow transcription that includes paralinguistic markers and hesitation phenomena. Source and target texts are aligned mainly to demonstrate structural features of the target texts, in particular use of verb tenses, passive, subordinate conjunctions and the structure of dependent clauses. Inter-cultural features of this variety of conference interpreting are not mentioned, but these are hardly likely to be absent, even if thematically, the source (and target) speakers are talking about the following: "economy, politics, diplomatic policy, national defence and related areas" (Hu & Tao, 2013, p. 628).

3.3.2   *Diplomatic interpreting*

The designation 'diplomatic interpreting' is based on the position of the interlocutors that the interpreter is working with: diplomats as a hypernym encompassing heads-of-state, members of the diplomatic corps and senior government officials. As stated, diplomatic interpreting can be considered a sub-set of conference interpreting because international conferences are a typical setting involving contact with diplomats. Diplomatic interpreting also has many similarities with media interpreting, as heads-of-state and senior officials most commonly communicate with the public via live spoken media.

Diplomatic interpreting is probably the most well-known interpreting setting. Anyone who has viewed meetings of state or diplomats without a common language assembled together will have noticed others who are either standing next to or slightly behind the dignitaries, whispering in to their ear in a lowered voice. Other familiar scenes are those interpreters sitting behind dignitaries with pencil and paper in hand, making notes to interpret consecutively, or sitting in a second row of chairs around a dining table and interpreting simultaneously. Being privy to such high level and confidential talks, and being able to seamlessly interpret in both simultaneous and long consecutive mode, diplomatic interpreters enjoy the admiration and curiosity of onlookers, and very often the focussed attention of intelligence services of not only their own country but of other countries as well.

We digress briefly here with details about or from diplomatic interpreters over the last seventy-five years. As in other forms of interpreting, it goes without saying that the principle of confidentiality is an assiduously observed principle. But that has not stopped some diplomatic interpreters from writing books about themselves, in part due to the market attractiveness of such an account from a key protagonist e.g. Berezhkov (1994) as Stalin's interpreter or Schmidt (2016) as Hitler's interpreter. These books market themselves as revealing the 'inside story' of world diplomacy. Of course, no diplomatic interpreter may reveal confidential details and these accounts fall short of revealing any secret information. This sub-genre of biographical literature contains a mix of personal reflections, carefully worded accounts of diplomats and politicians with whom the interpreter has worked, with occasional bylines on actual interpreting performance. Disappointingly for the trainee interpreter, these accounts usually devote little space to *how* they acquired their high-level skills. One exception to this is the account given by Harry Obst (2010), a German-English interpreter who was Head of the Office of Language Services of the Department of State in Washington from 1984 to 1997. He emphasizes natural academic curiosity as a pre-requisite, and the ability to absorb and build on acquired specialist knowledge in various areas as a key attribute for diplomatic interpreters. At times, Obst recalls being a key figure in not only language transfer, but also political decision-making:

> The president turned to me and asked, "Mr Interpreter, how shall we answer that?" Luckily, I had read and half memorized the military part of the briefing book for this meeting. I suggested an answer, and gave him the facts, numbers and names of weapons . . . [President Lyndon Baines] Johnson repeated what I had just told him, without missing a beat.
>
> (Obst, 2010, p. 227. Square brackets added.)

Diplomatic interpreters are also usually the only category of interpreters to gain popular media attention, either through alleged or real gaffs (Korchilov, 1997, pp. 300–306), or through their work that brings to public attention the semantic and discourse-pragmatic features of one language compared to another. Some popular attention has focussed on East Asian languages in particular, and the issue of how non-committal responses or polite refusals are conveyed and interpreted. For example, the Japanese term *zensho shimasu*, lit. gloss: 'I will dispose of this in a favourable way' was understood by American diplomats, at first, as an affirmative response. But, its closer meaning is a non-committal: 'I'll think about it' (Bumiller, 1991).

In diplomatic (and in non-diplomatic) interactions, euphemistic phrases such as 恐怕不太方便, lit. gloss 'Maybe it is inconvenient' are not uncommon. This phrase is a polite refusal to a question or request. In an attempt to consider an interpretation that optimally conveys the refusal contained in the euphemism Lü and Li (2012, p. 158) favour an interpretation such as 'No, I am not permitted to do that' as one that matches the illocutionary force of the source speech comment. A similarly euphemistic response such as 考虑考虑, lit. gloss '[I'll] think it over' is discussed by Setton (1994) and Lü and Li (2012). Lü and Li (2012, p. 159) suggest that an interpretation such as 'I am afraid we cannot agree at this time' matches the illocutionary force and register of the source speech more so than seemingly formal equivalents such as 'We'll think about it' or 'Your proposal needs further thought'.

Of particular interest are accounts from Chinese–English diplomatic interpreters such as Ji Chaozhu (2008) and Nancy Wensheng Tang (China Africa Magazine, 2017) who both grew up in the United States and returned to China in their early adulthood. Their familiarity with the political systems and the cultural mores of America and China endowed them with intercultural schemas that enabled them to recognize and understand discourse-pragmatic features specific to high-powered negotiations. An example of such types of discourse is a salutary speech. In Chinese culture, the celebratory nature of some high-level occasions can lead to quotes or even poems or prose being used in source speeches. One Chinese–English diplomatic interpreter, Chas Freeman, recalls the advance notice and preparation that he required before interpreting a celebratory toast to a high-level delegation that included Chairman Mao himself and senior US government officials where the Chinese source speech contained excerpts of Chairman Mao's poetry (Association of Diplomatic Studies and Training, 2013). Other accounts of diplomatic interpreting are provided by Ren (2000), Xu (2000) and Shi (2007).

We turn now to aspects of diplomatic interpreting in which interpreters employ their intercultural competence in rendering terms that are geo-politically sensitive. The following is an excerpt of a Chinese source speech and an English target speech from a press conference in March 2010. A question was posed in English by a Wall Street Journal journalist about the investment environment in China. After receiving an interpreted version of the journalist's question the then Chinese Premier, Wen Jiabao, responded with the following:

Example (1)

SS: 我们要从法律上为外国企业在中国的经营创造一个公平的环境，而且使外国的企业能够享受同中国企业一样的国民待遇。比如，在应对金融危机当中，我们实行了许多刺激经济的政策：家电下乡、汽车以旧换新，我们都采取公开招标的办法。参加招标的既有国内企业，也有国外企业，也有台商和港商。

Gloss: *We will create a level playing field in law for foreign businesses to do operations in China. Also, we will ensure that foreign businesses operating in China will enjoy the same national treatments as Chinese businesses. For example, we have implemented a series of policies to stimulate the economy to tackle the financial crisis. These policies include the subsidy program of home appliances in China's rural areas and the subsidy program for vehicle replacement. In the process of putting these programs into effect, we have organized public tendering. The public tendering process has been partici-pated in by domestic companies, and foreign companies, and companies from Taiwan and Hong Kong.*

(Xiong, 2010)

We focus our attention on the last sentence:

参加招标的既有国内企业，也有国外企业，也有台商和港商.

The public tendering process has been participated in by domestic compa-nies, and foreign companies, and companies from Taiwan and Hong Kong.

In this last sentence a division of companies according to those that are "domes-tic", "foreign" and those "from Taiwan and Hong Kong" could be understood as a statement that suggests Taiwan and Hong Kong are independent of (the People's Republic of) China. The interpreter, Ms Zhang Lu, was well aware of the political sensitivities about how the status of Taiwan and Hong Kong should be expressed in English, and the consequences of her interpretation on the source speaker with whom she was working, Premier Wen Jiabao, as well as for herself as an inter-preter. In her target speech, she re-ordered the sequencing of the groups, so that "companies from Taiwan and Hong Kong" were mentioned before foreign ones, and her target speech associates these as being akin to Chinese domestic ones:

TT: And these public tendering has been participated by both companies from the mainland, and from Hong Kong and Taiwan as well as foreign businesses.

The interpreter, Zhang Lu, was able to promptly recognize the intercultural frame pertaining to the source speech, and to employ a strategy to avert a potential loss of face to the speaker and to others. The following example (2) is taken from a press conference featuring China's Premier, Li Keqiang.

Example (2)

SS: 大家啊都有退休或者需要养老的一天，这里 . . . 我想做个安民告示，不过要准确的说.. 中国政府对中国公民保证养老金发放，从全面长期来看是没有问题的。我们去年.. 养老保险收支结余是 . . . 三千四百多亿，累计结余三万四千多亿。我们还有..全国的社会保障基金储备一万六千多亿.. 没有动啊，还 . . . 有能力划拨国有资产来充实这个.. 养老基金，所以.. 可以肯定的说老有所养，不会.. 也绝不能是一句空话，谢谢。

Gloss: *Everyone, er, will retire or need to live out life in retirement one day, here, I want to make an announcement to reassure the public. However to be precise, for the Chinese Government on ensuring pension payments for Chinese citizens, there will be no problem from a comprehensive and longterm perspective. Last year our pension security incoming and outgoing balance was some 340 billion, with accumulative balance at 3.4 trillion. We also have the national social security fund reserve at 1.6 trillion that has not been touched, er, and the ability to appropriate state-owned assets to substantiate this pension fund. Therefore it can be said with certainty that the elderlies will be provided for, these are not and can never be empty words. Thank you.*

(CCTV, 2016)

We focus on the following utterance at the start of the excerpt:

这里我想做个安民告示

Here, I want to make an announcement to reassure the public.

This utterance contains a well-known Chinese phrase that Chinese political leaders have been known to use in public speeches. Such idiomatic phrases (成语: chéngyǔ) consist of four characters, and these four-character phrases along with (excerpts from) classical poems, and Confucian sayings are common in speeches given by Chinese officials. In regard to rendering these cultural items into English, they inevitably require sense-for-sense rather than word-for-word equivalents. The four-character phrase,安民告示, lit. gloss: 'reassure populace notice' or more freely glossed as 'an announcement to reassure the public' was rendered in the target speech as 'the message of reassurance'. The last two characters, 告示, 'official notice' was rendered as 'message' instead of 'announcement', despite the latter being closer to the literal meaning of the source phrase.

An utterance towards the end of the excerpt contains the following phrase:

所以可以肯定的说老有所养，不会也绝不能是一句空话

Therefore it can be said with certainty that the elderlies will be provided for, these are not and can never be empty words.

In this utterance, the phrase 老有所养 lit. gloss: 'the old have their support', is another well-known Confucian saying in China, meaning that the elderly will be looked after. In the context of age pension policies, the target speech contains the following formulation: 'to ensure that the elderly will be provided for'. A full version of the actual target speech is given as follows:

TS: One day we will all get retired and live on pension benefits, so here is the message of reassurance, that is nationally speaking and in the long run, there will absolutely be no problem for meeting pension, um, payments by the Chinese um Government. Last year, the surplus of our pension insurance schemes stood at 340 billion RMB Yuan and the accumulative balance um, was some 3.4 trillion RMB Yuan. Moreover, we still have the central social security fund, which is worth 1.6 trillion RMB Yuan as a strategic reserve that has not been touched, and we can also, um, use state-owned assets . . . to replenish the social security, um, fund, so to ensure that the elderly will be provided for, cannot and will not be an empty promise. Thank you.

As we can see, four-character idioms present a number of inter-cultural challenges to interpreters. Bourne (2016, p. 19) cites an example of another one used by then Chinese premier, Wen Jiabao, and reminds us they are not only a rhetorical device with a certain metric, but expressions that mark a speaker as "knowledgeable and respected". She gives the following example (3) from a press conference on the topic of the relationship between mainland China and Taiwan where the opening phrase is a four-character saying:

Example (3)

Premier Wen's ST: 骨肉之亲，析而不殊。
Lit. gloss: *Bone and flesh's closeness, separated but not disconnected*
Interpreted TT: We are compatriots, and I believe brothers, though geo-
                      graphically apart will always be bound by their blood ties.

(Bourne, 2016, p. 20)

We conclude with an example (4) of source text produced by a non-native speaker of Chinese working for an international news agency who posed the following question to Chinese Wen Jiabao on the topic of China's position towards Syria and the war in that country. Yuan (2013, p. 109) notes that the journalist, as an L2-user of Chinese, appeared to have transferred pragmatic conventions from his L1 into the formulation of his question in Chinese, and ascertains "that the journalist made a bald-on record statement which posed a non-mitigated threat to the Premier' face and the image of Chinese government". This was the foreign journalist's question to the Chinese premier:

Example (4)

在中东问题，尤其是在叙利亚问题上，中国的立场与其它很多国家存在很大的 分歧。那么中方解决叙利亚问题的立场以及出发点是什么？

Gloss: *On the issue of the Middle East, in particular on the issue of Syria, China's position is in great discrepancy from that of many other countries. Then what is China's position and departure in resolving the Syrian issue?*

(Yuan, 2013, p. 108)

The question was addressed directly to the Chinese Premier who responded to it directly, and the interpretation was provided for those journalists present who had not understood the original question in Chinese. The face of these recipients of the target speech (i.e. the journalists present without proficiency in Chinese) was therefore not threatened as they were not the direct addressees of the question. Nonetheless, the TT contains examples of mitigation of the face-threatening effect of the question to its direct addressee, the Chinese premier. This is the interpretation into English provided by the interpreter present:

> TS: On the issue of Middle-East, in particular the issue of Syria, it seems that there is a wide gap between China's position and the position of many other countries in the world. I want to ask what exactly is China's position on the issue of Syria and what is China's consideration behind all these efforts surrounding the Syrian issue.
>
> (Yuan, 2013, p. 108)

Yuan (2013) analyses the TT in the following terms:

> in the interpretation, two negative politeness strategies of a hedge on illocutionary force ('it seems') and of impersonal structure ('there is') were adopted to communicate concerns of H's [the premier's] face. This could demonstrate the interpreter's intention to alleviate the strong tone featuring the journalist's utterances.
>
> (Yuan, 2013, p. 109. Original round brackets and punctuation. Square brackets added.)

The interpreter present shows knowledge of the intercultural schemas that apply in this example. These are: the contextual schema (appropriate behavioural parameters according to Chinese pragmatic norms); the strategy schema (the 'problem-solving' strategy is a mitigation of perceived face-threatening acts).

Elsewhere, a large corpus of data on Chinese–English interpreted interactions was examined by Wang (2012) who focuses on 11 interpreted press conferences led by the Chinese Premier of the time. Wang notes that the interpreters working in all recorded press conferences were themselves in-house interpreters of the Interpreting and Translation Section of China's Ministry of Foreign Affairs. This is something we noted previously. But Wang (2012) shows that the significance of this is twofold: as employees of the Ministry of Foreign Affairs, they are regularly in contact with the *content* of Chinese foreign policy; as employees to a state ministry, they occupy a dual role providing language transfer *and* upholding the interests of the state ministry, meaning that face-threatening speech emanating from, or directed towards, officials of the Ministry of Foreign Affairs may be mitigated in their interpretations. The following is an excerpt from a response from then-Premier Zhu:

Example (5)

SS: 朱总理：关于无限期的问题，我不知道英文该怎么翻译，有人告诉我应该用 *indefinitely*，还有人告诉我，应该用一个拉丁文，叫*sinedie*，我也不清楚我念清楚了没有，发音是不是准确，因为我不懂拉丁文。

Gloss: *As for the word "indefinitely," I do not know how to interpret it into English. Someone told me I should use "indefinitely," and someone also told me that a Latin word should be used, which is "sinedie". I'm not sure whether I said it clearly or the pronunciation is correct or not, because I do not know Latin.*

TS: As for the word "indefinitely," I do not know what is the best interpretation of the word in English. Someone told me the English version should be "indefinitely," and someone also come up with another recommendation. It was a Latin word, which is *sinedie*. I do not know whether I pronounce the term correctly in Latin, <u>because I do not have any knowledge about the language of Latin</u>.

(Wang, 2012, p. 207)

The interpretation contains a passage (here underlined) that seems to be a further explanation (and justification) for the Premier's lack of certainty about his pronunciation of Latin words. As such it appears that the interpreter has recognized the significance of the intercultural context schema (appropriate behavioural patterns) in the interaction which guided them in the justification strategy employed.

3.3.3 Media interpreting

We now shift to media interpreting which is a less studied and less conspicuous area of interpreting work, but with parallels and overlap with diplomatic and conference interpreting, as mentioned. Media interpreting refers to live interactions on radio, television or online forums where a compere or interviewer interacts with an allophone studio guest or interviewee who may be physically present or connected via audio- or video-link. The source speech is interpreted simultaneously via a 'voice-over' or interpreted consecutively. The interpreter may be an in-studio but off-screen 'target speech voice', or a physically present and visible mediator in their own right, or consecutive interpretation can be provided by the compare or interviewer. The latter has been studied by Straniero Sergio (1999) and Amato and Mack (2013) in Italy where this has something of a tradition.

We present a Chinese–English example of media interpreting as follows which is from an interview conducted with the Chinese-Singaporean Kung Fu actor Jet Li, born Li Lianjie, 李连杰. Jet Li is well known as a martial arts practitioner and an action movie star, but less known as a devout Buddhist who has been practising his religion for several years. The topic of the interview was philanthropy, with some questions specifically relating to his charity, named 'One Foundation'. Jet Li has been living for many years in Singapore and has receptive skills in English, and requested that questions asked to him in English need not be interpreted. The interpreter worked uni-directionally from Chinese into English only, interpreting his responses from Mandarin into English. The interpreter, Bernard Song, was seated behind Jet Li. It is clear from responses from the audience that many understood Jet Li's turns in Mandarin and signalled this through immediate applause or laughter.

The following excerpt is taken from a setting entitled, 'philanthropy breakfast' at a university in Singapore, where Jet Li talks about the effect that Buddhism has had on his life:

Example (6)

SS: 其实 . . . . 诶.. 我.. 经过七年的学习.. 佛教，其实我主要是在佛教，使我了解到宇宙的整个形成的状况，呃，所有的物理、化学，如何形成的这样的.. 一个世界。呃，包括宇宙，包括地球。也了解到人七情六欲、喜怒哀乐如何产生，如何快乐如何痛苦。所以当我想清了这个事情以后，我发现我是世界上最没事做的人。我不再 (laughs)，我不再需要更多的名，也不需要太多的钱，因为一日三餐，我相信我们家一家子到死都够了，所以生活的.. 真正需要的东西并不多。所以 . . . . 剩下什么？剩下的就是说， 全世界一直很爱护我，不管对我的武术还是电影。我如何把大家给予我的这个 . . . . 公 . . . . 众的一种 . . . . 一种观点，一种观点 (laughs)，李连杰这个，这三个字的value，怎么样用它创立一个平台回馈给世界，这才是我要做的。这也是我很enjoying在做的。

Gloss: *Actually, uh, after seven years studying Buddhism, actually I mainly study Buddhism, which makes me understand the formation of the whole universe, uh, everything about physics and chemistry, how the world was formed. Uh, including the universe, including the Earth. Also understanding how the seven emotions and six desires, being happy, angry, sad and joyful are created, how to be happy and how to bear suffering. Therefore after I have been thinking through these matters, I realise that I am a person with nothing to do in the world. I no longer (laughs), no longer need more fame, no longer need much money, people only need three meals a day. I believe my money will be sufficient enough until we all die in our family, so life does not really need a lot of things. So what's left? What's left is that, the whole world has always loved me. Kung Fu or the movies haven't mattered to me too much. How can I use the idea . . . the idea given to me by the public. The name Lianjie Li, the value of these three characters, is to build a platform to repay the world, this is what I will do. This is also what I am enjoying doing.*

TT: So, eh, through seven years of studying, um, Buddhism . . . I learned about the universe, how this chemistry, the, the physics is like in this universe . . . how this universe is formed. And I also learned how this . . . feelings from human beings are formed, like . . . how can you get happy? And how can you get sad or angry? And, when I learn all of these, I felt that, I'm the only one probably in this world that I have nothing to do [laughter from audience]. Because I have enough money. I have fame. And . . . my money can be enough for my family to live for the rest of their lives. So, but there is one thing that I can, I can do is to love back the people that I . . . who love me, whether it is for my martial arts, for my movies. I need to pay, pay them back. So . . . now I need to make use of the value of this . . . of my name, Jet Li, to pay back the world, pay back to the society, and to love them back.

(Youtube, 2016)

We focus on the first part of Jet Li's speech in which he mentions Buddhism, Buddhist principles, how the world was formed, and the Buddhist teachings of seven emotions and six desires, after which he lists four of the emotions and two of the desires. Numbers (as well as times, dates, proper names etc.) are often not easy to interpret (cf. 3.1.1 in which Seleskovitch's notion of deverbalization and form-to-sense conversion predicts that those items that cannot be deverbalized, such as numbers, are a challenge to the interpreter). The TT omits mention of the emotions and desires, together with their numerical value. This appears to be an omission. But, we should keep in mind that most examples of good interpreting contain 80% of the content of the source speech, so that a margin of 20% omissions is not an indication of inadequate interpreting. But we dwell briefly on the "the seven emotions and six desires" mentioned in the ST as these are culturally (and in this case religiously) specific terms. Such terms are likely to immediately represent an intercultural frame for the Chinese–English interpreter which brings up the question of what type of intercultural model will be found in the TT. As stated, "the seven emotions and six desires" and the topic of emotions are absent in the TT, and are represented by three of the four affective emotions given in the TT: "How can you get happy? And how can you get sad or angry?" As such, the interpreter's intercultural strategy used here is message reduction but with most of the ST content still rendered.

3.3.4   Business interpreting

Business interpreting refers to settings in which an interpreter works with other participants who are interacting with each other usually to secure a commercial or transactional agreement. There are very few studies on business interpreting, e.g. Takimoto (2006), Gavioli and Maxwell (2007) and Sandrelli (2011). A further reason for the lack of research is that most businesspeople are reluctant to allow recording of commercial business interactions that would enable the collection of empirical data needed for scientific research. Writing over 20 years ago about the reluctance of businesses to employ interpreters, Kondo et al. (1997) report the following:

> First, the interpreter is considered as an intruder, both physically and psychologically . . . Secondly, the interpreter is seen as a non-specialist, a generalist, above all with little understanding of corporate culture . . . [and], the client is not sure of the loyalty of the interpreter.

(Kondo et al., 1997, p. 162)

The issue of loyalty is a key one in business settings, while at the same time, most ethics codes contain standards of behaviour for interpreters that advocate impartiality and confidentiality, e.g. AUSIT Code of Ethics and Code of Conduct (2012, p. 5), CIoL Code of Professional Conduct (2015, p. 4). A Chinese–English interpreter reflects on their own experience working in business settings, which included information provision beyond that which occurred in verbal dealings with the other party:

> I would argue that my position as an employee of a corporation competing for business overseas meant that my primary loyalty when engaging in interpreting on behalf of the corporation was to the corporation. Therefore, my role was to provide as much information to my employer about what was being said (or not said) by the other side, even if it was not part of the actual formal dialogue being engaged in at the time. (Chi-Eng.inter.20)

The role enacted by the Chinese–English interpreter who gave the excerpt is a *dual* one: firstly, as an employee of one of the parties and who declares this so that the other party is informed that the interpreter they are working with is *not* impartial and has a loyalty to the employer; secondly, as an interpreter who is providing inter-lingual transfer for a business interaction. The same Chinese–English interpreter makes the following further comment about the role and actions of being an interpreter employed by one party to interpret *and* to act in that party's interests:

> My role as interpreter was not as a neutral party, in between the two parties. It was to ensure that the company for whom I was employed enjoyed the greatest advantage possible out of the relationship-building exercise that was the purpose of the meeting. Therefore, I deliberately "condensed" what our manager said to reflect the intent of what he said and including whatever non-controversial details I could.(Chi-Eng.inter. 20)

The sensitive nature of business interactions means that speech acts that are potentially face-threatening are to be avoided. We re-visit one of the examples provided by Lü and Li (2012) presented in Section 3.3.2 and show how an interpreter may view the intercultural frame of one part of the interaction, and what intercultural strategy is 'operationalised':

Example (7)

Eng.-sp. businessperson:	Could I have a name list of your employees?
Interpreter:	可以给我一份你们员工的名单吗？
Chi.-sp. businessperson:	恐怕不太方便。
Literal translation:	*Maybe it is inconvenient.*
Interpreter:	It might be a bit inconvenient to do that.
	(Adapted from: Lü & Li, 2012, p. 159)

In this interaction, the English speaker poses a yes-no question. The answer of the Chinese-speaking businessperson is 恐怕不太方便。 The nominal *locutionary* force of "Maybe it is inconvenient" is a non-committal statement, while its *illocutionary* force, in Chinese is that of a polite refusal. The response is therefore euphemistic which is in line with Chinese pragmatic norms in which a direct negative response is avoided as it is potentially face-threatening. The potential threat to the face of the other interlocutor is avoided through a formally unclear response, which is understood as a refusal. The illocutionary force of the direct *English* equivalent "Maybe it is inconvenient" is that of a response signalling reluctance in giving a firm answer, but is not a polite refusal. The interpreter uses their intercultural agency and a strategy of approximation in providing a polite refusal which captures the meaning and intent of the Chinese source response.

We turn now to some general descriptions of business meetings in both Chinese-speaking and English-speaking settings. Based on analysis of 20 business and administrative meetings in a public institution in Beijing, Gu and Zhu (2002) report that Chinese business meetings have up to 16 stages, with six occurring before the meeting itself (pre-stages), and up to seven taking place after it (post-stages). In a congruent study of a wide number of business and commercial interactions conducted in the UK Handford (2010, p. 69) reports that British business meetings usually have up to six stages, with up to two pre-stages. Figure 3.1 presents the stages identified by both sets of researchers from their corpora of recorded business meetings:

Pre-stage 1	Meeting initiation
Pre-stage 2	Agenda fixing
Pre-stage 3	Decision on participants
Pre-stage 4	Meeting site is *guan*-sensitive
Pre-stage 5	Meeting notification is no less *guan*-sensitive
Pre-stage 6	Seating arrangements
Stage 1	Opening of meeting
Stage 2	Settling agenda business
Stage 3	Closing
Post-stage 1	Further private discussions (unresolved due to shortage of time)
Post-stage 2	Private discussions on off-agenda business
Post-stage 3	Private discussions on things that could not be placed on the agenda
Post-stage 4	Further arrangements about how to execute meeting decisions
Post-stage 5	Follow-up minor meetings in break-up groups
Post-stage 6	Meals together and other forms of shared entertainment
Post-stage 7	Interpersonal networking – renewing old friendships or making new friends.

Figure 3.2 The pre-states, main stages and post-stages of Chinese business meetings

Source: (Adapted from: Gu & Zhu, 2002, pp. 102–114)

Pre-stage 2	Meeting preparation
Pre-stage 1	Pre-meeting
Stage 1	Opening of meeting
Stage 2	Discussion of the agenda
Stage 3	Closing of the meeting
Post-stage 1	Post-meeting effects

Figure 3.3 The pre-states, main stages and post-stage of British business meetings.
Source: (Adapted from: Handford, 2010, p. 69)

The structures identified by Gu and Zhu (2002) and Handford (2010) in their respective corpora reflect the maximum number of identifiable stages occurring across all recorded meetings, and they also reflect different intercultural event schemas. It is conceivable that business meetings in either country could have more stages than the numbers identified by them, but it is more likely, particular in the case of Chinese business meetings, that they will have fewer than 16 stages, and in the case of British business meetings, there may be fewer than two pre-stages.

The over-arching concept in the Chinese business meetings is that of *guān* (官) ('officialdom'). Observation of *guān*, i.e. inter-personal positioning determined by the Chinese socio-political system of officialdom and power relations necessitates careful planning of a business meeting as an enactment of the hierarchical relations that exist between interlocutors, depending on whether they wield *guān*, and if so, how much they wield. The six pre-stages are therefore important and we cite here Gu and Zhu's description of three of them as demonstrations of observation of *guān*:

> *Meeting initiation* is normally performed by one *guān*, who will consult his/her superior and his/her equal(s) for a second opinion. If s/he fails to do this, bad feelings are likely to be generated, and the latter's cooperation is likely to be in jeopardy.
>
> *Agenda fixing* is even more sensitive. What is to be put on the agenda, and what is to be left out, is a form of control. Some issues require prior negotiation behind the scenes before they are placed on the agenda. Others, particularly sensitive topics such as one that will discredit a co-*guān*, may be deliberately put on the agenda so that the co-*guān* will lose public confidence, or even find it difficult to maintain his/her post.
>
> *Decision on participants* should be carefully considered. Failure to invite those *guān's* whose presence is required by the prospective meeting means their serious disregard, and that the decisions reached at the end of the meeting are likely to be nullified.
>
> (Gu & Zhu, 2002, p. 102. Original italics)

In contrast, meetings in Britain may have one or two pre-stages preceding the main meeting. Some meetings may have a pre-arranged agenda composed by someone unrelated to the meeting, or there may be no agenda and the meeting is a regularly scheduled event to which attendees arrive with few preconceptions or informed only by the outcomes of a previous meeting. Stages 1–3 represent the core stages or the physical gathering of participants at the meeting (whether face-to-face or remote) who address the meeting's agenda. Interestingly, Gu and Zhu (2002, p. 103) describe the main section of the meeting as "settling agenda business" while Handford (2010) describes this as "discussion of the agenda". The former suggests that a pre-ordained series of decisions are 'delivered' to attendees, while the latter suggests a more horizontal and open-ended treatment of agenda items. At Chinese business meetings opening and closing stages are important as to who performs them (almost always the most senior person present) and what they say; at British business meetings, these are short formalities, sometimes even performed by those who wield little power hierarchically, e.g. a 'rotating' chairperson. With some variation, Handford (2010) locates a more 'levelled' (i.e. egalitarian) structure to UK business meetings: a person's presence at the meeting means that he/she can contribute thematically or procedurally to the meeting in more or less the same way as most others – the function of the business meeting is to discuss topic-relevant matters and the form of the meeting allows for a more or less equal opportunity for all to contribute, with less regard to status or position. A Chinese–English interpreter recalls some of the more demanding forms of discourse that they dealt with in the stages of business meetings themselves:

> I found having to deal with the hidden agendas of some of the people we were dealing with extremely hard. Often they would come up with elaborate schemes for skimming benefits from project contracts for themselves and I had a lot of trouble dealing with this in terms of understanding what they were trying to do, how they wanted to do it, and in particular with the moral dimensions of what they often wanted to do. Both language level and cultural factors played a big role in the hardship I experienced in this respect.
>
> (Chi-Eng.inter.20)

The three stages that constitute the Chinese business meeting itself may be much shorter than comparable British meetings, and they may contain less discussion and fewer contributions from lower-status attendees. This means that in the pre-stages, the interpreter (who may or may not be party to the organization of the agenda, notification and seating arrangement for the meeting etc.) needs to attend to the titles, role-relationships, honorifics and hierarchically laden discourse, regardless of whether the interaction takes place in a Chinese-speaking or English-speaking country. In China, where the pre-stages include interaction with speakers of other languages, the involvement of the interpreter, usually an *in-house interpreter*, can be instrumental for the status and role of possible attendees to be communicated and for there to be an elicitation of potential thematic points to be placed on the agenda. The interpreter may, in a quantitative sense, engage in a greater volume of inter-lingual transfer (via spoken language interpreting and sight translation) during these pre-stages than in the course of the actual meeting (stages -3) itself (see 3.3.4). To relate this to the work of interpreters who work in business settings in the UK or other English-speaking countries, depending on the function that an interpreter fulfils in his/her work, the interpreter may be present to interpret for interlocutors from pre-stage 2 to stage 3 as an *escort interpreter*, for stages 1–4 only as a *business interpreter*, or depending on his/her employment status he/she may be interpreting for all stages as an *in-house interpreter* or for stages 1–3 only as a *freelance interpreter*.

The 'time investment' for Chinese business meetings is also the following, differing from that in British or most Anglophone meetings: much power (and therefore decision-making) is invested at the pre-meeting stages or the post-stages of the meeting, and sometimes more than in the course of the meeting itself. After British meetings the post-stage serves the purpose of attending to matters agreed on at the meeting. At the post-stages of Chinese business meetings, Gu and Zhu (2002, p. 104) locate a number of phenomena not least of which is that at these stages, those wielding *guān* are less likely to behave as a *guān* and even take on a non-*guān* role as confidant or colleague:

> This offers one of the explanations of why post-meeting activities can be quite rich. Since the role of a post-meeting *guan* is less well-defined, less *guān*-like, so to speak, some decisions cannot be made during the meeting proper are reached through post-meeting activities.
>
> (Gu & Zhu, 2002, p. 104)

The structure of business interactions in China means that the post-stage interactions are as important as stages 1–3 in the performance of interpreting duties. The following is reported by an interpreter who worked in many business settings about the post-stages in China-based interactions:

> My experience in dealing with Chinese people in business is that they will maintain a distance during formal negotiations (often speaking through a chosen representative or deferring to a power-broker within the group), but will then adopt a much more personal approach during banquets and after-banquet activities (such as karaoke, spas, massage, etc.) which are sometimes (or often) fuelled by alcohol.
>
> (Chi-Eng.inter.20)

3.3.5   *Police, legal and court interpreting*

The area of police, legal and court interpreting is a large one. We focus on a number of dyads or constellations of interlocutors particular to this area. These include: police-witness interviews (3.3.5.1); and court interpreting (3.3.5.2). Interpreting in lawyer-client interactions, and prison interpreting are further legal settings but not discussed here.

3.3.5.1 Police-witness interviews

The heading for this sub-section features the term 'interview', although until recently, the term 'police interrogation' was widely used in most Anglophone countries (and it still remains a widely used term amongst many, cf. Berk-Seligson, 2011) and this term is also used in China. At a primary level, police interviews are usually conducted with alleged suspects or potential witnesses to a crime or suspected illegal activities. In criminal law matters the police are chronologically usually the first 'official' entity with whom suspects or witnesses have contact. In other words, contact with the 'executive' arm of state power usually precedes contact with the 'judicial' arm.

Information on police interviews, in general, whether interpreted or not, is not readily available in China. As foregrounded, this interaction in China is more commonly termed 'police interrogation' (警方审讯). We use this term when discussing this interaction in relation to China, and this term is used by Du (2015) and McConville (2011) whose data we draw on here. In Du's (2015) examination of courtroom discourse that otherwise focuses on the use of different languages (Hakka and Mandarin Pǔtōnghuà) and the role of the interpreter, there is reference to the events of the police interrogation given by defendants (Du, 2015, p. 514).

In other countries, the term 'police interrogation' has now been abandoned as it reflected a combative or confrontational approach that is no longer used in police-witness or police-suspect interactions. There has been a shift in the means that information is elicited by police officers and also more stringent conditions on the admissibility of police interviews as evidence. In many English-speaking countries today police interviewing practices are based on the Cognitive Interview technique (Geiselman et al., 1984) that seeks to enhance the interviewee's ability to recall and relate relevant details about an event that s/he has witnessed or which s/he is suspected of being involved in (Heydon & Lai, 2013). This technique in an extended form (Fisher & Geiselman, 1992) consists of four components: report everything (instructions to relate everything encourage more detailed and accurate descriptions), reinstate context (request to focus on the sights and sounds present at the scene/s), change order (recounting events in reverse or altered temporal order), change perspective (recounting the events from the perspective of another participant) (Heydon & Lai, 2013). The aim of the Cognitive Interview is to elicit free and uninterrupted narratives from the witness or suspect.

A free-form narrative is the variety of speech that a police officer will typically seek to elicit from an interviewee in English-speaking countries. In interpreted police interviews, the interpreter almost always works consecutively and the narrative that is being recounted by the interviewee is necessarily truncated at intervals by the interpreter who typically employs consecutive interpreting into the language of the police officer. Heydon and Lai (2013, p. 82) go as far as to say that this desired form of an interview "conflicts fundamentally with the cognitive requirements and linguistic operations of the interpreting process". Interpreters working consecutively need to attend not only to the overall meaning of interlocutors' utterances as in all interpreting work, but in many cases also to the *form* of items used in their utterances. It is important not to disregard discourse markers ('well', 'see', 'now'), tag questions (with variable intonation) and back-channelling forms ('right', 'I'm with you') as challenging to interpreter performance (Hale, 2004). Even a silent response in a police interview is meaning-carrying and may warrant verbal contribution from interpreters where a silent response is not perceived by an interlocutor from one speech community in the same way that it is intended by a speaker of another speech community. On this last point, Nakane (2014) locates differences in East Asian norms compared to those of most Anglophone countries in regard to silence, and interpreters' position to interviewee silence. She reports that some interpreters 'fill' a silent response from an interviewed suspect with a repair or re-statement of a previous rendition, thereby adding a response where this is otherwise absent.

As stated, a statement, as either a witness or suspect, is also usually prepared at the end of an interview. Typically, the police officer has been making notes based on information conveyed via interpretation and prepares a draft of a statement that the interpreter then sight translates into the other language. The interviewee is given the chance to signal their agreement or to make changes, which are relayed back to the police officer. The final version is prepared by the police officer, with the interviewee asked to sign it. This is the way in which most police interview protocols foresee the preparation of a statement via the interpreter. The interpreter is discouraged from preparing a statement in the language of the interviewee as this way of statement drafting needlessly excludes the police officer and greatly increases the volume of interpreting or sight translation that the interpreter has to perform as the final version must usually be prepared in the language used by the police officer (Fowler, 2003).

3.3.5.2   Court interpreting

Conventions of court interpreting and the work of the court interpreter rest very much on the structural organization of the legislative and judicial systems of a country. In contrast to police or lawyer-client interviews, interactions that take place in the courtroom are usually public and multi-party. The formal nature of the courtroom setting that represents one arm of state power in a society – the judiciary – is characterized by a number of features: distinct hierarchical relations between judge, jury, legal representatives (prosecution and defence), suspects, witnesses and members of the public gallery; dress codes; right to take the floor; language – terminology, register, discourse and rhetorical conventions. We focus on the language used in courtroom settings, but also pay attention to courtroom officials' roles and courtroom procedures and how these have an effect on the language used.

Studies on language in the courtroom have occurred typically in Anglophone countries with a common law tradition and adversarial system for courtroom proceedings. Both sides in the adversarial system employ their oratory skills to represent their parties' position before an impartial judge or jury and present their cases in the form of oral evidence.

For the interpreter, the courtroom presents a number of challenges. These include:

- interpersonal ones – others' misunderstanding of the role of the interpreter;
- preparational ones – a lack of information or briefing about the nature of proceedings and the purpose of the courtroom proceedings (answering a summons, guardianship claim, trial of a summary offence etc.) greatly hampers an interpreter's ability to be adequately equipped and ready to work;
- terminological ones – specialist terms, including Latin ones (*mens reus, corpus delicti*) may be frequently used in the speech of judges and lawyers, despite efforts to encourage those in court to use varieties more accessible to others, e.g. *plain English in law* (Australia) or *plain legal language* (USA);
- referential content ones – the meaning of interlocutors' speech may not be understood due to its complexity, the interlocutors' verbosity or long-windedness, and/or the interpreter's inability to match the interlocutor's speech with his/her existing knowledge of the relevant thematic area;
- discourse-rhetorical ones – the devices used by speakers, particularly lawyers, are not recognized as such and not rendered in interpretations, or they are misunderstood and rendered erroneously in target speech.

Berk-Seligson's (2002) study of interpreters in US courts reveals that the interpreter's role is misunderstood by most other courtroom participants, and that interpreters are hampered in rendering examiners' questions in the way these are intended. Further, the testimonies of witnesses or defendants are not rendered in the way that these wish them to be, and that interpreters often alter the pragmatic intent of source speakers' speech in general. In the latter case this relates to changes to what is perceived as a 'powerless testimony style' which has negative consequences on jurors' ratings of witnesses' credibility, intelligence and general competence (O'Barr, 1982; Hale, 2007).

The trial procedure for a criminal case in China has elements of both the adversarial and inquisitorial systems. Cases are heard before a collegial panel, comprising three judges, or a combination of judges and people's assessors with the latter having equal rights with judges. Interpreters are mentioned in the 1996 Criminal Procedure Law (CPL) along with other parties in court proceedings (Art. 154, 1996 CPL). The defendant and the victim (witness) are given the opportunity to present statements regarding the alleged offence/s. The defendant may be examined by the prosecutor *and* the judge. With the permission of the presiding judges witnesses may be questioned by the prosecutor, the defence and other parties. The judge is given express power to stop questioning that s/he considers irrelevant (Art. 156, 1996 CPL). Judges can adjourn the case if they have doubt about evidence, and have investigative powers to conduct an inquiry or inquest. Towards the end of the trial, a form of 'open debate' between parties may be allowed, "the evidence having been presented, the parties, prosecutor and defender may, with permission of the judge, 'state their views on the evidence and the case, they may debate with each other'" (McConville, 2011, p. 195). After the final statement of the defendant, the judge announces an adjournment for deliberation (Art. 160, 168, 1996 CPL). The verdict is announced in the form of 'guilty', 'innocent', 'innocent on account of the fact that the evidence is insufficient and the accusation unfounded' or may, in unusual or difficult cases, the judge may pass the case to the 'president of the court', i.e. a more senior judicial official.

Following are nine extracts, (8) to (16), of courtroom proceedings with an interpreter present. The first example is taken from an initial procedure in a criminal trial, that of a *Courtroom Enquiry*. Beforehand, the defendant is served with a translated version of the charges. Later on, when in the courtroom, courtroom officials usually presume that the translation of the charges has been read and understood by the defendant, which influences their attitude towards the need for interpretation. The issue of whether the defendant did read the translation, whether they understood it, and whether they can remember all details of it in court is touched on by Du (2016):

> When no interpreting is provided to him [the defendant] in court, there is no way to determine his level of understanding. In the situation in which there is a production of zero rendition [i.e. no interpretation], the implication is that reading the indictment in Chinese is done to fulfil the procedural requirement . . . to demonstrate that due process has been performed. To save time, the judge does not require an interpretation to be provided to the defendant, which leads to a situation in which he is given no support or information at this stage of the trial.
>
> (Du, 2016, p. 105. Square brackets added.)

The example (8) is taken from a drug-smuggling case during the examination of evidence. A procedural requirement of proceedings is that the indictment is read out in court. This is shortened in the excerpt given as follows which contains turns from the judge (J), prosecution (P), interpreter (I) and defendant (D):

Example (8)

1   J: 現在開始法庭調查（.）先由公訴人宣讀起訴書
        Now begins the courtroom investigation (.) first the prosecutor reads out the indictment
        [The first part of the prosecutor's presentation of the written indictment is omitted here due to its length.]
2   P: . . . 審判長（.）公訴人起訴書宣讀完畢
        Chief judge（.）the prosecutor rests with reading the indictment
3   J: 翻譯（.）你問一下他（.）對於起訴書的翻譯文本他能不能看懂
4   （.）明白什麼意思（.）
        Interpreter (.) you ask him (.) if he can understand the translated indictment (.) if he understands what it means
5   I: Have you read the indictment?
6   D: Yeah.

(Du, 2016, p. 108)

In example (8) a full version of the prosecutor's reading out of the indictment is not given as indicated in the square brackets between lines 1 and 2. The words of the prosecutor in line 2 here are his concluding ones. No part of the indictment is interpreted for the defendant. Instead, the judge in lines 3 and 4 addresses the interpreter, using 3.SG to refer to the defendant, to ask if he had understood the translated indictment. The interpreter does not interpret this prompt as such, and instead, in line 5, reproduces the judge's question as a *direct recapitulator*. In example (13), lines 1–4 are not interpreted by the interpreter. These uninterpreted turns appear to represent what is otherwise known as "zero renditions" (Wadensjö, 1998, p. 108) or "non-renditions" (Takimoto & Koshiba, 2009, p. 16). Zero renditions or non-renditions are not desirable from the perspective of interpreter performance or from the perspective of the other interlocutors as at least one party is left not knowing what the other party said. In a procedural sense, zero renditions undermine the interpreter's notion of his/her own role and capacity to provide inter-lingual transfer, and it undermines others' expectations that the interpreter is there to perform a certain role and that they can expect to be the recipients of his/ her inter-lingual renditions. Where zero renditions are a regular and apparently voluntary occurrence, we can conceive of the interpreter's footing as that of 'voluntary omitter' in not fulfilling his/her role of inter-lingual relayer. Where others interrupt, talk over or through other means disallow an interpreter from providing inter-lingual transfer, and notwithstanding the interpreter's explanation of his/her role to enable the achievement of a mediated interaction, we can conceive of the interpreter's footing as that of an 'involuntary omitter'.

On first glance it appears that courtroom speech that is either procedural and addressed to all present, as well as turns between the judge and the prosecution or defence are not interpreted. But as Du (2016, p. 9) remarks, sometimes these turns are interpreted, or at least a certain part of them: "[t]here is no definite and clear rule on when interpreting must be offered and how much information must be produced". Example (9) is a lengthier one. In some places interpretation is provided. In other places there are zero-renditions. This example contains turns from a further courtroom interlocutor, the defence lawyer (L).

Example (9)

1   J: 公訴人有沒有新的意見回應？
         Does the prosecutor have any new opinion to respond?
2   P: 回應一點吧（.）被告人的認罪態度並不是特別好（.）因為他在剛
3   查機關人員抓獲的時候承認　他的行為是一種違法行為（.）但
         從公
4   訴人提審直至今天的法庭審理階段均不承認他的行為是一種
5   違法行為（.）因此公訴人認為被告人的認罪態度並不是特別好
         Respond to one point (.) the defendant's attitude of confession was
         not very good (.) because when he was arrested by investigators he
         admitted his act was illegal (.) but from the time that the prosecutor
         interrogated him until today's trial he has been denying his act was

illegal (.) therefore the prosecutor is of the view that the defendant's
attitude of confession is not very good.

6 I: The prosecutor doesn't think pleading guilty of the defendant is true
7   (.) he told the police that his act is illegal but later in the interrogation
8   and in the courtroom he does not (.) He didn't admit that his act is
9   illegal (.) so his act of admitting the guilt is not very good.

10 J: 辯護人還有無新的意見提出？

Does the defence counsel have new defence opinion?

11 L: 雖然本案案情比較簡單（.）但是被告人的態度比較坦誠（.）並
12   是說走私毒品才叫違法（.）即使 被告人走私的不是毒品（.）
13   常的藥品進入我國國內（.）我國對進口的藥品也沒有免稅規定
14   （.）即使只是普通的藥品（.）也構成偷逃稅款（.）也是違法
15   為（.）因此不能把當事人誤以為的違法行為當做是他認為攜帶
16   是毒品（.）鑒於被告人本身文化 程度和他不是慣犯（.）不能
17   的表述想當然地理解成他是走私毒品（.）因此我認為他 的態度是
18   友好的（.）包括今天在法庭上從頭到尾（.）他 都沒有對公安司法
19   機關辦案過程的挑剔或者是反駁（.）我認為他的態度是良好真
20   的

*Though the fact of the case is simple (.) the defendant is honest (.) not
all illegal acts involve drug smuggling (.) even if the defendant did not
smuggle drugs (.) but ordinary medicines into our country (.) because
our country does not impose tax exemption s on imported medicines
(.) even if they were just ordinary medicines (.) it constituted tax eva-
sion (.) it is also illegal (.) therefore the illegal act defendant mistakenly believes he has committed cannot be interpreted as the act of
smuggling drugs (.) considering his poor education and he is not a
recidivist (.) it is inappropriate to interpret his statement as confess-
ing to drug smuggling (.) and so I think his attitude is good (.) including his behaviour in the court today (.) he did not criticize the police
or make a rebuttal (.) I think his attitude is sincere.*

21 J: 已經記錄在案了（.）控辯雙方的意見法庭都已經充分聽取了并
22   記錄在案（.）問一下被告有什麼要說的

*It is put into record (.) the prosecution and the defence opinions are
both received by the court in good record (.) now ask the defendant
whether he has anything to say.*

23 I: Defendant (.) do you have anything else to tell the court?
24: D: I'm sorry I don't know there are drugs inside.

(Adapted from: Du, 2016, pp. 108–109)

In example (9), the judge's questions to the prosecution in line 1 and to the defence
lawyer in line 10 are not interpreted, but the prosecutor's statement in lines 2–5 is
interpreted, while the defence lawyer's statement in lines 11–19 remains uninterpreted. The judge's statement in line 21 attracts a zero rendition, while the directive to the interpreter in line 22 that refers to the defendant in 3.SG is rendered via
2.SG as a *direct recapitulation*.

Examples (8) and (9) indicate that interpreting occurs when prompts to the interpreter are provided to do so, or at other moments, when statements *against* the defendant are made, usually from the prosecution. In Chinese criminal law trial proceedings, Du (2016, pp. 88–89) identifies the defendant as the "key player" in a process that she describes as having two purposes: "to ascertain the accused's guilt, and to decide on the punishment". In this excerpt, the prosecutor reads aloud a test conclusion report confirming that the material discharged from the defendant's body contained heroin. In example (10), the judge (J) appeared to understand some English, or at least signalled that he understood some of the responses of the defendant (D) (see line 8). In particular, we focus on the discourse of the interpreter (I), i.e. what he presents or re-presents to others, and what role he appears to be enacting according to Merlini and Favaron's (2005) more fine-grained categories of footing.

Example (10)

1 J: 問下他對上述證據有無意見
      Ask him whether he has any opinion about the foresaid evidence.
2 I: Do you agree?
3 D: I don't know what those things are.
4 I: 他說不知道   [那些是什麼東西
      He says he doesn't know [what those things are
5 J: [對這個鑑定的真實性有無>異議<
                     [To the truthfulness of the expert conclusion> if
                     there is any >objection<
6 I: Do you agree to the expert conclusion?
7 D: I said I don't know what those things are –
8 J: 他說他不知道吧?
      He said he didn't know right?
9 I   對
      Yes.
10 J 辯護人有沒有意見?
      Does the lawyer have any opinion?
11 L: 沒有意見
      No.

(Adapted from: Du, 2016, p. 100)

In line 1, the judge addresses the interpreter, not the defendant. The judge had directly addressed the interpreter, not the defendant, and uses 2.SG forms with the interpreter and 3.SG forms in relation to the defendant. The interpreter's interpretation is prompted by the judge, but the choice of words and the question asked by the interpreter is not a relayed version of the judge's words. Instead, the interpreter poses a question to the defendant that presupposes that the defendant is able to form an opinion on what he has heard. The interpreter's utterance in line 2, when interpreting into English, is an example of him occupying the role of the *principal*.

In line 4, he switches to the role of *indirect recapitulator* when interpreting into Chinese. In line 6 when interpreting into English, he is prompted by the judge's words, but asks a question not asked by the judge and therefore acts as *principal*. In line 8, the judge pre-empts the interpreter and states what he believes the defendant said, together with a tag question. This is consistent with the judge's convention of addressing the interpreter, and referring to the defendant with 3.SG. In line 9, the interpreter responds directly to the judge's question as a principal. The judge's question to the lawyer in line 10 is not interpreted, nor is the lawyer's response in line 11.

Example (11) features a first judge (J1), a second judge (J2), the defendant (D), an interpreter (I) and the defence lawyer (L):

Example (11)

1 J2 問一下被告人(.)就是對起訴書指控的犯罪事實(.)有沒有異議?
      Ask the defendant (.) to the fact of the alleged offence stated in the indictment (.) does he have any objection?
2 I: Do you have any objection to the facts charged in the indictment which
3   I read to you just now?
4 D   (1.0)
5 I: Do you have any objection to the contents of the indictment which I
6   read to you just now?
7 D: (4.0) I don't understand=
8 L: =可以翻譯的很簡單(.)不要用那個專業 –
      =Interpret it in a simple way (.) don't use technical –
9 I: Do you have any objection to what I read to you just now?
10 D: (0.5) Objection↑
11 I   Yes (.) to the charge
12 D: I don't understand
13 I: (0.4) Do you have any objection to the charges made by the
14   prosecution department=
15 J1: =那他这种是什麼語啊=
      =what language does he speak=
16 L: =說英語(.)他的英語特別好(.)跟他溝通的時候(.)用最簡單的(.)不
17   那種那種(.)正文的那種 –
      =Speaks English (.) his English was quite good (.) when talking to him (.) use the simplest (.) not that that (.) formal kind –
18 J1: =通俗   [的
      =Commo   [n
19 L: [通俗的口語化的(.)他們那 [邊說話口語化
                   [common colloquial (.) they   [speak colloquially
20 J2:   [問他有沒有意見(.)那個通俗點=
                          [Ask him if he has any opinion (.) use common=

```
21  J:   =盡           [量通俗
         =try          [to use common
22  L:                 [就問他有什么意见=
                       [Just ask him if he has any opinion=
23  I:   =Do you have any objection to the charges?
24  D:   (0.6) <objection>=
25  I:   (0.2) do you have any opinion about your –
26  D:   What <I want to say> is (.) I'm very sorry [XXX] the things are not
27       mine [XXX] it's my friend [XXX] gave me –
28  J1:  呃(.)詳細地就不用說了(.)就問他對於這個指控的事實和過程有
29       意見就行了(.)這個過程 –
         Er (.) no need to state the details (.) asking him about his viewpoint
         on the alleged fact and criminal process is enough (.) the process --
30  I:   =他對於指控的過程沒有意見(.)但是他想說非常抱歉因為那些東
31       不是他的
         He had no opinion about the process (.) but he wanted to say he's
         very sorry because those things did not belong to him.
32  J1:  這個等一会再說
         This can be stated later.
```

Line 1 from Judge 2 is interpreted by the interpreter adopting the footing of a direct recapitulator (lines 2–3). The defendant's silence leads to the interpreter repeating the interpretation (lines 5–6). A longer pause follows, with the defendant providing a response of not understanding what has been said. The defence lawyer issues a directive to the interpreter, and the interpreter in line 9 provides a third (this time shortened) rendition of the judge's source speech from line 1. Judges 1 and 2, and the defence lawyer engage in a side-conversation in lines 15 to 22 about the defendant's and the interpreter's language use. Lines 23 and 25 are fourth and fifth renditions of the Judge 1's directive from line 1. The defendant's response in lines 26 and 27 is not uninterpreted, and Judge 1, who appears to have understood the gist if not the words of the defendant's turn issues a directive with a 3.SG to the interpreter. The interpreter does not relay this directive to the defendant, but instead responds as a *narrator* of what the defendant said, using 3.SG in lines 30 and 31. Judge 1's response in line 32 is a dyad-like response to the interpreter, which is not interpreted. In example (11), there are 23 turns, and only one of them – the first turn in line 1 – is interpreted (albeit five times).

In one predominantly Chinese-speaking setting, namely Hong Kong, Chinese–English court interpreting is now a well-organized and conventionalised practice. Around 150 court interpreters are employed as full-time civil servants of the Court Language Section of the Judiciary of Hong Kong, leading Ng (2009, p. 120) to claim that Hong Kong's judicial processes are "one of the most 'interpreted' legal systems in the world". In Hong Kong, for a trial heard in English, interpreting is usually conducted in the consecutive mode between Cantonese and English, as chuchotage is not always a workable mode to use to larger numbers of Cantonese-speakers with little or no proficiency in English. Defendants and witnesses can equally access English-source speech (Ng, 2015, p. 247). While interpretation facilitates communication between those without sufficient proficiency in either English or Cantonese, there are usually others in the courtroom who have high proficiency in both languages. For these courtroom interlocutors, interpreting is not an activity enabling communication, but a form of 're-presented' speech to which they may or may not pay attention.

Court interpreters in Hong Kong are usually keenly aware of the presence of bilinguals who have heard the source speech of others, and who then listen to the interpreter's target speech, sometimes making their own judgement of the felicity of the interpretation. The constellation of other bilinguals being present in the interaction, occupying various roles, is termed adversarial interpreting by Kredens (2017, p. 17) "where an interpreter's output is monitored and/or challenged, either during the speech event or subsequently". Ng (2015, p. 247) recounts that "it is not uncommon for bilingual counsel or judges to criticize an interpreter's rendition", and refers to past examples such as Chow and Chin (1997) who quote a magistrate saying in open court that his interpreter's poor interpretation 'could rob the defendant of a fair trial'. The interpreter in question was unable to compose herself after this comment and had to be replaced. Ng (2015) comments that the presence of other bilinguals (and sometimes fellow interpreters) in the courtroom makes Hong Kong court interpreting more transparent and also more demanding. She gives an example from court proceedings featuring a defence counsel (DC), interpreter (I) and a witness (W) where the interpreter provides an interpretation of the term 'aggrieved' (marked here in bold) that the defence counsel considers to be too imprecise, motivating an intervention from him in line 7:

Example (12)

1   DC: Alright. Now, when you . . . after the sexual intercourse, you must
2   feel very **aggrieved.**
3   I: 噂，咁係呢，係你進行完性交之後呢，咁應該呢，就係呢，係覺
4   得呢，好辛苦，係咪？
           *Now, so after the sexual intercourse, you must have felt very **hard/bad**. Is that right?*
5   W: 係
           Yes.
6   I: Yes.
7   DC: No, "aggrieved", "aggrieved".
                    (Ng, 2015, p. 252. Cross-examination of W, Rape, High Court)

It is not clear if the interpreter then interpreted the defence counsel's interjection. The 'over-hearer status' of the defence counsel and the desire to challenge the interpreter is likely to be conditioned by the communicative event, that of cross-examination, in which a defence counsel typically employs a variety of means to disprove or discredit a witness's testimony. In the following example, the prosecution counsel (PC) is interrupted by the magistrate (M). The interpreter

(I) interprets this not as two turns from two speakers, but as a single turn with further added content:

Example (13)

1	PC:	So, em, now after she discard the wrappings-
2	M:	Well, hold on, hold on. After she took that, what did she do?
3	I:	佢攞咗哩一 . . . 哩一個子母袋之後，佢點呀？

Having taken a 2-in-1 bag, what did she do?

(Adapted from Ng, 2015, p. 255. Examination-in-chief of
W. Theft. Magistrates' Court)

The two turns from the prosecution counsel and the magistrate in English in example (13) are 'collapsed' into one turn in Cantonese provided by the interpreter. It appears that the interpreter had little chance to interpret what the prosecution counsel had said as the magistrate interjected. The interpretation into Cantonese does not appear to distinguish which interlocutor contributed which referential content. A similar example is shown following, which is taken from the examination-in-chief of a witness in a case dealing with charges of trafficking in dangerous goods, heard at a Hong Kong District Court. Here, the interpreter (I) does not interpret anything until a 'negotiated' or 'imposed' question form is agreed upon between the prosecution counsel (PC) and the judge (J). The defence counsel (DC) joins the interaction at the end while the witness (W) is present throughout:

Example (14)

1	PC:	During the, uh, time . . . during the time that . . . this video . . .
2		interview was being conducted, officer, did you have any contact from
3		outside the room?
4	J:	Well, that's not the allegation, is it? This is, it's video'd. It's before
5		there's an allegation that . . . they taught her what to say.
6	PC:	Yes, Your Honour, but, um, I don't need to lead that or, or, or I, what I
7		wish to establish is that during the interview, there was contact from
8		outside, if I may just put my question . . .
9		Were you given any instructions, whilst this interview was being
10		conducted, officer, whilst you were inside the room?
11	I:	拿咁當時當進行緊呢個嘅er會面嘅時候 呢，當你係間房裡面嘅
12		時候啦,當時係咪有俾過指示你㗎?

*So when you were conducting the interview, when you were inside
the room, were you given any instructions?*

13	J:	There's no such allegation
14	PC:	I'm not . . . it's nothing to do with allegation, Your Honour. I'm just
15		asking this question [if I may.
16	J:	[Why?

17	PC:	\<sigh> Because this is what happened during the (.) the proceedings,
18		Your Honour.
19	J:	. . . . . Was there an interruption?
20	DC:	I think that towards the end of the interview, someone [. . .] placed a
21		piece of the paper underneath the door and put it into the interview
22		room. Either this officer or the other officer [. . .], for the purpose of
23		their enquiry.
24	I:	[Interpreter provides a chuchotage interpretation of the DC's
25		comment to W.]
26	J:	I see. Sorry. Yes.

(Adapted from: Ng, 2015, p. 256)

In example (14) the prosecution counsel commences by directly addressing the witness. As in example (13), it appears that the judge then immediately took the floor, and the interpreter was reluctant to or unable to interpret the turn in lines 1–3. The judge interacts directly with the prosecution counsel (lines 4–5), and the prosecution counsel (lines 6–8) responds with a justification for the framing of the question to the witness. The interpreter's interpretation in line 11 reflects only the last part of the prosecution counsel's turn. Ng (2015, p. 257) observes that "access to the uninterpreted interaction between counsel and the judge has been effectively denied to the witness in the witness box, the defendant in the dock, as well as the spectators in the public gallery". In line 9, the prosecution counsel addresses the witness, which appears to be a cue to the interpreter to interpret the question into Cantonese (lines 11–12). The witness does not respond or is perhaps not given an opportunity to respond. The judge in line 13 disputes the content of the question put by the prosecution counsel. Lines 13 to 19 contain an exchange between the judge and the prosecution counsel, with the contribution from the defence counsel being interpreted via chuchotage to the witness only. Ng (2015, p. 257) notes that during one of the video recorded interviews that are used as evidence in the court, a piece of paper was slid underneath the door during the course of the interview.

The Hong Kong courtroom is a context in which not only the operationalisation of court interpreting services can be studied, but one in which a number of features of interpreter performance can be looked at.[1] A close examination of interpreting performance in two cases, both involving charges of sexual assault of teenage girls by adult males is undertaken by Leung and Gibbons (2008). The content of many of the testimonies and questions asked to witnesses and defendants posed a challenge to some interpreters whose interpretations were recorded. In the first place, interpreters are obliged to faithfully and without distortion interpret source speech into target speech retaining the illocutionary force of the source speech and the speaker's intent. This means that their target speech should not alter the propositional content of source speech in a way more positive or more negative compared to the way that it was delivered. At the same time, an interpreter requires the self-awareness to know if s/he may be unable to retain his/her role of impartiality due to the content of others' speech or due to other attributes of the interlocutors, notwithstanding his/her professional obligation *not* to allow these to influence his/her performance. In real terms this means that an interpreter should work in an unbiased way with all clients, regardless of whether they are school students, senior bureaucrats, cancer patients, police officers or suspected rapists.

Leung and Gibbons (2008) locate instances in which the interpreter's personal unease with the type of question being asked by a defence barrister (DB) to teenager witness becomes apparent in the interpretation provided by the interpreter (I).

Example (15)

1	DB:	. . . should because such never happened at all?
2	I:	. . . 嗱辯方話原因係因為根本無咁嘅事發生過你同唔同意啊
		. . . now the defence said that.. the reason is that such never happened at all, do you agree, ah?

(Adapted from: Leung & Gibbons, 2008, p. 181)

The interpreter otherwise uses first person in her interpretations, as recorded by Leung and Gibbons (2008). But in the aforementioned instance, she does not. In the trial, the defence barrister had been arguing that the witness had fabricated the claim of being raped. The question asked by the defence barrister is rendered in the Chinese interpretation with an addition at the start of the turn that overtly identifies the defence barrister as the source speaker, *not* the interpreter. It appears that the interpreter makes this addition to change her footing. The change to *narrator* makes it clear to the witness that the interpreter is not addressing the witness as the personally, but relaying another's words.

In the following instance the same defence barrister questions the same witness and why she accepted an invitation to go to her badminton coach's house where she was allegedly sexually assaulted. The defence barrister invokes Chinese notions of politeness in his question that contains the assumption that 礼貌 'politeness' in Chinese culture is expressed by repeated polite refusals to an offer, before an invitation is finally accepted. The defence barrister wishes to suggest in his question that the witness's first-time acceptance of the invitation is not congruent to traditional notions of how a teenager should behave. Leung and Gibbons (2008, p. 183) note that invocation of this politeness norm ignores another cultural norm: that a child or teenager cannot easily refuse an invitation from a person more senior to him/her without threatening the face of the senior person.

Example (16)

1	DB:	So, it never occurred to you on THAT phone chat . . . when he told you
2		come over to MY house. . . . to watch the video . . . about badminton
3		. . . that you should . . . at least . . . see if he . . . he could LEND you
4		the video and so that you can watch it at home.
5	I:	咁意思係咪即係話嗰次:eh響電話度當佢同你講呢話:叫你去佢

6   屋企一齊睇羽毛球帶嘅時候呢(.)當時你從來呢都無諗過就話eh:
7   問佢

   So . . . it means, at that time on the phone when he told you . . . to go
   to his house to watch the badminton video tape, together, at that
   time you never thought of . . . asking him.. to lend you the tape so
   that you could watch it at home. You never thought of that?
                        (Adapted from: Leung & Gibbons, 2008, p. 181)

The illocutionary force of the target speech in lines 5 and 6 contains some features
of note. The moralising tone of "you should at least see if" is rendered as 你無咁
諗過 'you never thought of asking him'. The omission of "at least" and the change
from "you should" lessens the force of the social assumptions concerning appropriate behaviour contained in the defence barrister's question. The defence barrister's
turn is nominally an interrogative, but the illocutionary force, as noted by Leung and
Gibbons (2008, p. 163) is one of casting doubt on the witness. These are neutralised
to some extent by the interpreter whose Chinese interpretations are more like elicitation questions, further exemplified by the addition of a final tag, 你無咁諗過 'you
have never thought of that'? Leung and Gibbons (2008, p. 183) conclude that the
defence barrister's speech is based on "an underlying ideology, and the discourse
through which it is manifested, is gendered, and culturally and legally laden".

It appears that the interpreter is aware of this, and her interpretations strongly
indicate that she is not unbiased towards the ideology represented by the defence
barrister. But it is hard to speculate on the degree that she knowingly changes the
illocutionary force in her target speech. One of the authors, Leung, herself a court
interpreter, reflects on

   her own experience of unconsciously making changes when interpreting an
   idea that she found hard to accept, resisting the adoption of the voice of the
   speaker. . . . This is in contradiction to guidelines and ethics for court interpreting.
                        (Leung & Gibbons, 2008, p. 182)

The reminder that Leung gives us is that changes and even distortions in an
interpreter's target speech may not be apparent to the interpreter him-/herself
where the position presented by the source speaker strongly diverges from the
interpreter's own worldview or personal values, notwithstanding the efforts of the
interpreter to still observe the profession's principles of impartiality and unbiasedness. We see here how professional ethics and the intercultural models employed
by the interpreter intersect and how the interpretation bears an intercultural strategy of self-rephrasing.

3.3.6   *Healthcare interpreting*

In many countries healthcare settings are now a common area for work for interpreters. In Canada and the United States, healthcare interpreting is a very large
area of work for interpreters' employment (Kelly & Stewart, 2010, pp. 15–17),

while a major supplier of interpreting services in Australia reports that at least 48% and up to 90% of requested interpreting assignments relate to healthcare (Hlavac, Gentile, Orlando, Pappas, & Zucchi, 2018, p. 77). The reason for the high volume of healthcare interpreting in some cases is a consequence of *health* policies, rather than *linguistic* policies.

A conceptualization of interpreting as an activity that enables the provision of healthcare is likely to have an effect on the operationalisation of medical interpreting. The growth in healthcare interpreting is reflective also of "ideological" changes in the provision of healthcare and to doctor-patient relations in which the needs (including the cultural-linguistic ones) of the patient play an important role. It is no accident that the provision of professional interpreting services in the healthcare sector has happened in concert with the development of a 'patient-centred' approach to healthcare, in which healthcare workers (initially) adopt open-ended discussions with patients, inform patients about their options and choices and guide them rather than present them with a diagnosis (see 4.2.3). Such a relationship with an allophone patient is achievable only through the use of professional interpreting services.

We identify here, in particular, in-house hospital employees, who in addition to the requirement to provide linguistic mediation for healthcare staff and patients, also have obligations to their employer to work towards ensuring the health and well-being of patients and in averting harm to them. What this means is that recorded examples of medical interpreters' discourse show that interpreters contain instances of expanding, adding or checking comprehension, and these occur as moves that interpreters make in serving the afore-mentioned goals: serving the patient's health and well-being and averting harm. Hsieh and Kramer (2012, p. 158) surmise on the basis of data from interpreted interactions that "interpreters actively and systematically intervene in provider-patient interactions to achieve effective, ethical, and culturally sensitive care".

Within the area of medical discourse, and the area of doctor-patient relations in general, we refer to the following statement made by Price, Perez-Stable, Nickleach, Lopez, and Karliner (2002, p. 226), "effective communication in clinical encounters depends on exchange of accurate information between clinician and patient and on interpersonal skills that foster understanding of patients' social or cultural backgrounds and development of patient-clinician rapport". Further, the ability to respond flexibly and dynamically in medical interactions is something that Penn and Watermeyer (2012, p. 396) locate in many interactions, leading them to state that "in a successful triad there appears to be a fluidity of role depending on topic, patient and stage of interaction. This flexibility seems to be an essential component of successful intercultural practice". Based on over 300 medical encounters Angelelli (2004, p. 78) finds that interpreters adopt different footings across different interactions and within the same interaction, from the 'classic' footing of *reporter* or *direct recapitulator*, re-presenting the speech of others, to other footings such as *pseudo co-principal, responder* or *principal*, where these aid the interpreter in "controlling the flow of traffic, exploring answers, expanding/summarizing, expressing solidarity/exercises power", and to further footings as a *principal* where the interpreter has complete 'text ownership' in "brokering cultural references, [showing] alignment/affect" and even "replacing the monolingual interlocutor". Angelelli (2004) uses the term "visibility of text ownership" and degrees thereof, where it is clear to at least one of the interlocutors if not both that the interpreter's words emanate from only the interpreter him-/herself, either wholly or partly.

A number of studies of medical interpreting record the interpreter adopting a "gatekeeper" position (Davidson, 2000) or that the interpreter is selective in what they transmit to the other person, including the possibility of omissions, direct responses and side-conversations as what Bolden (2000, p. 391) describes as characteristics of a "mediated interaction" (e.g. Kaufert & Putsch, 1997; Metzger, 1999; Bot, 2005). Bolden (2000) contrasts these interactions to "directly interpreted interaction" in which the interpreter faithfully interprets everything that is said, without additions or omissions. The "gate-keeping" approach, as described by Davidson (2000) results in two interposed conversations taking place: one between the healthcare provider and the patient; the other between the interpreter and the patient. The use of 3.SG pronoun forms is also a conspicuous feature of this approach that reinforces the impression that the interaction is structured as two parallel conversations.

Hale (2007) warns strongly against the gate-keeping approach where interpreters take on the role of deciding what is important or relevant to be relayed to others, and where they add to the healthcare professional's utterances. They appear to do this when they deem these to be insufficient or they may even respond directly to patients' questions, instead of allowing the healthcare professional to reply. She is critical of interpreters having an understanding of their role when:

> [i]nterpreters become pseudo-health care providers by holding separate but related conversations with the physician and the patient, later providing summaries of the original utterances in the other languages. . . . They argue that such an approach helps the doctor save valuable time.
>
> (Hale, 2007, p. 43)

A point mentioned in Price et al.'s (2002) description of doctor-patient relations is the development of patient-clinician rapport. It is hard to conceive how doctors can establish rapport with a patient when an interpreter engages in side-conversations with the patient that the doctor cannot understand, or when a doctor asks a question and then suspects from the patient's response that the question may not have been conveyed accurately to the patient. Further, it is not clear how a healthcare professional can gain an understanding of patients' social or cultural backgrounds if the interpreter edits or omits patients' responses to questions or narratives, or re-phrases them in a way they believe will be more easily understood by the healthcare professional. In the medical setting, the interpreter's knowledge of features of cultural backgrounds of both interlocutors is a resource that, in the first place, should optimise the quality of their *interpreting*, rather than compel them to censor or re-cast culturally specific discourse forms. Gentile et al.

(1996, pp. 60–61) explain that "cultural knowledge and contextual knowledge is used only to carry out the interpreting accurately, not to assist the NES [non-English speaker] as a cultural broker". Hale (2007) sums up a number of features relevant to healthcare interpreting and advocates the application of a conventional understanding of interpreting that allows all parties to communicate with each other without unsolicited interventions from the interpreter:

> By [interpreters] so doing, doctors maintain the responsibility for directing the consultation, as the appropriate questions, picking up on cues from seemingly irrelevant material provided by the patient, and attempting to build a rapport with the patient. Patients, on the other hand, maintain the right to decide on what they say and how to say it and to have their questions answered by a professional physician. The responsibility for effective communication still lies with the authors of the utterances.
>
> (Hale, 2007, p. 43)

Notwithstanding this clear description, we locate a number of instances when interpreters adopt footings other than that of reporter. We present three examples of Chinese–English medical interpreting taken from a corpus of 29 doctor-patient interactions that Zhan and Zeng (2017) recorded at a Guangzhou hospital. In this corpus, Zhan and Zeng (2017) record 2,914 turns (from all participating inter-locutors) in interactions with a total time length of over 4.5 hours (274 minutes). Approximately one half of the 2,914 turns would have come from interpreters, i.e. approx. 1,450 turns, amongst which, they record 129 that bear total or partial ownership of the interpreters only. These relate to turns where the interpreters take on the role of principal in initiating or re-casting verbal text that is relayed to either the doctor or the patient. In a statistical sense, these 'principal-enacted' turns account for less than 10% of all interpreter turns. Zhan and Zeng (2017) specifically focus on these, to examine how and why they occur. We draw on their examples to examine the changes in footing of the interpreter, and to see whether intercultural features play a role in these. All interpreters possessed a degree in Medical English, had passed specialist tests set by the hospital and had received intensive training in basic healthcare practices and medical interpreting. Their role is one of in-house interpreters.

In example (17), the Philippine patient (P) reports pain in her digestive tract and a bloating of her upper abdomen. The excerpt following is taken from a point early on in the interaction, where the patient has just listed her symptoms to the doctor (D) via the interpreter (I):

Example (17)

1 D: 没有明显的痛，但是不舒服，胀。完了吃完以后吐是吧？其他的
2   还有什么不舒服？
     No obvious pain, but feeling uncomfortable and bloated. You vomit after eating, right? Any other discomfort?

3 I: Besides the symptoms you mention, is there anything else?
4 P: No.
5 I: 没有。
       No.
6 P: [Only before when I had fever . . .]
7 D: [多长时间了?
       How long is that?
8 I: How long does it last?
9 P: My fever?
10 I: No. Your stomach upset.
11 P: Until now. In the morning, I also vomit.
12 I: Yes. How many days?
13 P: I think it's already one week.
14 I: 一个星期。
       One week.
15 D: 反酸，烧心，是吧?
       Acid reflux, burning in the heart, right?
16 I: 嗯。
       Yes.
       <Doctor examines patient>
17 I: So when the doctor presses, you feel pain?
18 P: No. No pain.
19 I: 不痛。
       No pain.
20 P: [I come . . . vomit.]
21 D: [这，这儿呢?]
       Here, what about here?
22 I: How about there?
       <Patient shakes her head>
23 P: No.
24 D: 其他的没问题，就是这地方不舒服，是吧?
       No other problems. You just feel uncomfortable here, right?
25 I: 她说按的时候也会有想吐的感觉。
       She says when it's pressed, she also feels like vomiting.
26 D: 想吐的感觉。哦。以前有什么病?
       Feels like vomiting. Well, any disease in the past?
27 I: Do you have any basic disease? For example, any problem in the
28   heart, lung, liver?
29 P: No. No.
30 I: 没有基础病。
       No basic disease.

(Adapted from Zhan & Zeng, 2017, pp. 105–106)

In line 3 the interpreter omits content from the doctor's question in lines 1 and 2 that he considers to be understood, and renders this via a shortened statement and an interrogative. In lines 9 and 13 the interpreter engages with the patient in a dyad, asking focused questions to elicit the length of time that the patient has been suffering the upset stomach, and provides the doctor with the time length in line 14. The interpreter does not interpret the doctor's description of the symptoms in line 15, and instead agrees in line 16 that these symptoms are present. In line 17 the interpreter initiates questioning about pain symptoms after the doctor started pressing her. The interpreter answers a question on the patient's behalf in line 25, and in line 27 omits the doctor's statement 'feels like vomiting', and renders the doctor's question, together with an additional question containing examples of internal organs that are prone to illness. In example (17) the interpreter adopts the role of reporter (as the 'faithful interpreter'), principal (in initiating questions or eliciting responses sought, but not actually verbalized by others) and responder (in private dyads with the doctor). This results in the turns in lines 9, 11, 15 and 24 remaining uninterpreted.

In the following example (18) a Philippine patient (P), accompanied by her daughter (P'sD) is visiting the cardiovascular department, to have results explained to her. A history of high blood pressure motivates the doctor (D) to take her blood pressure. The interpreter (I) was privy to information that the patient had had her blood pressure measured by a nurse just before coming to the cardiovascular department. The excerpt following is from near the start of the interaction:

Example (18)

 1 D: 给她量个血压看。
          Let me take her blood pressure.
 2 I: Take her blood pressure.   她其实有。刚刚在护士那里量的。
                                        She has in fact done it. Just now, the
                                        nurse took it.
 3 D: 好。
          Okay.
 4 I: 这是今天早上在那个，产科那边不是有自己量血压的那个仪器嘛
 5   量的
          This morning, there, at Obstetrics Department, they had a machine
          to take blood pressure. She did it.
          [The doctor starts to take the patient's blood pressure with a sphygmomanometer, despite the fact that she has an electronic device to measure blood pressure.]
 6 P'sD: And now, I bought her a vitamin. It is Centrum Silver.
 7 I: 哦，善存银片。
          Oh, Centrum silver.
 8 P'sD: For 50 years old, up. So, I just wanna ask if it's the vitamin good for
 9   her. Or, is there any vitamins that she needs to take?
10 I: I'll ask the doctor.
11 P'sD: OK.
12 I: Centrum, right?

13   P'sD: Yes. Centrum.
14   D: 血压现在降到新低啊，105
           Blood pressure has fallen to a new low, 105
15   I: 她还有吃那种五十岁以上的善存。
           She has been taking Centrum for people aged fifty years or over.
                                    (Adapted from: Zhan & Zeng, 2017, p. 107)

In line 2 the interpreter conveys to the patient (and her daughter) that the doctor intends to take her blood pressure as a *reporter*. In the same line, and in lines 4 and 5 the interpreter interacts with the doctor only, informing him in which hospital department the patient's blood pressure had been taken on that same day. In line 7 the interpreter interprets the title of the vitamins that the patient's daughter wants to show to the doctor, namely 哦，善存银片 'oh, Centrum Silver'. This is a partial rendition only of the English utterance in line 6. The patient's daughter's first utterance is not interpreted; it may be that the doctor could see from her actions that she had brought vitamins that her mother was taking. In line 8 the patient's daughter's utterances contain three pieces of information: the target age group of people for whom Centrum Silver is intended; if the vitamins are good for her mother; should the mother take any (further) tablets. Lines 10 to 13 contain dyads between the interpreter and the patient's daughter that include the interpreter checking the name of the tablets. None of this is interpreted to the doctor. The doctor intervenes with his announcement of the patient's blood pressure reading in line 14, and the interpreter's utterance in line 15 is a partial rendition of what was said in line 8. It is not clear if the doctor's utterance from line 14 on her blood pressure reading is interpreted. In all, there are only two pieces of information that are interpreted in this excerpt: the doctor's announcement that he will take her blood pressure (line 2) and the patient's daughter's information that her mother takes Centrum Silver for people aged 50 or over. The source speech in lines 4, 5, 7, most of 7, and all of 8, 9, 10, 11, 12 and possibly 13 remains uninterpreted.

The following example features a doctor who is a Traditional Chinese Medicine practitioner (D). An American patient (P) is seeking treatment from him for shoulder pain caused by the degeneration of cervical vertebrae. The doctor has spoken to the patient about the diagnosis and treatment options, which in this case involves the administration of acupuncture. The following excerpt is near the start of the interaction:

Example (19)

1   D: 如果是说，每天过来做治疗的时候 . . . . . . 你可以问一下他，他
2   来做过什么推拿呀跟针灸啊这些，做过没有。
         *If he comes for treatment every day . . . You can ask him, has he had
         massage or acupuncture before?*
3. I: Did you receive any acupuncture or massage?
4. P: Before?
5 I: Yes.

6 P: Er . . . Massage yes, but acupuncture no.

7 I: 他接受过那种推拿，然后，针灸没有。
       He has had some kind of massage. No acupuncture.

8 D: 针灸没有。那你跟他讲一下，针灸呢，因为我们是这个，这个针

9   插时有一些酸胀痛吧，这样的情况，但它不会说非常疼。<Doctor

10   turns to the patient> 所以如果要是说很疼的话，你可以适当地跟

11   们说。<Doctor turns to the interpreter> 让他不用紧张就是了。
       No acupuncture. Then you tell him, acupuncture, when a needle is
       inserted, he will feel a bit sour, swollen and painful, situation like
       this, but it won't be very painful. So if you feel great pain, you can
       tell us. Just tell him not to feel nervous.

12 I: When the doctor performs the acupuncture, there may be a little bit pain

13   and discomfort. So if you cannot, er, stand the pain, tell the doctor.

14 P: OK.

15 I: I took the acupuncture before, just a little bit . . . <gives a visual signal
        for a small amount using the thumb and index of his right hand.>

16 P: Hm. Is it necessary?

17 I: Yes, to promote your blood flow and help the nerve tissue to repair.

                        (Adapted from: Zhan & Zeng, 2017, p. 107)

In lines 1 and 2 the doctor uses a 3.SG pronoun about the patient, and then a
2.SG pronoun directly addressing the interpreter. In line 3 the interpreter transfers
the last part of the doctor's turn only, as a *direct recapitulator*. The interpreter
interprets the patient's response in line 6 to the doctor in line 7 as an *indirect
recapitulator*, using 3.SG. The doctor's turn in lines 8 to 11 switches in addressing first the interpreter, then the patient, then the interpreter, shown in the use of
3.SG and 2.SG as well as via the physical position of the doctor. The interpreter
interprets part of what was directed to him, as the interpreter, and all addressed to
the patient as a direct recapitulator in lines 12 and 13. What follows in line 15 is
a comment to the patient from the interpreter as a principal, in which he recounts
his own experience of having acupuncture. That is, the interpreter shares his own
experience as a patient receiving acupuncture, and his remark to the patient functions as a comforting statement in the manner of "Don't be afraid. I've had acupuncture too". The patient's question in line 16 is not interpreted, and instead, the
interpreter replies as a *responder* providing an explanation drawing on his own
medical knowledge.

As stated, the examples that we present from Zhan and Zeng (2017) focus on
'principal-enacted' turns from interpreters in a larger set of corpora in which these
are otherwise not so common and in which interpreters interpret as *reporters* or *direct
recapitulators* of others' speech. In addition to instances in which the interpreters
enact these roles in examples (22) and (24), the interpreter engages in private dyads
with the doctor where the interpreter believes that they have information to answer
the doctor's questions directly (example 23) or information to pre-empt activities
that the doctor is about to perform (examples 22, 24). In places the interpreter
directly asks questions to the patient where they believe that the response provided

will be of interest to the doctor. In other places, the interpreter engages in dyads or one-to-one conversations with the patient or the patient's family member and information from these dyads is only selectively relayed to the doctor. The zero-renditions and the 'principal-enacted' or 'responder-enacted' turns occur, in part, due to the in-house status of the interpreters with their (non-specialist) knowledge of medical procedures (Bolden, 2000). Further discussion on roles and mediation is provided in section 3.4.

3.4   Untrained interpreters and ad-hoc interpreting

Sections 3.3.1 to 3.3.5 outlined the settings in which interpreters most frequently work and examples were presented in each of these to show how professional and trained interpreters work with others. As outlined in section 3.2, the role(s) of the interpreter are often not well understood by others, and bilinguals can sometimes be asked to linguistically mediate for others without a clear idea of how to do this. This section focuses on such occurrences. The term 'untrained interpreters' refers to people who linguistic mediate for others without formal training and without obvious knowledge of the situations, discourse features, role-relations, turn-taking and interactional management protocols of interpreter-mediated interactions. Ad-hoc interpreting refers to a person performing linguistic mediation for others where they do not see this as their (main) occupation, regardless of whether they are remunerated for this or not. Often ad-hoc interpreting occurs when others call upon a bilingual person known to them to interpret as mentioned in Section 3.1.

Ad-hoc or impromptu interpreters are bilinguals without interpreter training who provide linguistic mediation for others. An absence of training and knowledge of the work and role of the interpreter usually has predictable (i.e. negative) consequences. In the study presented as follows, interpreting is required for six Chinese businessmen visiting business partners in Britain. Instead of an interpreter, the British hosts hired a local university student with Chinese as his L1, who was a technical expert in the relevant area of business. While the decision to employ a person with relevant technical knowledge is understandable, the student had no reported experience in interpreting and did not understand what the role of the interpreter is. The student had been in Britain some time and in addition to English-language skills had acquired proficiency in British pragmatic norms.

In the excerpt of the transcript given in example (20), taken from Spencer-Oatey and Xing's (2009) study of a Chinese–English business meeting, the ad-hoc interpreter employs his pragmatic knowledge on how business meetings are held by (British) English speakers and by Chinese speakers. The six visiting Chinese businessmen were engineers from a Chinese company who had been invited to Britain for a post-sales visit hosted by the partner company with which they trade. The setting is an introductory meeting where the British chairman welcomed the visitors, asked the British staff to introduce themselves, gave a brief introduction to the company and then asked the Chinese visitors to introduce themselves. The hosts of the meeting are British and the organization of the meeting proceeded according to British norms. Jack is the British host. Sun is the most senior of the Chinese visitors, and Shen, Chen, Xu and Ma are further members of the Chinese delegation. The interpreter is marked as (I), translations as (T), back translations as (BT), glosses of uninterpreted Chinese turns as (UCT) are marked in italics with non-verbal details given in angle brackets:

Example (20)

1	JACK:	Could I now ask if the members (.) could each introduce
2		themselves so that we can learn (.) um (.) who they are and what
3		their interests are.
4	I:	他说让你们就是自我介绍一下，就是一些兴趣或者就是一
5		些……呃……单位呀、一些呃……这个自己的兴趣爱好介绍一下？
	BT:	*He says that he wants you that is to introduce yourselves that is*
		your interests or that is something about your work unit or
		introduce some of your interests and hobbies.
6	SUN:	\<turns to colleagues and discusses with them and the interpreter
		in Chinese\>
7	SUN:	我们每个人都自我介绍一下.
		We each introduce ourselves.
8	SHEN:	如果你能代表我们做就最好了。
		It's best if you do it on our behalf.
9	SUN:	\<reading from a script\> 首先，亲爱的「X」公司
		First of all, to [X] Company. . .
10	I:	不是不是。他说先介绍一下。我是……就是说，是，就是说我
11		是公司的……，我是单位
		No. he said first you introduce yourself . . . I am that is, I am
		that is, I am from such and such a company, I am from such and
		such an organization.
12	SUN:	我是「姓」，我来自公司「名称」
		I am [surname] from Company [name].
13	I:	He is from [name of Company]
14	CHEN:	说你做了什么。
		Say what you do.
15	SUN:	我参与了设计。
		I'm involved in design.
16	XU:	说你的全名。全名。全名。说你是一名设计工程师。
		Give your full name. Full name. Full name. Say you're a design
		engineer.
17	SUN:	设计工程师
		Design engineer.
18	I:	His name is [name] and he is a design engineer.
19	MA:	我来自[公司名称]，[产品]部门经理
		I am from [name of company], and manager of the [product]
		department.
20	I:	He is the manager of the [name of Department] of [name of

21   Company]<Chinese delegation members continue to introduce themselves.>

(Adapted from: Spencer-Oatey & Xing, 2009, p. 227.
Chinese characters added.)

There are a number of features in the excerpt from the interaction that identify the student/technical expert as an ad-hoc interpreter: use of 3.SG. in rendering speech from source speeches in which they use 1.SG (lines 4,13,18,20), omissions of speakers' turns (lines 7,8,9,14,15,16). The most prominent instance of his interpreting practices is his interruption of the most senior member of the delegation, Sun, in line 10. The ad-hoc interpreter curtails what he believes will follow from Sun, namely a 'return' speech from the Chinese visitors to their British hosts. Spencer-Oatey and Xing (2003) later asked questions to most of the participants. They report that at the point when the head of the Chinese delegation was invited to introduce the members of his delegation, he:

> took it as an invitation to deliver a return speech, and started to express the group's appreciation to the hosts. However, he was cut short by the interpreter, who explained that they had been asked to introduce themselves, not give a return speech. After several minutes of uncomfortable discussion in Chinese by the visitors, each delegation member introduced himself.
>
> (Spencer-Oatey & Xing, 2003, pp. 39–40)

The ad-hoc interpreter is aware of the intercultural schemas that pertains here. These are: British and Chinese conventions of introducing oneself at a formal meeting where interlocutors meet for the first time: British and Chinese notions of hospitality and being a guest. The ad-hoc interpreter, of Chinese origin, also knew that in Chinese business meetings, it is customary after one party has delivered a speech for the other party to deliver a speech in return. The ad-hoc interpreter uses a strategy of interruption to avert a speech act that he believes will be unfamiliar to the British hosts. As stated, the ad-hoc interpreter possessed knowledge of the pragmatic norms pertaining to *both* groups of speakers, but did not use this knowledge to allow *one* group, the Chinese speakers, to exercise their norms.

He could have done this, with the possibility of briefly intervening to explain to the English speakers that the Chinese speakers viewed the moment as an opportune one for them to deliver a return speech. If the interpreter had done this, he would have allowed the Chinese speakers to perform an act that they consider *necessary* as guests to perform to their hosts, and to maintain face. This would have been acceptable to the British hosts, with the chairman later remarking in a follow-up interview that "if the interpreter said to me that they are just making a return speech, then it would have been fine" (Spencer-Oatey & Xing, 2003, p. 41).

Instead, the ad-hoc interpreter intervened to silence the Chinese guests, in the belief that the meeting should follow British English pragmatic norms only. This caused the Chinese guests to lose face, and to believe, together with other things that happened at the meeting, that "perhaps the British look down on us Chinese"

(Spencer-Oatey & Xing, 2003, p. 41), as stated by the Chinese delegation leader in a follow-up interview. Some of the delegation members blamed the ad-hoc interpreter for the lack of opportunity to give a return speech. The following exchange was recorded by the authors of the study with the Chinese businessmen after the introductory session:

Example (21)

1	MA:	这种时候「翻译员的名字」不应该打断他
		At moments like this [interpreter's name] shouldn't have interrupted.
2	LIN:	是的。
		That's right.
3	XU:	中国人觉得一次性说几句话很正常。
		From the Chinese point of view, it's normal to say a few words.
4	SUN:	需要说一些礼貌性的话。
		To say something out of courtesy.
5	MA:	事实上，我要说些不那么令人愉快的话了，「翻译」就只是翻，
6		仅此而已……他不应该参与任何其他事情。无论我说什么，他
7		不应该 插嘴。这是一个正式场合，他只需要翻译。
		In fact, let me say something not so pleasant, [interpreter] was just a translator, nothing more . . . He shouldn't have taken part in anything else. Whatever I said, he shouldn't have butted in. He should have just translated it, this was a formal occasion.
8	LIN:	没错，没错。重点就是翻译就应该只翻译。
		That's right, that's right. The key is to function as an interpreter.
9	SUN:	还有一种可能，也许他们不想让我说话。
		On the other hand, maybe they didn't want me to speak.
10	MA:	确实，他们没有让你说话。
		It's true that they didn't ask you to speak.

* * * * *

18	CHEN:	至于「翻译的名字」……此刻他至关重要……
		As far as [interpreter's name] . . . played a very important role at this moment . . .
19	LIN:	这才是重点。[Several chorus agreement]
		This is the point.
20	CHEN:	[翻译的名字] 的翻译太简单，而且有时他会把他自己的观点加
21		进他的 翻译里。那是不行的。翻译不该是这个样子的。
		[interpreter's name]'s interpreting was too brief, and some-times he put his own opinions into his interpreting. That won't do. This is not the way of interpreting.

(Adapted from: Spencer-Oatey & Xing, 2009, pp. 225–226. Chinese characters added.)

The delegation leader, Sun, believed that that the decision to disallow him from speaking came from the British hosts themselves, which was not the case. The

British host, Jack, gave his recollection of the welcome meeting to the researcher (R) in the following way:

Example (22)

```
 1  JACK:  This is where they went into total chaos, and it just didn't work out
 2         . . . I thought, well, you know, and that's where you wonder, well,
 3         what did the translator say?
 4  R:     He was trying to give a return speech. He was expressing their
 5         thanks to [British company name], then he was cut short by the
 6         interpreter. The interpreter allowed them just to introduce
 7         themselves, just tell their names, their position, their interests.
 8  JACK:  And that's interesting. So, it goes back to the point of our concern
 9         about interpretation, because if the interpreter had said to me that
10         they are just making a return speech, then it would have been fine.
```
                    (Adapted from: Spencer-Oatey & Xing, 2009, p. 226)

Unfortunately, the interpreter used his pragmatic knowledge of the norms for both groups of speakers in a way to inform one group that their norms were not appropriate to the situation, with disastrous consequences. The point of having pragmatic knowledge of two groups of speakers is for this intercultural frame to guide the interpreter in his choice of intercultural strategies and in managing the interaction in a way that is in line with the overall intentions of both groups of speakers. Both groups of speakers had the intention to perform a welcome meeting as an event that formally marks the arrival of an overseas delegation for a 10-day business visit. The interpreter's intervention is an example of an application of cultural-pragmatic knowledge in an inappropriate way that led to an almost total breakdown of the meeting.

Further to this, the business context of the interaction is one in which *rapport* (Spencer-Oatey, 2002) between parties is critical for the purpose and desired outcome of the interaction – a consolidation and deepening of the existing business relationship. Although business interpreters may be employed by one side only as an in-house interpreter, and even function as dual-role mediators who both interpret *and* work as 'team members' for one party, business interpreters are cognisant of the intention and purpose of the business meeting from both parties' perspectives and employ their cultural-pragmatic knowledge and intercultural schemas to allow the meeting to be conducted in a way that reflects the intentions of its participants.

There is no post-interaction interview with the ad-hoc interpreter available, and it is not clear why the ad-hoc interpreter intervened in this way. It is possible that the ad-hoc interpreter believed that his role was to serve one party's interests, those of the party that was employing and paying him. His lack of knowledge of the role of the interpreter led to a further encounter on the second last day of the visit when a representative of the British company wanted to see if the Chinese visitors wished to visit London. At the same time the Chinese visitors wished to enquire about the monetary allowance that they knew that they were entitled to. The British host in this interaction is Sajid. The names of the Chinese visitors are given individually. The researcher, Jianju Xing, marked as (R) joined the interaction at the end. The interpreter is marked as (I), back translations as (BT), glosses of uninterpreted Chinese turns as (UCT) are marked in italics with non-verbal details given in square brackets:

Example (23)

1 SAJID: Could you please ask them is there anything specific that they want
2   to do in London because obviously we don't have much time left
3   <gesturing to look at watch> (.) we must make plans (?)
4 I: 他说你们是不是有特殊的要求在伦敦
           He asked if you have anything specific to do in London.
5 SHEN: 他们要把我们的费用算一算的 (.) 要不然明天没有时间了。
   UCT: *They should work out our expenses otherwise there will be no*
           time for it tomorrow.
6 SAJID: Where do they want to go specifically? To Oxford Street?
7 I: 伦敦的话，他们比较大一点，牛津街，一条商业街。
           Well, London is a big city. Oxford Street, a shopping street.
8 SAJID: Because we want to make this visit as fruitful as possible for them.
9   But for now (.) what do they want to do specifically? They want
10   to go to the Bank of China to change money? Can you ask them?
11 I: 他的话就是说伦敦的话，也就说，要走路的话，从这边走
12   那边的话就稍微远一点。这样，你如果想在这儿，就是说
13   个地方购物，就是说，是吧，做完了之后他可以开车，再
           换 一个地儿
14 BT: In London, that is, if you walk, from this side to that side, it is a bit
           far. So if you decide to go shopping in one place, after you have
           finished, they can pick you up, and take you to another place.]
           [Chinese visitors discuss among themselves]
15 SUN: 就这样吧。他们要结算，结算完了以后把钱拿出来，他们好购
16   物。
   UCT: *It's like this. They want to settle the expenses, after they've set-*
           tled the expenses they can get the spending money so that they
           can go shopping.
17 XU: 走吧。
   UCT: *Let's go.*
18 CHEN: 你们不要走啦「指着Sajid」还有话说呢。还得算账。
   UCT: *No, wait a minute he [pointing to Sajid] hasn't finished yet. And*
           we have to settle the expenses.
19 SAJID: So where do they want to go? What do they want to do? They want
20   to go to the Bank of China? (.) To change your money (.) Yes? Can
21   you ask them?

22	I:	是不是先想到中国银行那儿？
	BT:	*Do you want to first go to the Bank of China?*
		[Chinese visitors discuss among themselves. Some say: 算了，不，忘了吧。 'no, forget it'.]
23	SUN:	不是的(.) 他们的意思是现在可以算账。（转向其他成员）我
24		意思是不是这个意思呀？结了账之后，能不能够把钱拿出来
25		那么他们好购物。是不是这个意思？
	UCT:	*No (.) they want to settle the expenses now. (turning to other members) is this what you want to say? After the settlement could they have the money so they can go shopping with it. Isn't it what you wanted to say?*
26	ALL CHINESE SPEAKERS:	是呀。
	UCT:	*Yes.*
27	R:	[to interpreter] 那你就问问他，是不是可以先拿那个 spending
28		money。可以问他（2）如果换不了钱的话。
	UCT:	*You could ask him if they could have their spending money. You can ask him that. (2) if they can't change their money.*
29	SAJID:	So they want to go to the Bank of China?
30	I:	No (.) they don't think they can change their money there.
31	SAJID:	So, what do they want to do?
32	R:	Well, actually they said if they can get eh (.) for example (.) the
33		spending money now (.) today (.) so that they can do some
34		shopping in London they don't need to change money.

(Adapted from: Spencer-Oatey & Xing, 2009, p. 299.
Chinese characters added.)

In the extract, the Chinese visitors requested four times that the money that they knew that they were entitled to be made available to them, i.e. for their 'expenses to be settled'. The ad-hoc interpreter did not interpret any of these requests. The confusion of the British host, Sajid, and the frustration of the Chinese visitors was so great, that the researcher present at the interaction, Jianyu Xing, a Chinese–English bilingual who was following the interaction, felt compelled to intervene. The ad-hoc interpreter still did not respond. This begs the question why a person employed to be an interpreter did not interpret multiple turns. This appears to be a case of the ad-hoc interpreter misunderstanding his role as to how to work as an interpreter, and this is understandable as he had received no formal training. As an ad-hoc interpreter, he allowed his personal discomfort with the topic and the speech acts of the Chinese speakers to override his responsibility to interpret between the two languages. It appears that he mistakenly felt that his interpretations represent his positionality to others, and refrained from interpreting when he found the content of others' turns awkward or potentially embarrassing. In doing so, he frustrated the Chinese speakers and confused the English speaker, leading to agitated responses from the former and more urgent questions from the latter. Both of these were face-threatening to the ad-hoc interpreter, and in the end, another – the Chinese–English researcher present – takes on the role of (second) ad-hoc interpreter which most probably led to a loss of face for the ad-hoc interpreter. On the last day of the visit, there are further requests from the Chinese speakers for the money allocation set aside for them to be made available. Spencer-Oatey and Xing (2009) recount what happened:

> Once again, the interpreter failed to interpret their request. Over a period of 50 minutes, the visitors repeated their request fourteen times, using the following terms and phrases: list of costs, proof, proof of cost, the basis of the expense calculations, how they worked out the figure. Yet the interpreter did not convey this to the British until Sun, the delegation leader, lost his temper with the interpreter saying, "this is not your business, you just translate what I say, translate what he says, don't worry about us, don't be afraid". Only then did he interpret what the Chinese were asking for.
>
> (Spencer-Oatey & Xing, 2009, p. 234. Original punctuation.)

An ad-hoc interpreter who refuses to interpret 14 separate turns between participants, despite pleas and complaints for him to do so, is *not* an interpreter. It appears that the ad-hoc interpreter for this business visit saw his roles primarily as the following: an associate of the British company – hence his interruption of the Chinese senior visitor when he sought to speak in a way not congruent to the local business discourse, and his ambivalence in conveying a request for money that would be paid by the British company; a Chinese speaker who avoids making direct requests to others that are face-threatening to him and to the recipient – hence his refusal to interpret the request for the money allocation; an intermediary that subordinates his instances of inter-lingual transfer to his own personal, occupational or cultural beliefs. The effect of the latter is that when these are in conflict with the requirement to interpret, he ceases to interpret and at least temporarily 'withdraws' from the interaction, even though he remains physically present and all others expect him to continue performing the role of interpreter.

3.5   Cultural mediation and interpreters

In the previous sections we have discussed how interpreters work across a number of settings and how each setting features specific groups of interlocutors, particular kinds of interactions, likely conventions of discourse. We can see that each setting brings with it its own intercultural discourse, such as frames, models, and intercultural agency of the participants in relation to their schemas and strategies. In this section we focus on the role of culture itself, and how interpreters and those working with interpreters view culture as being an overtly present feature of interpreter-mediated interactions.

In a large-scale survey of experienced interpreters in Australia, Chesher, Slatyer, Doubine, Jaric, and Lazzari (2003) report that detailed knowledge of each language group's socio-cultural features is listed as the second most important particular skill that interpreters believe they should possess. Knowledge of the cultural-pragmatic norms of speech communities is strongly recommended by

Niska (2005), while Rudvin and Tomassini (2011) now argue that intercultural competence is a pre-requisite for professional interpreting practice. What has always been a feature of accomplished interpreting performance – knowledge of the pragmatic features used by speakers of both languages and their faithful rendition in interpretations – is now becoming a recognized sub-discipline in training and testing.

As we have outlined in many places in this chapter, interpreting is not only the performance of inter-lingual transfer. Interpreting involves a number of forms of behaviour that are determined by situation, context, other individual participants, the structure and setting of the interaction and the (interpreter's) management thereof. Further, the linguistic norms and the forms of behaviour of all interlocutors (including the interpreter) are socially and culturally grounded. We have described in some of the sections presented so far in this chapter that the management of an interaction sometimes necessitates asides, requests or other instances of intervention. This raises the issue of whether the interpreter's management of the interaction includes interventions to elicit, provide or check on cultural features of interlocutors' speech or behaviour, and to draw the attention of the allophone interlocutors to these. To address this issue, we first refer to a survey that elicited responses on Chinese–English interpreters' self-descriptions of role, status and professional identity conducted by Setton and Guo (2009). They report most of the interpreters "downplaying cultural mediation", seeing it not as a part of their performed tasks (Setton & Guo, 2009, p. 210). One interpreter is quoted as saying: "I facilitate communication for company operations and business development. This doesn't have much of a national or cultural dimension" (Setton & Guo, 2009, p. 233). Some codes of ethics also see intercultural competence as an attribute to enable language transfer, and less so as an attribute that is drawn on or displayed overtly. For example, in the UK, the Chartered Institute of Linguists' *Code of professional conduct* subsumes 'culture' as an attribute within interpreters' 'linguistic competence':

> Members/Chartered Linguists will work only within their linguistic competence. Linguistic competence means their spoken and/or written command of the language(s) concerned, their awareness of dialects and other language variants, and their knowledge of the cultural, social and political features of the country or countries concerned.
>
> (CIoL, 2015, p. 3)

The AUSIT Code of Ethics and Code of Conduct has similar requirements. Within the principle of *professional conduct*, "[i]nterpreters and translators take responsibility for their work and conduct; they are committed to providing quality service in a respectful and culturally sensitive manner" (AUSIT, 2012, p. 12). Elsewhere in the same document, cultural knowledge is a skill-base that is maintained and extended: "[t]hey [interpreters and translators] continually upgrade their language and transfer skills and their contextual and cultural understanding" (AUSIT, 2012, p. 6).

A further conceptualization of intercultural competence is provided by the California Healthcare Interpreters Association (2002) in their *California Standards for Healthcare Interpreters. Ethical Principles, Protocols, and Guidance on Roles & Intervention* (hereafter; 'California Standards'). The California Standards list four roles as being within the realm of interpreter work: 'message converter', 'message clarifier', 'cultural clarifier' and 'patient advocate'. In these standards, alongside the principles of confidentiality, impartiality, professionalism and integrity, the ethical principle of 'cultural responsiveness' is outlined. This is defined as:

> Interpreters seek to understand how diversity and cultural similarities and differences have a fundamental impact on the healthcare encounter. Interpreters play a critical role in identifying cultural issues and considering how and when to move to a ***cultural clarifier*** role. Developing ***cultural sensitivity*** and ***cultural responsiveness*** is a life-long process that begins with an introspective look at oneself.
> (California Healthcare Interpreters Association, 2002, p. 11.
> Original emphasis and italics.)

Inter-lingual transfer is a 'base-line' activity that interpreters engage in. Alongside this the California Standards state how an interpreter may consider whether to "move to a[nother] role", where cultural sensitivity and cultural responsiveness are cumulatively rather than inductively gained skill sets. The definition of 'cultural clarifier' is given as:

> The cultural clarifier roles go beyond message clarification to include a range of actions that typically relate to an interpreter's ultimate purpose of facilitating communication between parties not sharing a common culture. Interpreters are alert to cultural words or concepts that might lead to misunderstanding and act to identify and assist the parties to clarify culturally specific ideas.
> (California Healthcare Interpreters Association, 2002, p. 13)

Also stated is that interpreters:

> [c]larify the meaning of non-verbal expressions and gestures that have a specific or unique meaning within the cultural context of the speaker.
> (California Healthcare Interpreters Association, 2002, p. 30)

The California Standards relate to healthcare interpreting only and to working with California's culturally and linguistically diverse residents, amongst whom there are beliefs about health and illness that may vary significantly from a Western and Anglophone biomedical perspective. Shifting to the role of 'cultural clarifier', beyond the conventional roles of message converter and clarifier, is explained in the following way:

> The patient may perceive a provider's questioning strategy or remarks as culturally inappropriate. The same is true of the provider's perception of

patient's comments. This occurs even though no disrespect was intended by either party. It happens more frequently when patient and provider do not share a common understanding of illness and medical treatment. When there is evidence that any of the parties, including the interpreter, may be confused by cultural differences, interpreters need to:

a   Interrupt the communication process with a word, comment, or a gesture, as appropriate.

b   Alert both parties to potential miscommunication or misunderstanding (Interpreters may say, for example, "As an interpreter I think that there may be potential danger for miscommunication/ misunderstanding").

c   Suggest cultural concerns that could be impeding mutual understanding.

d   Assist the patient in explaining the cultural concept to the provider, or the provider in explaining the biomedical concept. When requested, interpreters also need to explain the cultural custom, health belief or practice of the patient to the provider, or educate the patient on the biomedical concept.

(California Healthcare Interpreters Association, 2002, pp. 43–44. Original punctuation.)

As can be seen, the California Standards contain an explanation of how interpreters can and should deal with interlocutors' intercultural schemas that shape not only their discourse in a general sense and the ways in which illness and healing are related to others, but their conceptualization and knowledge of health and medical treatments. Where these are not congruent between interlocutors to the extent that miscommunication can occur, interpreters are advised to intervene and clarify.

The California Standards are one of the few examples of codes of ethics or professional conduct for interpreters that describe and positively sanction cultural clarification. This is in part due to the very wide variety of conceptualizations of health and the treatment of illnesses amongst California's population, and the occurrence of hospital interpreters intervening beyond message transfer and in critical medical situations where they see miscommunication or misdiagnosis as a greater danger than that of contravening ethical principles of impartiality.

Another document that is written from the perspective of interpreters working in healthcare in Australia affords the practice of cultural clarifier less prominence. The AUSIT Guidelines for Health Professionals working with Interpreters devotes some attention to what *others'* (i.e. non-interpreters') expectations of the place of cultural mediation within the interpreted interaction may be:

During the course of a session, the interpreter may become aware of cultural issues which are preventing clear communication (such as different beliefs about illness and treatment). You should allow the interpreter to briefly indicate what may be causing a cultural misunderstanding if this is impeding good communication with the patient. However, interpreters should not be expected to be cultural "experts", and lengthy explanations of a cultural nature should be avoided.

(AUSIT, 2006, p. 6. Original punctuation.)

These instructions are clear that culture is considered to be a relevant or important feature of interlocutors' behaviour where (verbal) communication is in some way impeded. At the same time, the recommendation that those working with interpreters 'should not expect' interpreters to function as cultural experts is strongly stated. The same document later on expands on the role of culture in interpreted interactions and makes a clearly worded recommendation.

> Under the normal circumstances of general health interpreting, you should not be asking interpreters to give information about the patient's culture, unless communication has broken down. The importance of culture can be over-emphasized. All patients have different personalities, temperaments and life experience, and may vary considerably in the way they manifest their cultural background. However, professional interpreters know that language expression does not happen in isolation from customs and beliefs, especially in the health area. Interpreters are not producing word-by-word renditions of the patients' messages, but are passing on information across cultures to each party. They provide the **full meaning** of what is said by all parties in the languages spoken and understood by them.
>
> There may be rare occasions when you need to request essential cultural information from the interpreter, or the interpreter may consider that without certain information the message (from either party) may be distorted or there may be a total breakdown in communication. Under these circumstances, the information given by the interpreter should be factual (i.e. verifiable) and generally applicable to the patient's cultural background. Where possible, the patient should be involved in the discussion via the interpreter.

(AUSIT, 2006, p. 6. Original emphasis and punctuation.)

There are a number of points that these two paragraphs touch on. Firstly, overt questions to an unfamiliar interlocutor about his/her cultural mores are likely to be highly marked in not only healthcare interactions but in many others, and a clear warning against doing so is issued here. The second point about culture being "over-emphasized" is based on responses from interpreters that some, usually English-speaking interlocutors, elicit information about LOTE-speaking interlocutors' cultural mores where the elicitation of such information may have little obvious relevance to the overall purpose or setting of the interaction, or where the forms of behaviour displayed by LOTE-speaking interlocutors appear to be attributed to their cultural background only, and not to other factors.

The tenet of the CIoL code, the AUSIT code and guidelines, as well as the California Standards is that intercultural discourse and intercultural agency are never absent from interpreter-mediated interactions, and that these, as stated by Gentile et al. (1996, pp. 60–61) over 20 years ago, *serve the purpose* of achieving faithful, felicitous interpreting. Explanations of cultural information as an overt and distinct feature of interpreter performance are recommended only where these threaten to lead to miscommunication between parties and where this cultural information cannot be readily or adequately conveyed in the illocutionary force of the interpretations themselves. In most interpreted interactions there may often be little or no time for these to be given anyway. Instead, where cultural features determine that the locutionary and illocutionary acts for a speech event in one language are represented in a way that is significantly different to the way that these acts are represented for the same speech event in the other language, the interpreter, using his/her knowledge of the intercultural frame that such an event presents, is guided by the illocutionary force in the source speech. The intercultural strategy that the interpreter follows is to provide a rendition in his/her target speech that has an illocutionary force equivalent to that in the source speech for this speech event. The interpreter cannot control the perlocutionary effect of the interpreted speech event and the interpreter uses his/her judgement and observation of others' reactions to assess how the intent or illocutionary act has been received. Judgement relates not only to the illocutionary force of individual utterances, but to a speaker's turn, their overall intentions, the setting, the position and status of other interlocutors, and the context. All of these are part of the intercultural frames which influence the interpreter in the selection of intercultural strategies.

In the following example, a business interpreter omitted a key utterance and altered another two utterances in his interpretation into Chinese. He did so, to be *faithful* to the content and the intent of the source speaker's speech, using his intercultural schemas of how invitations are issued and received in Australian English, and how invitations are issued and received in Chinese culture.

I remember interpreting at a very boozy dinner with senior government officials of a middle-sized city in China. We were in the city to promote our company to these officials in an effort to improve our chances of winning an upcoming project in the city. At a dinner one night hosted by the local officials under the influence of copious amounts of alcohol a senior manager from our company made a very serious *faux pas*. Everyone was in an extremely good mood. (Here may I say that I as the interpreter played an important role of being able to convey the various friendly jokes and comments from both sides effectively thus sustaining the very jovial atmosphere at the table).

One of the city officials was a woman in her mid-50s who was the head of one of the municipal bureaus. Our senior manager, in an attempt to convey the conviviality he felt towards the Chinese city officials, said to them that when they next came to Australia he would love to invite them to his home for a traditional barbecue lunch. From the Australian perspective this is a sign of the importance of the friendship between the two sides. He went on to tell the Chinese city officials (through me) that he had recently had a brand new swimming pool built in his back yard that they must come and have a look at. Then, in an attempt to express an even greater level of goodwill, he directly addressed the female bureau head and said that she would be more than welcome to have a swim in the new pool and that she would look wonderful in a bikini. Clearly, in many cultures, and most definitely in Chinese culture, this was a very inappropriate and even dangerous thing to say no matter how well intended. To be a woman and a director of a municipal bureau was no small achievement. The woman concerned would more than likely have to continually prove her worth to her male colleagues.

A comment like this would have degraded her a lot in the eyes of her male colleagues at the table that night. Add to this her age and the extremely conservative attitude of Chinese to anything of a sexual nature and you have a potentially disastrous situation. In the end, what I interpreted to the Chinese side was a modified version of what our senior manager had said. I told them that our manager warmly welcomed them to his home for lunch and to see the new pool that he had had recently built. The reaction from the Chinese side was very good and the convivial atmosphere of the night continued on. (Chi-Eng.inter.20)

The anecdote related by the Chinese–English interpreter shows his understanding of the intercultural schemas and frames at work, i.e. the juxtapositions of Chinese and Australian notions of gender relations, observing seniority, inviting others to one's home, what a guest can feel comfortable to do etc., and the intercultural strategies that he employed such as message reduction or topic avoidance to successfully mediate between the parties.

In general, empirical studies on interpreter performance in dialogue or multi-party situations show that interventions to clarify target speech that could be misunderstood can occur but are not usually frequent, regardless of whether they are based on cultural, situational or other features (Wadensjö, 1998). The interpreter co-negotiates meaning between interlocutors, but cannot attend to all possible perceptions of speech and paralinguistic features occurring in an interaction. As one experienced interpreter puts it:

If the interpreter is hired through an agency purely as a professional interpreter to interpret then they should not be responsible for clearing up cross-cultural (mis-) communications. The only exception might be where it is agreed by both parties that the interpreter should play this role at the beginning. (Chi-Eng.inter.30)

The second line in the excerpt points to the 'cultural broker' (in terms of how Gentile et al., 1996 view this), or cultural clarifier (cf. California Standards), which is a role *distinguishable* from that of the interpreter or translator, and which can be enacted *alongside* this role, through making overt reference to a switch in role, e.g. "Let me clarify a possible misunderstanding here that appears to be culturally based" or, "Stepping out of my role as the interpreter, I would like to draw your attention to . . .". This is an instance of inter-professional discourse that can be precipitated by intercultural frames that are not shared by all interlocutors. The interpreter may employ intercultural strategies such as circumlocution or paraphrase to address these.

In interpreted healthcare interactions, doctors (and interpreters) are mindful that undistorted renditions of all parties' speech are vital for symptom description, diagnosis and treatment. But further to the "word-for-word" or verbatim interpretations that doctors sometimes expect from interpreters, in a recent qualitative study on 12 healthcare interpreters' practices, the importance of the information transfer that effectively conveys the cultural-pragmatic information of all interlocutors is described as the second most important feature of healthcare interpreters' work (Bischoff, Kurt, & Henley, 2012). In the words of one healthcare interpreter:

> I want to explain things at the patient's level. [. . .] The doctors, too, expect not simply word-for-word but intercultural translation. Sometimes doctors have said to me, "We don't want word-for-word translation. The patient has to have intercultural understanding. You need to explain the cultural things a bit: how it is in our culture and how it is in your culture".
>
> (Bischoff et al., 2012, p. 11. Original punctuation.)

A comment from a Chinese–English interpreter in healthcare settings touches on the challenges working with Chinese speakers whose experiences of doctor-patient communication and treatment procedures differ from the practices followed by the English-speaking doctors with whom they are also working:

> 要看场合。比如讨论到坐月子的时候我会有所解释。由于制度和文化的不同导致沟通出现障碍。比如西方医疗制度注重个人权利和个人选择，相信个人判断力，会要求病人作出对于自己治疗方法的选择。但由于新移民对于制度的不熟悉和教育程度问题，以及习惯性对医生的依赖性，不愿意自己做出选择，而希望医生采取适合自己的方案。故沟通出现障碍。

> It depends on the occasions. For instance, when discussing "postpartum confinement" I will share my opinions. Sometimes miscommunications are caused by differences in systems and cultures. For example, Western healthcare system pays more attention to individual rights and the freedom for an individual to make their own choice. It rests on a system of individuals using their personal discretion. Therefore, doctors ask patients to choose their preferred method of treatment. But newly arrived migrants are not familiar with the host culture and its systems and have varied levels of education. They're more accustomed to a system that is doctor-centred, and are unwilling to make their own choices. They would prefer for the doctor to choose what is best for them. Those are points of possible miscommunication. (Chi-Eng. inter.22)

When it is appropriate for cultural information to be given, either requested from the interpreter or directly volunteered by them according to the situation, most guidelines (CIoL, AUSIT, California Standards) recommend that such information should be given in a way that relates to the specific situation.

3.6   Conclusion

This chapter has given an overview of the main features and most frequently encountered settings of interpreter-mediated interactions. We have traced how descriptions of interpreting and the interpreter have developed from notions of 'word-rescrambling into another language' and 'conduit', to 'message transfer' and 'message transferrer', to 'interactional management' and 'situational intermediate', to 'intercultural discourse management' and 'inter-lingual and intercultural mediator'. The latter notions have arisen as a result of the 'social turn' in Interpreting Studies that represented an 'opening of the discipline's eyes' to things that had always been present in interpreter-mediated interactions. These things are, amongst others: interpreters' self-perceptions of their role and others' notion of their role; (socio-political) status; role-relationship to others in a given situation, context and setting; differences in the socio-economic status, situational position and worldview of allophone interlocutors; interlocutors' cultural background(s) and the enactment of discourse-pragmatic features; the interpreter as a 'relayer', as a co-interlocutor and/or as a co-negotiator of 'dyad or multi-party talk'; the interpreter as a key protagonist (but not the only one) with intercultural competence; the re-presentation of others' messages cognisant of the intercultural frames that arise through the matching of source language speech to target language speech.

To the theoretical frameworks that were introduced in Chapter 1 including the Inter-Culturality Framework, we add Merlini and Favaron's (2005) description of the voice and position that interpreters adopt that distinguishes seven different footings, as a fine-grained extension of Goffman's three-way distinction of 'animator', 'author' and 'principal'. We find from the examples drawn on in this chapter that interpreters usually adopt the sanctioned roles of 'reporter', or 'direct' or 'indirect recapitulator' when providing inter-lingual transfer. We also find that interpreters adopt other footings, depending on the setting, constellation, assumed and/or shared knowledge of interlocutors, and in some instances act as 'initiators' (or 'principals' in Goffman's terms), responder or narrator. These footings can be adopted on the basis of interactional-management features in which the interpreter employs these moves to work towards the 'achievement' of the interaction.

Our description of the various settings and fields that interpreters work in encompasses the following: conference interpreting, including the associated settings of diplomatic and media interpreting; business interpreting; interpreting in police, legal and court settings; and healthcare settings. All of these settings feature intercultural discourse, i.e. "cultural variation in the incidence of particular speech acts and the way in which they are performed" (Clyne, 1994, pp. 48–49). We summarize here the main features of each setting and locate how interpreters negotiate the intercultural frames that occur in each.

Conference interpreting settings typically feature interlocutors with similar or congruent knowledge bases, and educational and occupational profiles. There is common agreement and alignment towards the format and purpose of the conference setting – the well-known challenges for interpreters are specialist terminology and the formal register used which can include specific and marked rhetorical forms. At this point the interpreter is using his/her linguistic resources to recognize and understand forms used in topic-specific idiolects and to reproduce target language forms equivalent to these via intercultural strategies, some of which could be approximation, circumlocution or even foreignizing. At the same time the interpreter needs also to recognize and understand the rhetorical features – e.g. inductive vs. deductive argumentative styles, use of metaphor or analogy – which themselves are an intercultural frame that the interpreter manages online via intercultural strategies such as restructuring, paraphrase or 'use of all-purpose words'.

Diplomatic and media interpreting share many similarities with each other, not least the 'high stakes' setting common to both. Diplomatic interpreting at Sino-American or Sino-British meetings involving heads-of-state or senior government officials carries with it the challenge of moving not only between two typologically different languages, but between different conceptualizations of societal organization. The specific characteristics of the political and economic system found in China compared to that found in most predominantly English-speaking countries led to intercultural strategies such as literal translation of terms, e.g. 'The Great Leap Forward' （大跃进） into English as forms that are part of the terminological repertoire of Chinese–English interpreters working in the area of diplomacy. Diplomatic interpreters employ their pragmatic knowledge including that of face threatening acts to ensure that their interpretations do not contain these. Euphemistic or opaque metaphors may be forms that occur conspicuously in interlocutors' source speech and the interpreter applies his/her knowledge of intercultural schemas to provide target speech forms that capture the illocutionary force, without this offending the face of the recipient of the target speech. The notion of face extends also beyond the local level of the interaction to that of what is expected of a head-of-state and what the official policy of that country is. Example (1) shows how re-ordering of key terms in the interpreter's target speech served to uphold national policy on the status of political entities.

Media interpreting is no less demanding as the target language audience is usually infinitely bigger, along with the potential number of bilinguals who follow the source speech and match it to the target speech. Concepts that are more characteristic of the religious-cultural heritage of one language group can posit challenges for the interpreter. The interpreter considers which strategies can be drawn on to convey these in the target language, e.g. approximation, work-coinage, code-switching. Example (6) shows that omission is used to avoid the online difficulty of rendering specific concepts, and instead examples of the concept are used as a compensatory strategy. In a similar way, Chinese four-character phrases present similar difficulties and examples (2) and (3) show how circumlocution or paraphrase are employed to deal with these when working into English.

In regard to business settings, we identify a significant difference in the structure and performance of business meetings in China compared to those in Britain. Where interpreters working in these settings occupy a role further to that of inter-lingual transfer, i.e. as a team member or employee for one of the parties, this should be disclosed to the other party, and the interpreter should explain what activities as an interpreter they will be performing, and where they occupy a dual-role, the interpreter should state what activities beyond this they will be performing. Role-explanation can be an intercultural frame in itself where there are different notions of what role an interpreter can or should adopt in business interactions based on different cultural conceptualizations of business interpreters, and indeed for the very need for there to an explanation of these. Recalled examples show that the moves and devices that interlocutors from both parties may employ, e.g. greetings, exchanging cards, introductory small talk, welcome speeches, hedging, bluffing etc. can present challenges for interpreters. These are not only at the level of the utterance and its referential content that may contain situation-specific, theme-specific, or culturally specific features that may be difficult to render felicitously in the target language. These may be the occurrence of a *whole* speech act, such as a gregarious compliment or a celebratory thank you response that does not conform to the discourse-pragmatic conventions of the other group. Interpreters rely on their knowledge of intercultural discourse and intercultural agency in adopting strategies appropriate to the situation. We note, as shown in 3.4, how an intervention based on an ad-hoc interpreter's knowledge of both groups' pragmatic conventions, was made in an inappropriate and face-threatening way, leading to the non-achievement of a number of business-related interactions.

Differences exist in the functioning of the executive and judicial arms of state power in both Chinese-speaking and English-speaking countries. Differences also exist amongst all predominantly English-speaking countries. Thus there are hierarchical, organizational and procedural features that speakers of Chinese and English will conceive of in different ways. The executive and the judiciary are strongly influenced by the social and cultural features of each society, and we can see this in the way that English terms such as *contest mention* or *bail* or actions such as giving an *oath* or *affirmation* can make demands not only of the interpreter's knowledge of terminology but ability to convey terms that do not have ready equivalents in the other language's legal culture. From the courtroom data presented in 3.3.5.3, we see that Chinese–English interpreters working in courts in mainland China adopt a number of footings according to Merlini and Favaron's (2005) model. These are *direct recapitulator* and *indirect recapitulator*, which are both relaying roles, but also *narrator, principal* and *omitter*. The latter occurs when the interpreter gives zero renditions. Elsewhere in examples (13) to (16) we note that the interpreter is often directly addressed to obtain information from the defendant. This shows that the interpreter is not a 'forgotten' or 'invisible' presence in the courtroom, and makes us question what agency s/he is exercising when zero renditions occur, i.e. as a *voluntary omitter* or as an *involuntary omitter*. That court officials address the interpreter also suggests that the interpreter may be seen by them as a fellow inquisitor with bilingual skills, rather than as a non-aligned interpreter. Interpreters do not consistently relay speech into the other language in these given examples, and they appear to subordinate this role to the role of bilingual court official partial to the demands of the presiding judge(s) and/ or prosecution.

There are a gamut of intercultural frames in these examples that present challenges to any legal or court interpreter: procedural ones (i.e. nature of court proceedings and the sequential order of speech acts that characterize court proceedings); discourse ones (i.e. register, topic content, terminology, rhetoric and positionality of interlocutor) and macro-legal ones (i.e. code law inquisitorial system vs. common law adversarial system). It appears that the interpreters do not exercise agency in a way that would yield English-language interpretations that reflect the content, intent and positionality of the Chinese-language source speech. Alongside omitting and relaying (recapitulating), there are strategies of interpretive summary, possibly message replacement, comprehension checks.

Of all areas of interpreting, particularly public-service interpreting, it has been the field of healthcare interpreting that has witnessed the widest variety of interpreter constellations. These range from a conduit that provides inter-lingual transfer to an informed interpreter who, after touching base with the healthcare professional at a pre-interactional briefing as to the role interpreter and features of the interaction, introduces him-/herself and his/her role to the patient, and who works with all parties towards the achievement of the healthcare interaction. Agency and activism have also had a more conspicuous presence in healthcare interpreting compared to other fields. This can be accounted for by the situation in many Western countries where there can be major differences in the socio-economic situation, education level, world views on health and wellbeing, and in the level of health literacy between the healthcare provider and the patient who is typically a migrant (or refugee) unfamiliar with healthcare practices of their new place of residence. The most prominent example of agency and activism amongst interpreters is to be found in the 'California Standards for Healthcare Interpreters' (2002) that was developed by in-house interpreters (but not only in-house interpreters) with a dual role of providing inter-lingual transfer *and* working towards advancing the general health of patients. The implication of the 'California Standards' is that interpreters are not only aware of the intercultural frames that can likely occur in such interactions, but also of the intercultural schemas and strategies that are open to them to provide both inter-lingual transfer and remediate possible misunderstanding. To be sure, not all guideline documents for interpreters advocate an activist or interventionist position. There are compelling reasons why interpreters should consider intervening only in certain circumstances, not least is the need for the patient and the healthcare provider to build rapport with each other and to communicate directly with each other. But we see across a number of samples that interpreters adopt footings that show their own agency and interventions. The data from a hospital in China shows evidence that in-house interpreters enact roles that are congruent to some of those listed in the 'California Standards'.

Lastly, this chapter has looked at the relationship between the designated role of interpreter vis-à-vis roles bearing the title of cultural mediator. As stated, the role of 'cultural clarifier' is a sanctioned one in the 'California Standards'. Elsewhere, there are recommendations that interpreters refrain from intervening to address cultural issues except where this may serve the overall aim of providing optimal message transfer. The settings in which this is likely to occur vary: in conference, diplomatic and media interpreting, intercultural strategies that optimise the understanding of source speakers' turns are likely to be covert and embedded in the target speech itself; in business interpreting intercultural strategies employed by the interpreter are also likely to be covert and embedded, but there is greater scope for those to be overt due to the more dialogic nature of business exchanges and the differing protocols of formality; in police, legal and court interpreting, the form as well as the content of source speech is important and here intercultural strategies may include explicit references to the non-congruence of formal, procedures, rhetorical and/or discourse-pragmatic features across languages that are relevant to the achievement of the interaction for all parties; in healthcare interpreting, as outlined, an array of covert and overt intercultural strategies may be found in interpreter-mediated interactions. Healthcare interpreting is the setting in which we situate our multi-perspective examination of intercultural communication with data from groups of informants.

This chapter has focused on fields, modes, roles and settings and followed on from the presentation of theoretical models provided in chapter one and the discussion of Chinese and English speakers, and of the communicative practices of both groups. In the following chapter, we present data from both Chinese and English speakers on key situational aspects of interpreter-mediated interactions. Further, we present data from Chinese–English interpreters and apply concepts and models introduced in the two opening chapters, including the Inter-Culturality Framework.

Note

1 In Hong Kong, all court proceedings are recorded. Recordings of court proceedings containing interpreted discourse offer a comprehensive corpus of real-life interpreting performance that can be used for research as well as teaching purposes (Ng, 2015).

References

Amato, A., & Mack, G. (2013). Interpreting the Oscar night on Italian TV: An interpreters' nightmare? *The Interpreters' Newsletter*, *16*, 37–60.

Angelelli, C. (2000). Interpreting as a communicative event: A look through Hymes' lenses. *Meta*, *45*(4), 580–592. https://doi.org/10.7202/001891ar

Angelelli, C. (2004). *Medical interpreting and cross-cultural communication*. Cambridge, UK: Cambridge University Press.

Association of Diplomatic Studies and Training. (2013). *The Chinese interpreter who said 'no' to president Nixon*. Retrieved from https://adst.org/2013/05/the-interpreter-who-said-to-no-to-president-nixon/

AUSIT [Australian Institute of Interpreters and Translators]. (2006). *Guidelines for health professionals working with interpreters*. Retrieved from http://ausit.org/AUSIT/Documents/Guidelines_For_Health_Professionals.pdf

AUSIT [Australian Institute of Interpreters and Translators]. (2012). *AUSIT code of ethics and code of conduct*. Retrieved from https://ausit.org/AUSIT/Documents/Code_Of_Ethics_Full.pdf

Baraldi, C., & Gavioli, L. (2012). Understanding coordination in interpreter-mediated interaction. In C. Baraldi & L. Gavioli (Eds.), *Coordinating participation in dialogue interpreting* (pp. 1–21). Amsterdam and Philadelphia: John Benjamins. https://doi.org/10.1075/btl.102.01intro

Berezhkov, V. (1994). At Stalin's side: His interpreter's memoirs from the October revolution to the fall of the dictator's empire. Ann Arbor: Carol Publishing/University of Michigan.

Berk-Seligson, S. (2002). *The bilingual courtroom. Court interpreters in the judicial process*. Chicago and London: University of Chicago Press.

Berk-Seligson, S. (2011). Negotiation and communicative accommodation in bilingual police interrogations: A critical interactional sociolinguistic perspective. *International Journal of the Sociology of Language*, *207*, 29–58. https://doi.org/10.1515/ijsl.2011.002

Bischoff, A., Kurth, E., & Henley, A. (2012). Staying in the middle: A qualitative study of health care interpreters' perceptions of their work. *Interpreting*, *14*(1), 1–22. https://doi.org/10.1075/intp.14.1.01bis

Bolden, G. (2000). Toward understanding practices of medical interpreting: Interpreters' involvement in history-taking. *Discourse Studies*, *2*(4), 387–419. https://doi.org/10.1177/1461445600002004001

Bot, H. (2005). *Dialogue interpreting in mental health*. Amsterdam: Rodopi.

Bourne, J. S. (2016). Exploring intercultural communication challenges: A case study on Chinese–English interpreting. *China Media Research*, *12*(1), 14–24.

Bumiller, E. (1991, March 14). Japan's master interpreter. *Washington Post*. Retrieved from www.washingtonpost.com/archive/lifestyle/1991/03/14/japans-master-interpreter/0237dcfe-ec6f-4d1d-b29f-27a52ae86348/?noredirect=on&utm_term=.0bdce9ac5acf

California Healthcare Interpreters Association. (2002). *California standards for healthcare interpreters ethical principles, protocols, and guidance on roles & intervention*. Retrieved from www.chia.ws/standards.htm

Carr, S., Roberts, R., Dufour, A., & Steyn, D. (1997). *The critical link: Interpreters in the community*. Amsterdam and Philadelphia: John Benjamins.

CCTV. (2016). 【两会】2016 年李克强总理答中外记者问（张璐交传视频+总理金句+双语全文 (CCTV, 2016) [China's Two Sessions] Chinese Premier Li Keqiang responded to questions from domestic and foreign reporters at a news conference in 2016 (Ms Zhang Lu interpreting video + Premier's remarks + Bilingual full-text). Retrieved from www.youtube.com/watch?v=CVsTNJxi_wg&index=1&list=PLfAyWd GHnLdED3yyB2F0jXiqVomzgKHvp

Chesher, T., Slatyer, H., Doubine, V., Jaric, L., & Lazzari, R. (2003). Community-based interpreting: The interpreters' perspective. In L. Brunette, G. L. Bastin, I. Hemlin, & H. Clarke (Eds.), *The critical link 3: Interpreters in the community* (pp. 273–292). Amsterdam: John Benjamins. https://doi.org/10.1075/btl.46.28che

China Africa Magazine. (2017). *Tang Wensheng, an eyewitness of US president Richard Nixon's visit to China*. Retrieved from www.youtube.com/watch?v=4OX6YeQ9Ayo

Chow, M., & Chin, M. (1997, May 30). Bad translation could undermine justice, magistrate tells weeping interpreter. *South China Morning Post*, p. 3.

CIoL [Chartered Institute of Linguists]. (2015). *Code of professional conduct*. Retrieved from http://ciolweb.nfpservices.co.uk/sites/default/files/CPC15.pdf

Clyne, M. (1994). *Inter-cultural communication at work: Cultural values in discourse*. Cambridge: Cambridge University Press.

Corsellis, A. (2008). *Public service interpreting: The first steps*. Houndmills and Basingstoke: Palgrave Macmillan.

Davidson, B. (2000). The interpreter as institutional gatekeeper: The social-linguistic role of interpreters in Spanish-English medical discourse. *Journal of Sociolinguistics, 4*(3), 379–405. https://doi.org/10.1111/1467-9481.00121

Dawrant, A., & Jiang, H. (2001). *Conference interpreting in mainland China*. Retrieved from http://aiic.net/p/365

Drugan, J., & Tipton, R. (2017). Translation, ethics and social responsibility. *The Translator, 23*(2), 119–125. https://doi.org/10.1080/13556509.2017.1327008

Du, B. (2015). The silenced interpreter: A case study of language and ideology in the Chinese criminal court. *International Journal of Semiotic Law, 28*, 507–524. https://doi.org/10.1007/s11196-015-9431-z

Du, B. (2016). *The bilingual trial: Access to interpreting, communication and participation in Chinese criminal courts* (PhD thesis), University of Hong Kong, Pokfulam, Hong Kong SAR. Retrieved from http://dx.doi.org/10.5353/th_b5807309

Edmonson, W. (1986). Cognition, conversing and interpreting. In J. House & S. Blum-Kulka (Eds.), *Interlingual and intercultural communication* (pp. 129–138). Tübingen: Gunter Narr.

Fisher, R. F., & Geiselman, R. E. (1992). *Memory-enhancing techniques for investigative interviewing: The cognitive interview*. Springfield: Charles C. Thomas Publisher.

Fowler, Y. (2003). Taking an interpreted witness statement at the police station: What did the witness actually say? In L. Brunette, G. L. Bastin, I. Hemlin, & H. Clarke (Eds.), *The critical link 3: Interpreters in the community* (pp. 195–209). Amsterdam: John Benjamins. https://doi.org/10.1075/btl.46.21fow

Garzone, G., & Viezzi, M. (2002). Introduction. In G. Garzone & M. Viezzi (Eds.), *Interpreting in the 21st century: Challenges and opportunities. Selected papers from the 1st Forlì conference on interpreting studies, 9–11 November 2000* (pp. 1–14). Amsterdam and Philadelphia: John Benjamins.

Gavioli, L., & Maxwell, N. (2007). Interpreter intervention in mediated business talk. In H. Bowles & P. Seedhouse (Eds.), *Conversation analysis and language for specific purposes* (pp. 141–182). Frankfurt: Peter Lang.

Geiselman, R. E., Fisher, R. P., Firstenberg, I., Hutton, L. A., Sullivan, S., Avetissian, I., & Prosk, A. (1984). Enhancement of eyewitness memory: An empirical evaluation of the cognitive interview. *Journal of Police Science and Administration, 12*, 74–80. https://doi.org/10.2307/1422492

Gentile, A., Ozolins, U., & Vasilakakos, M. (1996). *Liaison interpreting*. Melbourne: Melbourne University Press.

Gerver, D. (1976). Empirical studies of simultaneous interpretation: A review and a model. In R. Brislin (Ed.), *Translation: Applications and research* (pp. 165–207). New York: Gardner Press.

Gile, D. (1995a). *Basic concepts and models for interpreter and translator training*. Amsterdam and Philadelphia: John Benjamins.

Gile, D. (1995b). Interpretation research: A new impetus? *Hermes, Journal of Linguistics, 14*, 15–29. https://doi.org/10.7146/hjlcb.v8i14.25100

Gile, D. (1999). Testing the effort model's tightrope hypothesis in simultaneous interpretation – A contribution. *Hermes, 23*, 153–172.

Gile, D. (2009). *Basic concepts and models for interpreter and translator training* (Rev. ed.). Amsterdam and Philadelphia: John Benjamins.

Ginori, L., & Scimone, E. (1995). *Introduction to interpreting*. Sydney: Lantern.

Goffman, E. (1961). *Encounters: Two studies in the sociology of interaction*. Indianapolis and New York: Bobbs-Merrill.

Goffman, E. (1981). *Forms of talk*. Philadelphia: University of Pennsylvania Press.

Gu, Y., & Zhu, W. (2002). Chinese officialdom (Guan) at work in discourse. In C. Barron, N. Bruce, & D. Nuna (Eds.), *Knowledge and discourse: Towards an ecology of language* (pp. 97–115). London: Pearson.

Hale, S. (2004). *The discourse of court interpreting*. Amsterdam and Philadelphia: John Benjamins.

Hale, S. (2007). *Community interpreting*. Basingstoke: Palgrave Macmillan.

Handford, M. (2010). The business-meeting genre: Stages and practices. In M. Handford (Ed.), *The language of business meetings* (pp. 60–94). Cambridge, UK: Cambridge University Press. https://doi.org/10.1017/cbo9781139525329.005

Harris, B., & Sherwood, B. (1978). Translating as an innate skill. In D. Gerber & H. W. Sinaiko (Eds.), *Language interpretation and communication* (pp. 155–170). New York and London: Plenum Press. https://doi.org/10.1007/978-1-4615-9077-4_15

Herbert, J. (1952). *The interpreter's handbook: How to become a conference interpreter*. Geneva: Georg.

Heydon, G., & Lai, M. (2013). Police interviews mediated by interpreters: An exercise in diminishment? *Investigative Interviewing: Research and Practice*, 5(2), 82–98. https://doi.org/10.1057/9781137443199.0006

Hlavac, J. (2015). Formalizing community interpreting standards: A cross-national comparison of testing systems, certification conventions and recent ISO guidelines. *International Journal of Interpreter Education*, 7(2), 21–38.

Hlavac, J., Gentile, A., Orlando, M., Pappas, A., & Zucchi, E. (2018). Translation as a subset of public and social policy and a consequence of multiculturalism: The provision of translation and interpreting services in Australia. *International Journal of the Sociology of Language*, 251, 55–88. https://doi.org/10.1515/ijsl-2018-0004

Hsieh, E., & Kramer, E. M. (2012). Medical interpreters as tools: Dangers and challenges in the utilitarian approach to interpreters' roles and functions. *Patient Education and Counseling*, 89, 158–162. https://doi.org/10.1016/j.pec.2012.07.001

Hu, K., & Tao, Q. (2013). The Chinese–English conference interpreting corpus: Uses and limitations. *Meta*, 58(3), 626–642. https://doi.org/10.7202/1025055ar

Inghilleri, M. (2003). Habitus, field and discourse: Interpreting as a socially situated activity. *Target*, 15(2), 243–268. https://doi.org/10.1075/target.15.2.03ing

Ji, C. (2008). *The man on Mao's right: From Harvard yard to Tiananmen square. My life inside China's foreign ministry*. New York: Random House.

Kade, O. (1967). Zu einigen Besonderheiten des Simultandolmetschens. *Fremdsprachen*, 11(1), 8–17.

Kaufert, J. M., & Putsch, R. W. (1997). Communication through interpreters in healthcare: Ethical dilemmas arising from differences in class, culture, language, and power. *Journal of Clinical Ethics*, 8, 71–87.

Kelly, N., & Stewart, R. (2010). *The language services market: 2010. An annual review of the translation, localization, and interpreting services industry*. Common Sense Advisory. Retrieved from www.commonsenseadvisory.com/Research.aspx?AuthorID=9

Kirchhoff, H. (1976/2002). Simultaneous interpreting: Interdependence of variables in the interpreting process, interpreting models and interpreting strategies. In F. Pöchhacker & M. Shlesinger (Eds.), *The interpreting studies reader* (pp. 110–119). London and New York: Routledge.

Knapp-Potthoff, A., & Knapp, K. (1986). Interweaving two discourses – The difficult task of the non-professional interpreter. In K. Knapp, W. Enninger, & A. Knapp-Potthoff (Eds.), *Analyzing intercultural communication* (pp. 181–211). Berlin: Mouton de Gruyter.

Kondo, M., Tebble, H., Alexieva, B., van Dam, H., Katan, D., Mizuno, A., . . . Zalka, I. (1997). Intercultural communication, negotiation, and interpreting. In Y. Gambier, D. Gile, & C. Taylor (Eds.), *Conference interpreting: Current trends in research* (pp. 149–166). Amsterdam: John Benjamins. https://doi.org/10.1075/btl.23.10kon

Korchilov, I. (1997). *Translating history: Thirty years on the front lines of diplomacy with a to Russian interpreter*. New York: Scribner.

Kredens, K. (2017). Making sense of adversarial interpreting. *Language and Law*, *4*(1), 17–33.

Lai, M. (2017). Chinese public service interpreting. In C. Shei & Z. Gao (Eds.), *The Routledge handbook of Chinese translation* (pp. 336–354). London: Routledge. https://doi.org/10.4324/9781315675725-20

Lederer, M. (1978/2002). Simultaneous interpretation: Units of meaning and other features. In F. Pöchhacker & M. Shlesinger (Eds.), *The interpreting studies reader* (pp. 130–140). London and New York: Routledge. https://doi.org/10.1007/978-1-4615-9077-4_28

Leung, E., & Gibbons, J. (2008). Who is responsible? Participant roles in legal interpreting cases. *Multilingua*, *27*, 177–191. https://doi.org/10.1515/multi.2008.010

Levinson, S. (1988). Putting linguistics on a proper footing: Exploration in Goffman's concepts of participation. In P. Drew & A. Wooton (Eds.), *Erving Goffman exploring the interaction order* (pp. 161–227). Cambridge, UK: Polity Press.

Llewellyn-Jones, P., & Lee, R. (2014). *Redefining the role of the community interpreter: The concept of 'role-space'*. Lincoln: SLI Press.

Lü, S., & Li, S. (2012). The role shift of the interpreter to a cultural mediator: From the perspective of cultural orientations and contexting. *Babel*, *58*(2), 145–163. https://doi.org/10.1075/babel.58.2.02lu

Mason, I. (2009). Role, positioning and discourse in face-to-face interpreting. In R. de Pedro Ricoy, I. Perez, & C. Wilson (Eds.), *Interpreting and translating in public service settings: Policy, practice, pedagogy* (pp. 52–73). Manchester: St. Jerome Press.

McConville, M. (2011). *Criminal justice in China. An empirical enquiry*. Cheltenham, UK and Northampton, MA: Edward Elgar.

Mead, G. (1965). *Mind, self, and society from the standpoint of a social behaviourist*. Chicago and London: University of Chicago Press.

Merlini, R., & Favaron, R. (2005). Examining the 'voice of interpreting' in speech pathology. *Interpreting*, *7*(2), 263–302. https://doi.org/10.1075/bct.9.08mer

Metzger, M. (1999). *Sign language interpreting: Deconstructing the myth of neutrality*. Washington, DC: Gallaudet University Press.

Müller, F. (1989). Translation in bilingual conversation: Pragmatic aspects of translator interaction. *Journal of Pragmatics*, *13*, 713–739. https://doi.org/10.1016/0378-2166(89)90075-1

Nakane, I. (2014). *Interpreter-mediated police interviews: A discourse-pragmatic approach*. Basingstoke: Palgrave Macmillan.

Napier, J. (2004). Sign language interpreter training, testing, and accreditation: An international comparison. *American Annals of the Deaf*, *149*(4), 350–359. https://doi.org/10.1353/aad.2005.0007

Ng, E. (2015). Teaching and research on legal interpreting: A Hong Kong perspective. *MonTI Monographs in Translation and Interpreting*, *7*, 243–270. https://doi.org/10.6035/monti.2015.7.9

Ng, K. H. (2009). *The common law in two voices: Language, law and the postcolonial dilemma in Hong Kong*. Stanford: Stanford University Press.

Niska, H. (2005). Training interpreters: Programmes, curricula, practices. In M. Tenent (Ed.), *Training for the new millenium* (pp. 35–64). Amsterdam and Philadelphia: John Benjamins. https://doi.org/10.1075/btl.60.07nis

O'Barr, W. (1982). *Linguistics evidence: Language, power and strategy in the courtroom.* New York: Academic Press.

Obst, H. (2010). *White House interpreter: The art of interpretation.* Bloomington, IN: Author House.

Orlando, M. (2016). *Training 21st century translators and interpreters: At the crossroads of practice, research and pedagogy.* Berlin: Frank & Timme.

Penn, C., & Watermeyer, J. (2012). When asides become central: Small talk and big talk in interpreted health interactions. *Patient Education and Counselling, 88,* 391–398. https://doi.org/10.1016/j.pec.2012.06.016

Pöchhacker, F. (2006). Going social? On pathways and paradigms in interpreting studies. In A. Pym, M. Shlesinger, & Z. Jettmarová (Eds.), *Sociocultural aspects of translating and interpreting* (pp. 215–232). Amsterdam and Philadelphia: John Benjamins. https://doi.org/10.1075/btl.67.27poc

Pöchhacker, F. (2012). Interpreting participation: Conceptual analysis and illustration of the interpreter's role in interaction. In C. Baraldi & L. Gavioli (Eds.), *Coordinating participation in dialogue interpreting* (pp. 45–69). Amsterdam and Philadelphia: John Benjamins. https://doi.org/10.1075/btl.102.03poch

Pöchhacker, F. (2016). *Introducing interpreting studies* (2nd ed.). London and New York: Routledge.

Pokorn, N. (2015). Positioning. In F. Pöchhacker (Ed.), *Routledge encyclopaedia of interpreting studies* (pp. 312–314). London: Routledge.

Price, E. L., Perez-Stable, E. J., Nickleach, D., Lopez, M., & Karliner, L. S. (2002). Interpreter perspectives of in-person, telephonic, and videoconferencing medical interpretation in clinical encounters. *Patient Education and Counselling, 87,* 226–232. doi:10.1016/j.pec.2011.08.006

Ren, X. (2000). 外交口译的灵活度 [Flexibility in diplomatic interpretation]. *Chinese Translators Journal* (中国翻译) (5).

Roy, C. B. (2000). *Interpreting as a discourse process.* Oxford: Oxford University Press.

Rudvin, M., & Tomassini, E. (2011). *Interpreting in the community and workplace.* Houndmills, UK: Palgrave Macmillan.

Sandrelli, A. (2011). Training in business interpreting and the role of technology. In M. Montero, J. Francisco, & S. Tripepi Winteringham (Eds.), *Interpretazione e mediazione. Un'opposizione inconciliabile?* (pp. 209–233). Rome: Aracne.

Schmidt, P. (2016). *Hitler's interpreter. The memoirs of Paul Schmidt* (R. Steed, Trans.). Port Stroud, Gloucestershire: History Press.

Seleskovitch, D. (1962). L'Interprétation de conférence. *Babel, 8*(1), 13–18.

Seleskovitch, D. (1978). *Interpreting for international conferences* (S. Dailey & E. McMillan, Trans.). Leesburg, VA: Pen & Booth.

Setton, R. (1993). Is non-intra-IE interpretation different? European models and Chinese–English realities. *Meta, 38*(2), 238–256. https://doi.org/10.7202/004115ar

Setton, R. (1994). Training conference interpreters with Chinese – Problems and prospects. In R. K. Seymour & C. C. Liu (Eds.), *Translation and interpreting: Bridging East and West* (pp. 180–189). Honolulu: University of Hawaii Press.

Setton, R., & Darwant, A. (2016). *Conference interpreting. A complete course.* Amsterdam: John Benjamins.

Setton, R., & Guo, A. L. (2009). Attitudes to role, status and professional identity in interpreters and translators with Chinese in Shanghai and Taipei. *Translation and Interpreting Studies, 4*(2), 210–238. https://doi.org/10.1075/bct.32.07set

Shi, Y. (2007). 怎样做好外交口译工作 ['How to perform diplomatic interpreting well'] *Chinese Translators Journal* (3).

Spencer-Oatey, H. (2002). Managing rapport in talk: Using rapport sensitive incidents to explore the motivational concerns underlying the management of relations. *Journal of Pragmatics, 34*, 529–545. https://doi.org/10.1016/s0378-2166(01)00039-x

Spencer-Oatey, H., & Xing, J. (2003). Managing rapport in intercultural business interactions: A comparison of two Chinese-British welcome meetings. *Journal of Intercultural Studies, 24*(1), 33–46. https://doi.org/10.1080/07256860305788

Spencer-Oatey, H., & Xing, J. (2009). The impact of culture on interpreter behaviour. In H. Kotthoff & H. Spencer-Oatey (Eds.), *Handbook of intercultural communication* (pp. 219–236). Berlin: Mouton de Gruyter. https://doi.org/10.1515/9783110198584.2.219

Straniero Sergio, F. (1999). The interpreter on the (talk) show: Interaction and participation frameworks. *The Translator, 5*(2), 303–326. https://doi.org/10.1080/13556509.1999.10799046

Takimoto, M. (2006). Interpreters' role perceptions in business dialogue interpreting situations. *Monash University Linguistics Papers, 5*(1), 47–57.

Takimoto, M., & Koshiba, K. (2009). Interpreter's non-rendition behaviour and its effect on interaction: A case study of a multi-party interpreting situation. *Translation & Interpreting, 1*(1), 15–26.

Valdés, G., & Angelelli, C. (2003). Interpreters, interpreting and the study of bilingualism. *Annual Review of Applied Linguistics, 23*, 58–78. https://doi.org/10.1017/s0267190503000199

Valero-Garcés, C. (2014). *Communicating across cultures: A coursebook on interpreting and translating in public services and institutions*. Lanham, MA: University Press of America.

Wadensjö, C. (1998). *Interpreting as interaction*. London, NY: Longman.

Wadensjö, C. (2001). Interpreting in crises: The interpreter's position in therapeutic encounters. In I. Mason (Ed.), *Triadic exchanges: Studies in dialogue interpreting* (pp. 71–87). Manchester, UK: St. Jerome Publishing.

Wang, B. (2012). A descriptive study of norms in interpreting: Based on the Chinese–English consecutive interpreting corpus of Chinese premier press conferences. *Meta, 57*(1), 198–212. https://doi.org/10.7202/1012749ar

Wiener, E., & Rivera, M. (2004). Bridging language barriers: How to work with an interpreter. *Clinical Pediatric Emergency Medicine, 5*, 93–101. https://doi.org/10.1016/j.cpem.2004.01.007

Xiao, X., & Li, F. (2013). Sign language interpreting on Chinese TV: A survey on user perspectives. *Perspectives, 21*(1), 100–116. https://doi.org/10.4324/9781315228723-18

Xiao, X., & Yu, R. (2009). Survey on sign language interpreting in China. *Interpreting, 11*(2), 137–163. https://doi.org/10.1075/bct.29.04xia

Xiong, Y. (2010). *Professional interpreters' qualities as mirrored in premier Wen Jiabao's press conference during the 2010 NPC & CPPCC sessions*. Xiamen: College of Foreign Languages and Cultures, Xiamen University.

Xu, Y. (2000). Features in diplomatic interpretation of translation and diplomatic interpreters' qualities [外交翻译的特点以及对外交翻译的要求]. *Chinese Translators Journal, 141*, 35–38.

Youtube. (2016). *NUS-UBS philanthropy breakfast with Jet Li (Part 3) with mandarin Chinese interpretation*. Retrieved from www.youtube.com/watch?v=3KiCeShZY4g

Yuan, X. (2013). Face representation in interpreting politician-journalist interactions. *China Media Research, 9*(4), 102–113.

Zhan, C., & Zeng, L. (2017). Chinese medical interpreters' visibility through text owner-ship: An empirical study on interpreted dialogues at a hospital in Guangzhou. *Interpreting, 19*(1), 97–117. https://doi.org/10.1075/intp.19.1.05zha

4 Chinese–English interpreter-mediated interactions

The previous chapter provided an overview of the settings and contexts within Chinese–English interpreters' work. This chapter builds on our discussion of models and frameworks applied in research on intercultural communication in chapter one and on our presentation of Chinese and English speakers in Chapter 2. This chapter has a multi-perspective focus that presents the reported views of the three groups of participants in interpreter-mediated interactions: Chinese speakers, English speakers and Chinese–English interpreters. Complementing the presentation of linguistic, situational and discursive data provided in Chapter 3, this chapter presents reported responses, reflected experiences and stated attitudes about interpreter-mediated Chinese–English interactions.

This chapter seeks to bring cultural-pragmatic features to the foreground and to study Chinese and English speakers' self-reported perceptions of their linguistic and paralinguistic behaviour, and to match these with those from a group of professional interpreters. To analyse the research data, we apply the Inter-Culturality Framework (ICF) as the main theoretical framework, but also incorporate a number of relevant concepts and theories into our analysis. These include speech acts (Searle, 1969; Austin, 1975), politeness theory (Brown & Levinson, 1987; Gu, 1990), the cooperative principle (Grice, 1975), low versus high context cultures (Hall, 1976), intercultural speaker and interactional competence (Celce-Murcia, 2007; House, 2007), cultural pragmatic schemas (Sharifian, 2011; Sharifian & Jamarani, 2011), the dialogue features of interpreted interactions (Mason, 2006) and the dynamic roles of interpreters (Mullamaa, 2009; Setton & Guo, 2009) with a focus on Chinese and English speakers.

4.1 Multi-perspective data of Chinese–English interpreted interactions

We first look at the two groups of interlocutors who employ Chinese and English respectively: Chinese speakers and English speakers. We present responses from both two groups on the following:

responses about themselves;
responses about members of the other group;

responses about themselves when interacting with members of the other group;
both groups' responses about themselves when interacting with interpreters;
both groups' responses about interpreters when interacting with them.

We present responses from Chinese–English interpreters on the following:

responses about themselves;
responses about attributes of Chinese and English speakers separately;
responses from interpreters about themselves interacting with each group;

In this way, this chapter presents data not only on the perspectives that speakers
and interpreters have of each other, but also of speakers' and interpreters' *ideographic dimension* (i.e. the way how they see themselves) and their *nomothetic
dimension* (i.e. how they believe others see them). We diagrammatically describe
the perspectives of their responses in Figure 4.1.

Figure 4.1 has double-pointed arrows connecting all human protagonists and
these relate to the bi-directional, reciprocal relations which we present throughout
this chapter. The single-pointed arrows relate to the directionality of language
transfer from source speaker's speech to interpreted target speech provided by the
interpreter to the target listener.

4.1.1   *'Chinese speakers', 'English speakers' and 'Chinese–English interpreters'*

Chapter 2 provided a comprehensive description of 'Chinese speakers' and 'English speakers' and showed that both terms are hypernyms for two very heterogeneous groups. To re-list some of the characteristics of that group identified as
'Chinese speakers', we see that while most have *Pŭtōnghuà* within their linguistic
repertoire, and numerically most have Mandarin as their L1, there are very large

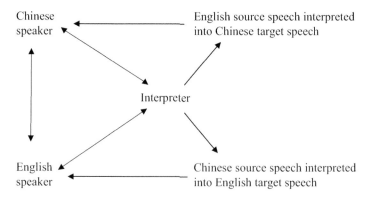

Figure 4.1 Ideographic and nomothetic dimensions of the protagonists of Chinese–English
interpreter-mediated interactions and directionality of language transfer

numbers of bi- and multi-lingual Chinese speakers with proficiency in Cantonese, Hakka, Hokkien, Shanghainese and/or other languages. There are different acquisition paths and patterns of functional use of Chinese languages in predominantly Chinese-speaking countries compared to countries in which Chinese languages are used in a transposed, diaspora or immigrant setting. There is wide variation in the discourse-pragmatic norms of Chinese speakers across both homeland and diaspora settings. The term 'English speakers' encompasses an even more diverse group of people. Most of them are not L1, but L2 (or L-subsequent) users of English, with even greater variation in the linguistic forms employed by not only L1 speakers across the span of 'inner-circle' countries who are users of a pluricentric language with similar, but distinct national standard varieties, to all over the world where lexical, phonological, grammatical and/or pragmatic features of speakers' other languages may be transferred into their varieties of English.

Chinese–English interpreters are, by definition, speakers of both languages and they therefore belong to both groups. As both of these groups are heterogeneous, it is reasonable to expect that there will be variety in their acquisition of their languages, their use of them, and in their knowledge of the cultural and discourse-pragmatic features of those two very large groups of speakers with whom they work: Chinese speakers and English speakers. Chinese–English interpreters are a diverse group. Most are located in mainland China, Hong Kong, Macau and Taiwan. The most conspicuous areas of work there are business and diplomatic interpreting. Significant numbers of Chinese–English interpreters work in diaspora settings in predominantly Anglophone countries, mostly in healthcare, police/legal/court or welfare settings that make up the most common areas of public service interpreting. Common to the overwhelming majority of Chinese–English interpreters is their L1, which is usually Mandarin, or another Chinese language such as Cantonese, Hakka or Hokkien. Ten years ago, Setton (2009, p. 109) observed that "perhaps 98% of interpreters of Chinese are Chinese native-speakers, and few than one in five have lived for more than a month or two outside China". While the proportion of Chinese–English interpreters who have resided outside China has probably increased since 2009 – in part due to the large number of Chinese-nationals undertaking translation and interpreting training outside China – it is still likely that a large number of those residing in the People's Republic of China have had little or no significant experience of living in allophone environments. That the majority of Chinese–English interpreters acquired Chinese as their L1 in countries or environments in which Chinese is the dominant socio-political language means that they are conversant in Chinese cultural-pragmatic norms, at least in relation to those that predominate in the area or environment in which they acquired Chinese. Those working in predominantly Anglophone countries who relocated from Chinese-speaking countries are likely to have commenced their acquisition of English before emigration and have gained a higher proficiency of English and familiarity with the cultural norms of the recipient country. At the same time, the number of 'overseas-born' or 'second-generation' speakers of Chinese, is increasing, and some from this group who acquired both languages in their early years (i.e. 'bilingual first language acquisition', see De Houwer, 2009) have joined the ranks of interpreters working in Anglophone countries, or in Chinese-speaking ones. (See section 3.3.2 for details on the biographies of Ji Chaozhu and Nancy Wensheng Tang.)

4.1.2   *Informants and samples*

This chapter presents responses from a data sample. The data sample consists of elicited answers to questions collected from three groups of informants by way of electronic or paper-copy survey. The first group consists of 25 Chinese speakers whose limited proficiency in English necessitates their use of Chinese–English interpreting services in healthcare (and other) settings. These informants were interviewed in spoken Mandarin and/or completed written Chinese survey forms. The second group consists of 24 English speakers who lack proficiency in Chinese and who rely on the use of Chinese–English interpreting services to communicate with Chinese-speaking patients. These informants completed an electronic survey in English. The third group consists of 33 Chinese–English interpreters. This group had the choice to complete an electronic survey in either Chinese or English. Of the group of 33 Chinese–English interpreters, eight of them agreed to be interviewed individually, responding in more detail to the same questions asked in the electronic survey [1]. All informants were residents of Melbourne at the time of data collection (June-August, 2012).

Chinese speakers were drawn from social Chinese-speaking associations situated close to a major metropolitan hospital and all Chinese-speaking informants had experience in using the services of Chinese–English interpreters at this or other hospitals. All English speakers are employees of a major metropolitan hospital in Melbourne. The Chinese–English interpreters were contacted through online directories of the professional association for interpreters (AUSIT) and the accrediting authority for interpreters, i.e. NAATI in Australia, as well as through the Chinese Interpreters and Translators Association of Australia. As stated, the healthcare sector is the major provider of interpreting work not only in the US, but in Australia as well (Chesher, Slatyer, Doubine, Jaric, & Lazzari, 2003, p. 278), and almost all of the Chinese–English interpreters reported having worked in this field.

The Chinese speakers completed an 18-question survey in Chinese, which elicited quantitative and qualitative responses. English speakers completed a similar 18-question online survey distributed to staff through a hospital-internal source; the Chinese–English interpreters completed a 17-question survey that was supplied to them in both Chinese and English through an online survey portal. Table 4.1 contains details of the numbers of informants and their assumed proficiency levels in the two languages.

The Chinese speakers migrated to Australia as adults and are linguistically dominant in Chinese. The English speakers are made up of three groups – monolingual Anglo-Australians; English-dominant bilinguals born and/or raised in Australia, L2- or L3-speakers with high proficiency in English. Thirty two of the 33 Chinese–English interpreters are tertiary-educated ethnic Chinese with

Table 4.1 Number and linguistic proficiency profiles of Chinese speakers, English speakers and Chinese–English interpreters.

	Number	Chinese proficiency	English proficiency
Chinese speakers	25	L1	L2 (limited proficiency)
English speakers	24	No information	L1
			L2 or L3 (high proficiency)
Chinese–English	33	L1	L2 (high proficiency)
interpreters		L2 (high proficiency)	L1

Chinese as their L1, while one is an English L1 speaker who has resided for lengthy periods in China and who has post-graduate level training as an interpreter and translator. All Chinese–English interpreters are holders of certification in interpreting. All are conversant in Chinese cultural-pragmatic norms. Length of residence in Australia varies, but all are likely to have a high level of familiarity with (Australian) English cultural-pragmatic norms.

Data from the three groups of informants are presented in the following way. Responses from Chinese speakers are provided first, with the Chinese wording used in the questions that were put to them. English glosses of these are supplied in square brackets. Responses from English speakers are provided second, with the English wording used in the questions put to them. The responses are combined into the same tables as both groups were asked the same or conversely equivalent questions. Responses from Chinese–English interpreters are sometimes given in separate tables, sometimes in tables combined with the responses of the Chinese and English speakers. The Chinese–English interpreters were asked equivalent questions that elicited responses about themselves and about both groups of speakers. As stated, the Chinese–English interpreters were given the choice of completing the survey in either Chinese or English. The questions asked to the interpreters are given in both languages: first English, then Chinese in the tables from sections 4.2 to 4.6. Excerpts from the interviews with the eight Chinese–English interpreters who participated are given in the language that they were provided in; Chinese quotes are followed by English glosses in single quotation marks. The following conventions for identifying informants according to which group they belong to are used: Chi-sp.inf.3 (Chinese speaker, informant no. 3); Eng-sp.inf.3 (English speaker, informant no. 3); Chi-Eng.inter.3 (Chinese–English interpreter no. 3). Figures given in tables are percentages.

This data sample is a quantitative-based corpus of informants' recollections of general features of interpreted interactions. The data sample is therefore indicative of informants' 'summative' and self-reported experiences, without the capacity to describe in detail informants' actual behaviour in particular interactions. In many cases, and for some features (e.g. small talk, leave-taking), informants' reported enactments of these features are dependent on or reactive to the behaviour of the other interlocutor/s and the same informant may vary greatly in their performance of these features from interaction to interaction. The responses provided by informants are therefore to be regarded as reflective of their recollections of events, rather than as systematically studied events, documented by an observer-researcher. The strength of the sample lies in the elicitation of situational features from informants who come from all three groups of interlocutors present in Chinese–English interpreter-mediated interactions.

As shown in Figure 4.1, the responses given by the Chinese and English speakers relate to: their own reported behaviour in general and when interacting with others; perceived behaviour of speakers of the other language; perceived behaviour of interpreters. The Chinese–English interpreters also provide responses about themselves; about speakers of each group in a general sense; and when interacting with each other in interpreter-mediated interactions. The presentation of responses in sections 4.2 to 4.6 is descriptive and interpretive, bringing together responses from different perspectives to the same or related features. The multi-perspective data is presented in a comparative but also integrative way referencing the descriptive tools of the Inter-Culturality Framework introduced in Chapter 1.

4.1.3   Situational features within the interpreter-mediated interaction

This chapter presents data on the situational features of interpreter-mediated interactions. These are grouped according to their chronological occurrence and thematic relationship: introduction, role explanation, pre-interactional briefing on features relevant to intercultural communication (4.2); physical proximity, small talk as an opener, body language (4.3); information presentation and elicitation (4.4); leave taking (4.5); metalinguistic awareness and language-transfer features (4.6). The features presented in sections 4.2 to 4.4 have been identified and examined in studies of healthcare settings (e.g. Sarangi & Roberts, 1999; Angelelli, 2004; Cordella, 2004; Tebble, 2013).

Further, healthcare settings are the most common settings in which the Chinese speakers interact with English speakers with an interpreter. They are the settings in which the English speakers almost always encounter Chinese speakers when working with an interpreter. As stated, for Chinese–English interpreters, the healthcare sector is the largest area of work and one that most informants reported working in regularly.

4.2   Introductions, role explanation, pre-interactional briefings

This section presents data on introductions, role explanations and pre-interactional briefings on features relevant to intercultural communication. These three elements are ones that characterize the *genre* of the interpreter-mediated medical consultation, or at least the initial components of it (Tebble, 2014). They usually occur as separate and distinct speaker turns in which interlocutors firstly introduce themselves, then explain their role, job title or position to others, followed by a briefing on any anticipated cultural differences that may impact on the interaction.

We distinguish between the three and present responses relating to each in the sections: introductions (4.2.1), role explanations (4.2.2), pre-interactional briefings (4.2.3). Following these, a summary of findings (4.2.4.) is provided.

4.2.1   Introductions

In doctor-patient interactions in China, it is common for neither interlocutor to introduce themselves. Instead, doctors usually verify the patient's name, based on written records supplied to the doctor, and the patient responds to this request (Zhang & Shang, 2002, p. 338). Tsai (2005) identifies time-constraints as a reason for the absence for self-introductions, and reports from 30 observed consultations in Taiwan that personal rapport, where sought, typically occurs at a later point in the interaction. Patients do not typically ask for the doctor's name, and when addressing the doctor directly, may use respectful terms which emphasize the seniority or expertise of the doctor, (Zhang & Shang, 2002). In English, self-introductions from both the doctor and the patient at their first meeting are common (Cordella, 2004, p. 56) while a doctor's verification of a patient's name is something more typical for mental health consultations than for general health interactions (Ribeiro & de Souza Pinto, 2005, p. 662). Table 4.2 contains Chinese and English speakers' responses on their self-introduction conventions.

Table 4.2 shows that roughly equal percentages of Chinese speakers always or sometimes introduce themselves by name. Over half of the English speakers always do this, 21% do this sometimes, and a further 21% do not usually do this. Self-introductions are considered obligatory for roughly half of the Chinese- and English-speaking informants. For some other Chinese-speaking informants, a self-introduction is optional, while for smaller numbers of English speakers, it is either optional or left out, probably due to perceived time constraints. Time constraints and the personal name badges worn by many doctors may lead to some doctors believing that they need not introduce themselves to the patient or inform them of their name. This may be a factor in accounting for the variation in English speakers' variation of responses. It is hard to contextualise the responses

Table 4.2 Chinese speakers' and English speakers' frequency of self-introduction.

	Chi-sp. informants	Eng-sp. informants	
你会正式介绍自己，在必要时告知自己的全名 (和职业吗)? [Do you formally introduce yourself, giving your full name (and occupation where relevant)?]		Do you formally introduce yourself, giving your full name, work title or other role?	
是的总是 [Yes, always]	44	58	Yes, always
有时 [Sometimes]	52	21	Sometimes
通常不会 [Not usually]	0	21	Not usually
未回答 [No answer]	4	0	No answer

of Chinese speakers with Zhang and Shang's (2002) and Tsai's (2005) data that showed that self-introductions are uncommon. The converse implication from Hall's (1976) "low" vs. "high" culture framework is that English speakers would be more likely to establish their role (through explication of their identity). But no more than 58% do this. One interpreter remarks on the openers of healthcare interactions:

> Chinese speakers sometimes provide a greeting and introduce themselves. English speakers always do this, and sometimes the whole greeting lasts a long time. (Chi-Eng.inter.32)

We are mindful that the responses given relate to the situation of Chinese and English speakers introducing themselves to each other *via* an interpreter. The English speaker, as the key protagonist with whom the Chinese speaker is interacting, is the one who commences the interaction by introducing him-/herself:

> It is my responsibility as a clinician to initiate all the introductions at the start of the interview, not the interpreter's role. (Eng-sp.inf.8)

The comment from this English speaker is congruent to guideline documents. Procedurally, some contemporary guides on working with interpreters recommend that the representative of a service should take the initiative to "introduce all parties to one another" (CCEH, 2014). The implication of this is that the English speaker commences the interaction by introducing him-/herself and then the interpreter, and the interpreter interprets this self-introduction of the English speaker and the English speaker's introduction of the interpreter. If this does not occur, the interpreter should introduce him-/herself. This is not only a situational courtesy but an element of interpreter practice (Hale, 2007; CCEH, 2014). The self-introduction can contain the interpreter's name, e.g. "Hello, I'm Vera, your Chinese–English interpreter working with you today". Alternatively, it need not contain a personal name where security or other measures justify the interpreter not identifying him-/herself, e.g. "Hello, I'm your interpreter for today. Please address me as Ms Interpreter". The interpreter is working with at least two interlocutors and the introduction should be made in *both* languages, to *all* parties. Table 4.3 contains responses from all three groups of informants.

The most frequent response from both Chinese and English speakers is that interpreters "usually" introduce themselves to them, and both groups report that the interpreter does this "usually" to the other (i.e. allophone) interlocutor. We hypothesized that interpreters reporting on themselves would record an even higher rate of self-introduction, due to them being the enactors of such a self-introduction. But their responses required a lower level of frequency than the other two groups, and the Chinese–English interpreters most commonly report that they "sometimes" provide a self-introduction. It is possible that others' introductions of the interpreter, e.g. "Today Vera is your Chinese–English interpreter

Table 4.3 Chinese and English speakers' responses on the frequency of Chinese–English interpreters' introductions to them and the other group; Chinese–English interpreters' responses on frequency of their own self-introductions.

	Chi-sp. informants		Chi-Eng. interpreters	Eng-sp. informants		
汉英译员会正式介绍自己吗 [Does the Chinese–English interpreter formally introduce him- or herself?]			Do you formally introduce yourself? 你会正式介绍自己，告知自己的全名、？	Does the Chinese–English interpreter formally introduce him- or herself?		
	对我 [To me]	对英语人士 [To the Eng-sp. person]		To the Chi-sp. person	To me	
经常 [Usually]	55	58	42	78	68	Usually
有时 [Sometimes]	45	42	55	11	26	Sometimes
很少 [Rarely]	0	0	6	0	0	Rarely
不知道 / 未留意 [Don't know/ Don't notice]	0	0	0	11	6	Don't know/ Don't notice

and we'll be working together" had the effect that some interpreters felt that they didn't always need to perform an introduction themselves.

4.2.2 Role explanation

As outlined in section 3.2.1, role is an implicit notion in work-related settings and it is a central construct in social science research. In a metaphoric sense, a *role* is "the part each person is called on to play in the social drama" (Calhoun, 2002). Narrowing 'role' down to formal interactions, including medical ones, Baert (2006, p. 524) describes it as "a set of expectations society has of individuals in a given social position or status". These expectations are both self-applied and applied to others, and in an interactional sense, these provide the 'script' for "particular behaviour in a particular situation, staged in front of an audience" (Pöllabauer, 2015, p. 355). Setting and characteristics of protagonists may render their roles obvious. In medical interactions, the roles of patient and healthcare professional are usually obvious. Nonetheless, role explanation, can occur, e.g.

I'm new here as a patient, but I've heard lots of good things about this clinic from my friends.
I'm the occupational therapist working with you today. Did the rehabilitation nurse explain to you how we would be working together to look at your mobility and safety around the house?

These turns mention the speaker's role, but little further information on how the speaker will enact this role. In the first instance the speaker adds a compliment and signals confidence that s/he will receive good medical care. In the second instance, the speaker is seeking to know if the patient knows what can be achieved with the help of an occupational therapist.

For those with little or no previous experience working with interpreters, an introduction such as 'I'm your interpreter' may not evoke a clear expectation of what the interpreter will do (and not do – see section 3.2.1). In Australia, the authoritative guide for the professional conduct of interpreters in Australia, the AUSIT Code of Ethics and Code of Conduct (2012, p. 12) sets out the interpreter's explanation of their role as an ethical principle: "clarity of role boundaries" is one of the nine principles that interpreters are advised to follow. Thus, there is a normative requirement for interpreters to explain their role to others, as well as evidence from discourse-focussed studies that identify the role explanation as *the* key step that represents a "contract" enabling all interlocutors to know how the interpreter will work with them (e.g. Tebble, 2014). Within this role explanation, there are attributes about their role that interpreters outline such as their credentials, use of first person, interpreting *everything* that is said by all interlocutors, assurances of confidentiality, directing one's gaze at each other etc. Table 4.4 presents both groups' reported experience of this being conveyed to them, and Chinese–English interpreters' self-reported role explanation to speakers from both groups.

Table 4.4 shows that all informants report that the interpreter 'usually' explains his/her role to both Chinese speakers and English speakers as reported by both groups, and in reference to their perception that this is provided for the other group. The Chinese–English interpreters also report this, with 73% responding that they 'usually' provide an explanation of their role for Chinese speakers (73%) while 52% do so for English speakers. This difference is more marked amongst English speakers, and can be accounted for by many English speakers' frequent and ongoing contact with the same interpreters, leading to these omitting the role explanation.

Chinese speakers appear to readily register whether role explanation is being provided to English speakers, despite most of them having limited English proficiency. The absence of Chinese proficiency amongst the English speakers accounts for why 22% do not know if the interpreter is explaining his/her role to the Chinese speaker. (Interpreter training programs typically recommend that the interpreter's explanation of role in both languages should include mention that the same explanation has been or will be provided to the speaker of the other language.) The following comment is recorded from an interpreter that accords with the responses from (and about) English speakers in regard to a lower reported incidence of role explanation to them:

> 使用翻译的英语人士通常已经习惯于使用翻译服务，所以不是每一次都需要向他们介绍翻译的角色。汉语人士虽然也使用翻译，但对于翻译角色的界定不是完全明白，并且由于汉语人士与翻译来自同样的背景，所以倾向于向翻译寻求帮助或者聊天，所以通常需要向他们解释翻译是做什么的，什么不能做。Usually English speakers who work with

Table 4.4 Chinese and English speakers' responses on the frequency of Chinese–English interpreters' explanation of role to them and the other group; Chinese–English interpreters' response on frequency of their own role-explanation to members of both groups.

	Chi-sp. informants		Chi-Eng. interpreters		Eng-sp. informants	
	汉英译员会说明自己的角色吗? [Does the Chinese–English interpreter explain his/her role?]		Do you explain your role (as an interpreter) to others? 你会向别人说明自己的角色吗?		Does the Chinese–English interpreter explain his/her role?	
	对我 [To me]	对英语人士 [To Eng-sp. person]	To Chinese speakers 汉语人士	To English speakers 英语人士	To Chi-sp. person	To me
经常 [Usually]	65	67	73	52	61	37
有时 [Sometimes]	30	28	21	35	17	26
很少 [Rarely]	5	6	6	13	0	26
不知道／未留意 [Don't know/ Don't notice]	0	0			22	11

interpreters are used to working with interpreters. Therefore, they do not need interpreters to explain their roles each time when they are present. Chinese speakers also use interpreters. However, they are not always completely clear about the role that interpreters play. Also, as Chinese speakers and interpreters share a certain common background, Chinese speakers tend to seek support from interpreters or chat with them, which is the very reason interpreters need to explain to them what they do and what they don't do. (Chi-Eng.inter.3)

Another comment from a Chinese–English interpreter contrasts English speakers' and Chinese speakers' perceptions of the interpreter's role in the following way:

> English speakers talk directly and frankly. They treat you and your work impartially and objectively. For Chinese speakers the opposite might be the case. They often treat interpreters very subjectively. 开始向你示好，希望对他们有好处。背后又会对你和其他当事者做出主观评论，考虑下次是否还用同样的传译员。
>
> English speakers talk directly and frankly. They treat you and your work impartially and objectively. For Chinese speakers the opposite might be the case. They often treat interpreters very subjectively. They try to make friends with you in order to gain something to their favour. Later, they may often make very subjective comments about you behind your back, considering if they will hire the same interpreter next time. (Chi-Eng.inter.7)

4.2.3   *Pre-interactional briefing on features relevant to intercultural communication*

A briefing is typically an exchange between an interpreter and a member of a particular occupational group held in private before the latter person (here, a healthcare professional) commences interacting with interlocutors who are allophone to him/her (here, Chinese-speaking patients). The briefing enables the interpreter to check how s/he will work, which mode of interpreting will be used (consecutive vs. simultaneous), previous experience with interpreters, an outline of the purpose or structure of the interaction, procedural or terminological features of other interlocutors' speech etc. It enables the healthcare professional to check on features such as physical configuration, the administration of diagnostic or treatment procedures, how to interact with family members etc. The briefing is considered an important requirement for health interactions by both health practitioners (e.g. Tribe, 1999; Tribe & Lane, 2009; O'Hara & Akinsulure-Smith, 2011; Costa, 2017) and interpreters (Bührig, Kliche, Meyer, & Pawlack, 2012; Crezee, 2013; Dabić, 2010; Pollard, 1998). Guidelines from both healthcare authorities (Phillips, 2010, p. 191) and interpreter professional associations (AUSIT, 2006, p. 2) advocate a briefing.

The briefing also enables the healthcare professional and the interpreter to exchange information on cultural aspects: for the healthcare professional to enquire if there are things to do or avoid to enable them to work with the patient; for the interpreter to provide advice on how the interaction can be optimally

Table 4.5 Chinese and English speakers' reported frequency of briefing on potential cultural differences from Chinese–English interpreters.

	Chi-sp. informants	Eng-sp. informants	
	在通过口译媒介进行交流时，汉英译员会将与此次交流相关的文化方面的注意事项告知你吗？ [Do Chinese–English interpreters brief you or provide you with information during an interpreted interaction about cultural aspects that are relevant to the interaction?]	Do Chinese–English interpreters brief you or provide you with information during an interpreted interaction about cultural aspects that are relevant to the interaction?	
经常 [Usually]	42	25	Usually
有时 [Sometimes]	29	25	Sometimes
很少 [Rarely]	29	50	Rarely

structured for the healthcare professional to work with Chinese speakers. The notion of a briefing also applies to contact between the interpreter and the patient before the interaction with the healthcare professional: interpreters may provide information to Chinese speakers about healthcare interactions in general, or about features specific to a consultation or procedure of which they have prior knowledge, but not information that amounts to medical advice. Table 4.5 presents Chinese and English speakers' responses of being briefed by the interpreter about cultural aspects that could be relevant to the interaction, about talking to the interpreter about possible cultural differences, and about asking the interpreter questions about the other group's culture.

The questions shown in Table 4.5 elicited Chinese and English speakers' responses in regard to the Chinese–English interpreter as a protagonist for the explication of cultural differences. Interpreters are often viewed as intercultural experts by others and this question relates to intercultural discourse as a feature of the interpreted interaction. Interpreters may locate potential intercultural schemas that could occur in the interaction, and foreground what strategies they may employ. These strategies may serve the purpose of averting miscommunication where the basis for this could be different cultural norms (Davies, 2014). Over 40% of Chinese speakers report that they are briefed by interpreters about cultural aspects relevant to the interaction, while a quarter of English speakers report this. Both figures are seemingly high, as it is often difficult (and perhaps not always possible) for an interpreter to anticipate which aspects of an interaction can pose possible challenges to effective communication. Chinese speakers are more commonly reported to be the recipients of this information.

It is possible that Chinese–English interpreters view Chinese speakers as being in greater need of instructive information; it is possible that they consider English-speakers, particularly experienced healthcare professionals, as being culturally competent (Garrett, 2009; Hlavac, Beagley, & Zucchi, 2018), and therefore in less need of such information. In any case, the reported rate of being briefed by an interpreter is less frequent amongst English speakers. An English-speaking clinician makes the following remark:

> If one does not speak the language, it is hard to gauge accurately how information is being provided and what information may be vetted due to the interpreter's own values. I prefer to elicit information about a person's cultural values and needs directly by asking the patient, as I do not want second opinions or to go in with a pre-conceived idea about how a person may think/feel, based on an interpreter's opinions. (Eng-sp.inf.8)

Responses from Chinese and English speakers are presented showing how often *they* interact with an interpreter to touch on cultural matters before the start of the interpreted interaction.

Table 4.6 shows a lower level of contact between the Chinese or English speaker and the interpreter where it is unclear who initiates the contact. This suggests that higher levels of pre-interactional contact occur when this is sought by the interpreter. Table 4.7 presents responses on the Chinese and English speakers as seekers of information on cultural features of the other group.

Table 4.7 shows that most commonly, Chinese speakers "rarely" ask interpreters questions about Australian culture, and English speakers only "sometimes" ask about Chinese culture. The responses indicate relatively low frequencies of elicitations of cultural differences in general. The following comment is from an English-speaking clinician:

> Interpreters are not cultural experts and cannot speak on behalf of everyone in the community. I have a very good knowledge of the concept of culture and particularly intra-cultural differences. (Eng-sp.inf.11)

Table 4.6 Chinese and English speakers' responses in regard to discussing possible cultural differences with the Chinese–English interpreters.

	Chi-sp. informants	*Eng-sp. informants*	
	互动之前，你会向汉英译员就可能的文化差异方面问题进行询问吗？ [Do you talk to the Chinese–English interpreter before an interaction to ask about possible cultural differences?]	Do you talk to the Chinese–English interpreter before an interaction to ask about possible cultural differences?	
经常 [Usually]	14	15	Usually
有时 [Sometimes]	67	50	Sometimes
很少 [Rarely]	19	35	Rarely

Table 4.7 Chinese and English speakers' reported frequency of asking questions to Chinese–English interpreters in pre-interaction briefing about potential cultural differences.

	Chi-sp. informants	*Eng-sp. informants*	
	你会问汉英译员有关澳大利亚文化的问题吗? [Do you ever ask Chinese–English interpreters questions about Australian culture?]	Do you ever ask Chinese–English interpreters questions about Chinese culture?	
是的 [Yes]	24	11	Yes
有时 [Sometimes]	29	48	Sometimes
很少 [Rarely]	47	42	Rarely

Table 4.8 Chinese and English speakers' reported frequency of being asked questions by Chinese–English interpreters in pre-interaction briefings about their knowledge of the culture of the other group.

	Chi-sp. Informants	*Eng-sp. informants*	
	汉英译员有没有问过你有关澳大利亚文化的知识? Do Chinese–English interpreters ever ask you questions about your knowledge of Australian culture?	Do Chinese–English interpreters ever ask you questions about your knowledge of Chinese culture?	
经常 [Usually]	0	5	Usually
有时 [Sometimes]	29	60	Sometimes
很少 [Rarely]	71	35	Rarely

As we can see, there are responses that show that the interpreter is not always viewed as the sole or most informed protagonist in regard to intercultural communication. Table 4.8 presents responses from Chinese and English speakers about interpreters asking them questions about the speakers' knowledge of the other group's culture.

Looking at the results shown in Table 4.8, the context of interpreters asking others questions about their knowledge of the other group's culture can be seen as an indirect offer for the *interpreter* to provide information. This may occur where a Chinese or English speaker signals that they lack knowledge on the other group and would welcome the provision of information from the interpreter. There are differences in the reported frequencies of this occurring between the two groups: Chinese speakers report this less frequently – perhaps as their knowledge of Australian culture is less likely to be questioned by interpreters; English speakers report this "sometimes" – perhaps as interpreters know that Chinese speakers are but one group that English speakers work with, and they are less likely to have knowledge specific to one other group in the way that Chinese speakers are likely

Table 4.9 Chinese–English interpreters' reported frequency of being asked questions by Chinese and English speakers about the culture of the other group.

	Chi-Eng interpreters	
	Do Chinese speakers view you as an expert on Australian culture and readily ask you about it? 汉语人士认为你很熟悉澳大利亚文化习俗并很乐意向你咨询吗？	Do English speakers view you as an expert on Chinese culture and readily ask you about it? 英语人士认为你很熟悉澳大利亚文化习俗并很乐意向你咨询吗？
经常 Quite often	55	27	Quite often
有时 Sometimes	42	24	Sometimes
很少 Rarely	3	49	Rarely

to have a knowledge of Australian culture. The same issue of cultural information being elicited or provided is shown in Table 4.9, this time as reported by Chinese–English interpreters.

Table 4.9 shows that 97% of the Chinese–English interpreters are "quite often" or "sometimes" asked by Chinese speakers about aspects of Australian culture. This is an overwhelming response reported about Chinese speakers. It would appear that for many, the interpreter may be the main or even only person available to answer such questions. One interpreter reports that this is a quite frequent occurrence:

> Many of the Chinese clients I assist are quite communication savvy, i.e. possess a proper understanding of communication know-hows. But for some of them when they come across culturally specific phenomena in the Australian culture, particularly those they have misperception on, they tend to break away from the communication process and ask me to get a clear picture. (Chi-Eng.inter.9)

Responses about English speakers show a lower but still sizeable level of frequency of enquiry. The responses clearly show that both groups call upon interpreters as intercultural experts. The following comments are related by an in-house interpreter:

> 会被问到文化方面的事情。比如"坐月子"或"喝温水"，还有新移民方面的问题。但是作为in-house interpreter会被问到更多问题，因为大家都对译员很熟悉，医生会问文化的问题，病人会问医院制度的问题。当别人觉得这个问题你应该能够更好或更快解决的时候会问。After explaining the cultural issue for one party, I would give a summary to the other party to explain what the conversation was about.
>
> Interpreters might be approached for inquiries on cultural issues, such as "postpartum confinement" or "drink warm water", and issues related to newly arrived migrants. But an in-house interpreter might be asked more questions as everyone is familiar with him or her. Doctors will ask questions

regarding cultural aspects, while patients might ask questions related to hospital regulations. People will ask you these things when they think you're better informed or can easily solve their concerns. After explaining the cultural issue for one party, I would give a summary to the other party to explain what the conversation was about. (Chi-Eng.inter.22)

The informant also adds that when questions by one party are asked within the mediated interaction itself, that the content of this 'side-conversation' is conveyed to the other party as well by the interpreter.

4.2.4 Summary of findings

In regard to self-introductions, Chinese and English speakers, as well as Chinese–English interpreters report high levels of providing these. Chinese and English speakers, in fact, report a frequency of interpreter self-introductions that is higher than that of the Chinese–English interpreters reporting on themselves. To account for this, we are reminded that all three groups of informants are unlikely to have been part of the same interactions. Role explanation is even more frequently provided by Chinese–English interpreters than self-introductions. This is confirmed by both this group, and Chinese and English speakers. There are occupation-based protocols as well as situational circumstances – e.g. how the interpreter interacts with patients' family members who may also be present and participating in the interaction (and who may believe that they should interpret for the patient) – that may foreground the role explanation more strongly than the self-introduction.

Role explanation is an important part of the preliminary stages of an interaction, as this informs both healthcare professional and patient on the protocols of a mediated interaction. From all three groups, most informants report that this "usually" happens. Chinese speakers report this in relation to themselves and also in relation to the way that they report witnessing the interpreter doing this for the other party. English speakers report that role-explanation is more likely to be provided to Chinese speakers than to themselves. Chinese–English interpreters report a very high frequency (73%) of doing this for the Chinese speaker, but still a high frequency for the English speaker (52%). The role-explanation is itself an example of a situational protocol and of an intercultural frame, as it draws both parties' attention to the bilingual, procedural and relayed nature of the communicative event.

Responses on the frequency of a briefing that includes mention of cultural features that could be relevant to the interaction are varied. Chinese speakers report a higher frequency of this "usually" occurring (42%) than English speakers (25%) where the interpreter is identified as the provider of information on cultural features. Where it is left open that this information could be brought up by either party, both Chinese and English speakers generally state that it happens "sometimes" (67% and 50% respectively). This is an example of intercultural frames and models being the focus of exchanges between the interpreter and the respective groups of speakers. Where Chinese speakers and English speakers are identified as the initiators of such a briefing, both groups record that this occurs less frequently. While 71% of Chinese speakers report that interpreters rarely ask them questions about their knowledge of Australian culture, 60% of English speakers report that interpreters ask them about their knowledge of Chinese culture.

There is a contrast in forms of behaviour reported by Chinese speakers compared to English speakers vis-à-vis the Chinese–English interpreter and intercultural knowledge: Chinese speakers report that interpreters more frequently brief them, that Chinese speakers ask interpreters to do this, and this view is confirmed by Chinese–English interpreters. Fifty-five percent of the interpreters report that they believe that Chinese speakers view them as experts on Australian culture. Amongst the English speakers the converse situation of them being briefed by the interpreter or asking the interpreter about cultural features is something that pertains to a lesser degree. The responses from interpreters corroborate this: almost half report that English speakers "rarely" view them as a cultural expert asking them questions about Chinese culture. We can see that intercultural discourse is commonly present in briefings or pre-interaction exchanges and the protagonist of this is usually, but not exclusively, the interpreter.

4.3   Physical proximity and proxemics, small talk as an opener, body language

The previous section discussed introduction, role-explanation and the elicitation of cultural information relevant to the interaction. This section sets out responses that relate to the initial stages of the interpreter-mediated interaction and focuses on physical space, whether small talk occurs as an opener, and perceptions of one's own and others' body language.

4.3.1   Physical proximity and proxemics

The doctor-patient situation is one that is marked by stark contrasts in body space conventions: the power-hierarchical difference obliges the patient to maintain "polite" distance from the doctor; the conditions that patients may suffer from can necessitate a doctor's intervention in intimate areas of their body. Gadit (2010) argues that such interventions, in some cultures, need to be negotiated very carefully not only to respect patients' personal space but also to protect a professional's reputation. Table 4.10 presents responses on speakers' perceived proximity vis-à-vis speakers of the other group.

Notions of 'closeness' and 'distance' to others are notoriously subjective, and there is likely to be considerable variation amongst speakers of the same group about what it means to position oneself 'closely' to others or not. Table 4.10 shows that nearly two-thirds of Chinese speakers believe they occupy a 'neutral' physical space in relation to English speakers, while nearly a quarter believe that they sit closely to them. Closeness may be motivated by the desire to hear English speakers more clearly. The English-speaking healthcare staff overwhelmingly select the "neither closely nor distantly" response. This is unsurprising where healthcare workers position themselves to be both engaged with the care of patients and mindful of patients' autonomy.

Table 4.10 Chinese and English speakers' reported physical proximity to members of the other group.

	Chi-sp. informants	Eng-sp. informants	
	在与英语人士交谈时，你会如何站位？ [How do you position yourself when you speak to an English-speaking person?]	How do you position yourself when you speak to a person from the other group?	
靠得较近 [Closely]	24	5	Closely
考得不近也不远 [Neither closely nor distantly]	64	95	Neither closely nor distantly
不确定 [Distantly]	12	0	Distantly

The interpreters were not asked a congruent question about how closely speakers of each group position themselves vis-à-vis speakers of the other group. Instead, interpreters were invited to provide general comments about their perceptions of the proxemics of both groups of speakers. The selected responses from interpreters show variation from those of these two groups. Interpreters perceive that Chinese speakers occupy a more proximate position than Chinese speakers themselves, while they also report that a quarter of English speakers position themselves closely to Chinese-speaking patients. While the first comment from an interpreter as follows is congruent to this former view, the remaining two views reflect a less clear-cut perception of cross-cultural proxemics:

> It depends on the circumstances. I do think that Chinese speakers position themselves a bit too closely to others, in particular, elder Chinese speakers. (Chi-Eng.inter.30)
> I agree that Chinese speakers position themselves neither too close nor too distant in healthcare interactions. (Chi-Eng.inter.3)
> 我觉得是 'neither closely nor distantly'. 有的西方人也会离得很近，尤其在生活中对话的时候。
>
> I think Chinese speakers position themselves "neither closely nor distantly." Sometimes Westerners can get very close to you also, especially when it's a casual and daily conversation. (Chi-Eng.inter.24)
> There are different notions of personal space. This may also be related to insider versus outsider perspectives. (Chi-Eng.inter.21)

The last comment again underlines the fact that self-reported estimations of proximity to others are imprecise indicators of actual (measured) space between interlocutors due to the different subjective notions of space. Table 4.11 presents Chinese–English interpreters' responses on the perceived proximity of Chinese and English speakers to them.

Table 4.11 Chinese–English interpreters' perceptions of others' physical proximity to them.

	Chi-Eng. interpreters	
	How do others position themselves to you when you work as an interpreter? 你担任译员时，别人怎么对待你？	
	Chi-speakers to me 汉语人士	Eng-speakers to me 英语人士
Closely靠得较近	48	20
Neither closely nor distantly 考得不近也不远	48	77
Distantly不确定	4	3

In general, Chinese–English interpreters report that Chinese speakers position themselves more closely to them than English speakers. In part, physical circumstances that do not enable a triangular and equidistant configuration (Wadensjö, 2001; Mason, 2009, 2012) can lead to the Chinese speaker (i.e. patient) being positioned more closely to the interpreter than the English speaker (i.e. healthcare professional).

In general, the responses are in line with Jones's (1971) and Beaulieu's (2004) findings in regard to Chinese and English speakers: the interpreters (as co-participants in but also expert observers of intercultural interactions) report "neutral" rather than "proximal" positions about both groups, with a slightly higher number of Chinese speakers reported to position themselves in a more proximal position than English speakers.

Multiple causations are at work, some of which function in concert with, some in opposition to each other. Chinese notions of politeness, i.e. 礼貌 (*lǐmào*) and 客气 (*kèqi*) as illustrated in Chapter 2, are based on interlocutors' desire not to display distance to others where a degree of personal investment has been established. 'Distance' need not be a physically measured quantity, but in the context of the informants surveyed here it could be that displays of politeness may include a reduction in physical distance. The presence of an interpreter can also have mixed consequences: the presence of another in a confined space may alter speakers' self-perceptions of closeness and distance; the presence of an interpreter can sometimes cause either or both allophone interlocutors to "withdraw" from the other and engage only through the interpreter. This last course of actions is one which trainee interpreters are taught to avoid through the adoption of a pro-active approach in the seating and eye-contact arrangements at the commencement of the interpreted interaction. Notwithstanding such an approach, interlocutors can and do adopt their own postures towards others.

4.3.2   *Small talk as an opener*

Phatic language typically performs the function of a "social lubricant" in (re-)forming social relations between interlocutors, where these relations are considered to pertain. Small talk, although thematically considered unimportant, is an aspect of conversation that provides a means of "easing things along" (Schneider, 1988, p. 17). It has been widely taken to be a "conventionalized and peripheral mode of talk" (Coupland, 2000, p. 1) that has been found on boundaries of conversation such as openings and closings but also in free and "aimless" social intercourse. Small talk is viewed derogatorily by some due to folk-linguistic perceptions that it is redundant. Nor does it fit easily into some linguistic analyses of talk that posit that the maxims of efficiency, expedience and truth must always pertain (cf. Grice, 1975). However, small talk can be used as a pragmatic device in conversation, and as such can represent an "intercultural schema" in which there may be shared or distinct cultural conceptual structures.

Differences in the use of small talk according to relationship to interlocutor and setting are ascertainable between Chinese and English speakers. In informal settings between mainland Chinese interlocutors familiar to each other, telephone small talk "may accomplish propitiatory, initiatory and exploratory functions simultaneously" (Sun, 2004, p. 1461). Its functions in English-speaking, including English lingua franca conversation, appear to be broader: small talk is used as an "ice-breaker" amongst unfamiliar interlocutors (in business or some commercial or service transactions); as a means of social cohesion at the workplace amongst people who are familiar but not close to each other (cf. Clyne, 1994, p. 84); and as a "re-establishment of ties" device between friends, similar to Sun's (2004) example.

Moving to healthcare scenarios, small talk or non-formal conversational routines between female healthcare professionals and female patients that included self-disclosure and empathetic comment were shown to lead to greater patient co-operation (Ragan, 2000). In a study of doctor-patient encounters at a small hospital in England, Coupland, Robinson, and Coupland (1994, p. 104) recorded compliments, banter and teasing in consultation openings and opined that "doctors' willingness to pursue non-medical topics [was] strikingly at odds with the findings of our previous studies". From research on the occurrence of small talk in interpreted health interactions, Penn and Watermeyer (2012) report that patients can direct such phatic speech at interpreters personally, while interpreted small talk from healthcare professionals performs an important function in framing comfort levels and offering guidance to patients.

Table 4.12 presents informants' selected responses in regard to the occurrence of "small talk", rendered as 闲聊 (*xiánliáo*) in the version supplied to Chinese speakers. It is worth noting that "small talk" can be rendered in Chinese as either 闲聊 or 寒暄 (*hánxuān*), both of which bear the meaning of "small talk", or light informal conversation for social occasions. However, the former rendition 闲聊 (*xiánliáo*) implies sustained conversation with successive turns or exchanges, while the latter 寒暄 (*hánxuān*) implies a short exchange of utterances to 'break the ice' before more content-based components of a social interaction are outlined. Tables 4.12 and 4.13 present Chinese and English speakers' and Chinese–English interpreters' responses to the importance of 'small talk'.

There is similarity between the responses provided by Chinese speakers and interpreters about Chinese speakers. Just over half of the informants from both groups state that "small talk" is "quite important", while similar percentages are reported from both groups in relation to a "neutral response". Most English speakers claim that "small talk" is "somewhat important" while Chinese–English interpreters evenly select responses to indicate that they believe that English speakers

Table 4.12 Chinese and English speakers' perceptions of the importance of 'small talk' with members of the other group.

	Chi-sp. informants	Eng-sp. informants	
	与英语人士正式会谈前，"闲聊"重要吗？ [Is it important to have 'small talk' with English-speakers before you come to the more formal part of the interaction?]	How important is 'small talk' with Chinese speakers before you come to the point of your meeting with them?	
非常重要 [Quite important]	52	24	Quite important
有些重要 [Somewhat important]	40	57	Somewhat important
不怎么重要 [Not very important]	8	19	Not very important

Table 4.13 Chinese–English interpreters' perceptions of the importance of 'small talk' amongst both groups of speakers.

	Chi-Eng. interpreters	
	How important is 'small talk' as a way for people to 'warm up to each other'? "闲聊"作为人们"拉近彼此间关系"的一种途径的重要性如何？	
	For Chinese speakers 汉语人士	For English speakers 英语人士
Quite important 非常重要	53	42
Somewhat important 有些重要	35	42
Not very important 不怎么重要	12	16

consider that "small talk" is either "quite important" or "somewhat important". The higher number of responses from Chinese speakers in regards to the importance of "small talk" can be partially accounted for by the relative greater salience that Chinese speakers attribute to the Chinese phrase闲聊in comparison to the salience that English speakers attach to 'small talk'. The following comment from an interpreter suggests that "small talk" is more likely to come from the Chinese speaker, as a strategy to present and establish their face:

汉语人士顾及面子。需要更多"闲谈"来拉近关系。情绪主导性。

Chinese speakers are more likely to care about their "face". That's why they may have a greater need for "small talk" in order to establish a closer relationship. It could be emotion-driven as well. (Chi-Eng.inter.1)

The importance that half of the Chinese speakers and the Chinese–English inter-preters attach to small talk is of note. This is contrary to the data from Smith, Dixon, Lam, and Lam (1999) which identified Chinese speakers' preference for a doctor-centred approach that usually does away with small talk and it is contrary to the high context expectations which require little or no establishing of roles that is often performed by small talk. English speakers believe that small talk is less important, perhaps restricted to its instrumental function as an icebreaker, after which a clear juncture follows to usher in problem reporting/elicitation. Inter-estingly, Chinese–English interpreters perceive its importance to be *greater* for English speakers than this group itself considers it to be. The following comment from an interpreter relates this to the specific context of the healthcare situation, and it is clear that the interpreter is referring to a conversational feature typical of the patient-centred, rather than doctor-centred approach:

> Small talk engaged in by the English-speaking health professional can actu-ally play a very important role that acts not only as a warm-up, but it helps the whole communication to run more smoothly later on. However, small talk sometimes can sometimes feel awkward and I find it a bit tedious at times. And I find it challenging as well – it's not easy to translate what is said some-times. (Chi-Eng.inter.30)

This interpreter is keenly aware that small talk is an intercultural frame that is enacted in a particular way in Australian English and that its function is for the healthcare professional to establish rapport with the patient (and hopefully vice versa). While this may now be a predictable and repetitive speech act that the interpreter relays into Chinese, its form in English and rendering that speech act with not only equivalent, but pragmatically appropriate forms in Chinese can be a challenge. Another interpreter remarks on the difficulties that ice-breakers can present when these contain idiomatic and culturally specific expressions:

> 我感觉small talks是just a warm-up formality。但是small talks不太好翻译，因为有很多笑话，有时会达不到效果。比如说在妇产科门诊医生会说：I have met you before! I like meeting someone I used to know. 比如在说完手术风险之后医生有时候会说：Touch wood!并摸桌子。这个时候我会解释Touch wood是希望坏运气被木头带走。
>
> I think instances of small talk are just like a warm-up formality. But small talk can be tough to interpret as there are many jokes or funny anecdotes that are not easy to convey into the other language. For example, in Obstetrics and Gynaecology, an outpatient doctor may say "I have met you before! I like meeting someone I used to know." Another example is, after explaining the risks of an operation, a surgeon may say "Touch wood!" while actually touch-ing the table, which I will then explain as a sign to say "By touching wood I hope this will ward off bad luck, and that only good things happen to you". (Chi.Eng.inter.27)

This interpreter addresses the small talk intercultural frame by employing a strategy of literal translation, sometimes with transfer and foreignizing. To return to the 'high' vs. 'low' context framework, the overall figures suggest that Chinese speakers are more likely to attach greater importance to talk which is instrumental in relationship-building only. This correlates with expectations from Hall's model in relation to the two language groups. But this correlation may be, on the basis of the afore-mentioned, circumstantial and accidental and it is perhaps tenuous to suggest that the figures in Table 4.13 conform to the expectations of the 'high' vs. 'low' framework.

4.3.3   *Body language and facial expressions*

In section 4.3.1 we outlined responses and views on the physical proximity of speakers to one another. This section elicits responses in relation to kinesics which refers to the study of physical movement and gesture, including facial expression, smiling and eye contact. Mention is also made here of haptics – the study of space between people and physical contact with others.

In general, gesture and body language perform a restricted number of functions in Chinese culture, e.g. finger counting on one hand; or the practice of *zuòyī* (作揖), covering one's right fist with the left hand to show gratitude or good wishes (Bi, 1998, p. 34). Otherwise, physical gesticulation, including head-nodding as a back-channelling strategy in dialogue conversation, is uncommon. This contrasts with the kinesic features of most speakers of Australian English (and of speakers in most other predominantly Anglophone societies) who commonly use non-verbal markers such as nodding and shaking of the head, polite smiles, shoulder shrugging, raised eyebrows, friendly or mock laughter, as well as body movements and subdued hand gestures to communicate with others.

In contrast to this combination of paralinguistic and haptic features, in Chinese culture it is facial expressions, in particular the appearance of the lower part of the face, especially the mouth and partly also the eyes, that are the most commonly employed paralinguistic markers. We outline here the role of *xiào* (笑) which can be translated as either a 'smile' or 'laugh'. The functions that *xiào* perform go beyond those of happiness and humour that the terms 'smile' or 'laugh' in English suggest, and this can lead to misunderstanding between Chinese and English speakers. The most common form of *xiào* is a 'gentle smile', *wēixiào* (微笑), which can express a speaker's positive feelings towards others, such as admiration. But *wēixiào* can also be a neutral response, showing another person's good intentions are acknowledged or understood. It can also be an evasive device or one conveying a person's non-commitment. Lastly, it can also express a person's dis-preference for something, expressing disagreement or even disdain at what the other interlocutor has expressed (Chen, 1987; Bi, 1998; Vargas-Urpi, 2013). The setting and interlocutors' relations to each other and to the context determine what emotional state is being expressed via a display of *wēixiào*.

Another variation of *xiào* is *péixiào* (赔笑) or a 'compensating smile' that is used to reconcile different positions or re-establish harmony, that is usually recognisable to non-Chinese speakers as a strained but conciliatory smile. A further variation is *kǔxiào* (苦笑) or 'bitter smile' that expresses a person's disappointment or powerlessness to address a frustrating situation (Bi, 1998; Sun, 2010). This is usually recognisable as a forced smile that masks a person's dismay. The overall intention of using such smiles is to avoid a loss of face for the other person and to preserve harmony in relationships, *héxié guānxì* (和谐关系) (Brick, 2004; Vargas-Urpi, 2013).

As can be seen, facial expressions involving the mouth and eyes convey information in Chinese which in English may be conveyed not only by facial expressions, but also by contemporaneous body movements and verbal text. This raises the question of Chinese and English speakers' perceptions of their own body language and facial expressions when interacting with speakers of the other group. We hypothesized that Chinese speakers would employ few gestures, few examples of body language and less animated facial expressions according to Chinese cultural mores in which these are less pronounced and less frequent. The influence of these, we considered, would override what is sometimes observed in many interactions in which interlocutors attempt to communicate with each other without a common language (Kim, 2008), which can still occur alongside the inter-lingual transfer provided by the interpreter. In relation to English speakers we hypothesized that they may amplify their body language and/or facial expressions, where paralinguistic markers are 'pressed into service' to function as 'means to communicate directly' where spoken texts are otherwise relayed via the interpreter. This intercultural strategy is what some speakers are reported to employ when communicating with others without a common language (cf. the use of 'foreigner talk', Rodriguez-Cuadrado, Baus, & Costa, 2018). Table 4.14 presents the Chinese and English speakers' selections of set responses in regard to their own body language and facial expressions.

Our hypothesis in relation to Chinese speakers was confirmed. The majority of Chinese speakers claimed no change in their kinesics. Where a change occurs on the basis of interacting with English speakers, 24% report toning down their body language and facial expressions. Only 12% claimed that they did the opposite. Amongst the English speakers, the overwhelming majority reported no change. This can be accounted for by their position as professional healthcare providers whose role is to be consistent and equal-minded when interacting with others regardless of their ethnolinguistic background (Krystallidou, 2014).

Our question to Chinese–English interpreters on this topic was phrased in a slightly different way. The selections, shown in Table 4.15, that interpreters could make related to the question of frequency of use of language and facial expressions as exhibited by both groups in general, and not specific to English–Chinese interpreted interactions. Thus, the responses reflect interpreters' views on the presence of these features as communicative tools in general.

The responses recorded by interpreters about speakers from both groups are congruent to research that records that body movements and facial expressions are less frequently employed by Chinese speakers compared to other groups (Brick,

Table 4.14 Chinese and English speakers' perceptions of their own body language when interacting with speakers of the other language.

	Chi-sp. informants	Eng-sp. speakers	
	与英语人士交谈时，你的肢体语言和面部表情会有所改变吗？Do your body language and facial expressions change when you speak to English speakers?	Do your body language and facial expressions change when you speak to Chinese speakers?	
是的。我会变得矜持，肢体语言和面部表情会缓和些。[Yes, I become more reserved and tone down my body language and facial expressions.]	24	5	Yes, I become more reserved and tone down my body language and facial expressions.
不会。我的肢体语言和面部表情不会有变化。[No, I do not change my body language or facial expressions.]	64	95	No, I do not change my body language or facial expressions.
是的。我会更加活跃，加大肢体语言和面部表情 [Yes, I become more animated and I amplify my body language and facial expressions.]	12	0	Yes, I become more animated and I amplify my body language and facial expressions.

Table 4.15 Chinese–English interpreters' perceptions of each group's use of body language and facial expressions when interacting with others.

	Chinese–English interpreters	
	How often do people use body language and facial expressions when talking to members of the other group? 人们在与别人交谈时使用肢体语言和面部表情的频率如何？	
	Enacted by Chi-speakers 汉语人士	Enacted by Eng-speakers 英语人士
Quite often 经常	24	70
Sometimes 有时	56	30
Rarely 很少	20	0

2004; Vargas-Urpi, 2013). The interpreters select responses that most Chinese speakers "sometimes" use these kinesic and paralinguistic tools. We are reminded of the different smiles and other facial gestures that can be a part of communication norms in Chinese:

> 汉语人士交流的时候一般不会有太多的语言交流，而是用手势或者肢体语言来代替
>
> Chinese speakers generally use gestures or body language when they communicate, instead of having too many language exchanges. (Chi-Eng.inter.2)

At the same time, most Chinese–English interpreters consider that English speakers "quite often" employ gestures etc.

> 英语人士交流的时候会有很多的眼神交流，表情非常丰富还有很多的肢体语言。English people will have a lot of eye contact when they communicate. Their expressions can be very rich and there can be a lot of use of body language. (Chi-Eng. inter.16)

This is reported from one interpreter who describes the incidence of 'foreigner talk' amongst those who have had less contact with speakers of other languages:

> I think that many English speakers can become more animated, particularly if they are mono-lingual and if they have limited or no experience communicating through another language. They try to convey more meaning through their gestures as they may assume this assists the interpreter to get their message across. (Chi-Eng.inter.20)

It is hard to compare how the same speaker interacts with others from other cultural backgrounds, but one interpreter makes the following observation where this information has been available to them:

> What I noticed is that the English speakers usually change their body language and facial expressions slightly. For example there is less use of arm movements when English speakers talk to Chinese speakers. (Chi-Eng.inter.31)

4.3.4 Summary of findings

Responses on proxemics show that the vast majority of Chinese and English speakers believe that they occupy a position that is "neither close, nor distant" to speakers of the other language. In general, Chinese–English interpreters also report that English speakers mostly adopt a position that is "neither close, nor distant" to them, while 48% of Chinese-speakers are reported also to position themselves "closely" to the interpreter. Small talk is reported by both Chinese speakers and Chinese–English interpreters to be an introductory 'warmer' that occupies more importance for Chinese speakers than for English speakers.

The importance of small talk attracts different ratings from Chinese-compared to English speakers, with the former group attaching greater importance to it than the latter group. Chinese–English interpreters also agree that small talk is more important for Chinese speakers, but also slightly more important for English speakers than this group itself claims. There are multiple, and perhaps conflicting intercultural frames at work here. The inductive and relational approach of Chinese, high-context discourse would suggest that phatic language such as small talk would be a common occurrence, which it is as reported by the Chinese speakers and interpreters. But the doctor-centred approach to medicine believed to be favoured by most Chinese speakers suggests to us that small talk would be a needless activity that delays the doctor from performing his/her duties. The patient-centred approach adopted by most English-speaking healthcare professionals encourages small talk as a means of establishing rapport and to develop a fuller picture of the patient's situation; and yet English speakers attach lesser importance to it than Chinese speakers. It is clear that there may be different notions of the meaning and importance of small talk to both groups, but it may be that the situational dynamics in individual interactions may be the decisive factor in whether it occurs or not, as a 'transition' stage following the introductions and openers (including the interpreter's role-explanation) and preceding the initial questions from the healthcare professional.

The vast majority of both Chinese and English speakers report that they make no change to their usual use of body language or facial expressions in a Chinese–English interpreted interaction compared to other interactions. Where changes occur, some Chinese speakers report that they become more animated, more so than less. These responses are based on speakers' perceptions of their paralinguistic behaviour, and on changes to it. In overall terms, these responses yield perceptions of change, rather than absolute descriptions of level of use of body language and facial expressions. The Chinese–English interpreters' responses relate to frequency, i.e. a description of how often these paralinguistic features are conspicuous in the behaviour of both Chinese and English speakers. The Chinese–English interpreters record a much higher frequency of use of paralinguistic markers amongst English speakers compared to the frequency that English-speakers record about themselves.

4.4   Information presentation and elicitation, and discursive 'directness'

The means through which a speaker "states a problem" and the linguistic means that serve him or her in doing this – speech acts – were posited to operate by universal principles (Austin, 1975; Searle, 1975). At the same time, mechanisms such as co-operation (Grice, 1975) and politeness (Brown & Levinson, 1987) have offered accounts for the forms that speakers choose to use with each other. Brown and Levinson's (1987) politeness model posited that the concept of speech acts can be applied in a universal way to interactions in all languages. In relation to Chinese Gu's (1990) analysis of politeness phenomena does not call into question a framework of speech acts that speakers draw on, but Gu argues that politeness and face-saving strategies are not only instrumental but normative (i.e. group-sanctioned) and that the number of maxims that Leech (1983) includes in his Politeness Principle should be extended to include a further number of maxims that reflect Chinese culture and the pragmatics of Chinese communication. Others disagree with a universalistic predictability of speech acts, and argue that groups' cultural norms and values determine the circumstances in which speech acts are employed (e.g. Wierzbicka, 1991).

Congruent to Wierzbicka's reservations that speech acts across cultures can be universally accounted for, Hall's (1976) concept of "high-context" and "low-context" for communication, based on the socio-cultural features of a speech community, provides a more abstract and top-down account for speakers' language behaviour. Researchers of intercultural communication who adopt this model (e.g. Ting-Toomey, 1994; Liu, 2002) describe Chinese culture as a high-context one, in which interactions feature "pre-programmed information that is in the receiver and in the setting" (Ting-Toomey & Chung, 2005, p. 368), with minimal information needed in utterance exchanges. "Indirect verbal negotiation, subtle nonverbal nuances and response intention inference" are examples of the strategies that speakers in high-context cultures engage in, according to Ting-Toomey and Chung (2005, p. 368). In contrast, speakers of (Australian) English belong to a low-context culture, in which direct and even upfront verbal styles are more apparent. These macro-level differences in discourse-pragmatic conventions are likely to lead to situations in which there are identifiable intercultural frames and our aim is to see how Chinese and English speakers may describe these, and which intercultural models and strategies may be identified by Chinese–English interpreters.

Information exchange and elicitation rests greatly on speakers' and hearers' notions of whether a communicative situation is "free conversation" (and usually "social") or more formal and focussed (e.g. "occupational" or "transactional"). In general, information presentation in Chinese tends to unfold gradually, with the listener being taken through the speaker's steps, so that the position, or in healthcare contexts, the speaker's symptoms of illness, are 'arrived at together', towards the end of the turn (Brick, 2004). This is a typically inductive approach to the organization of discourse. In contrast, information presentation in (Australian) English tends to feature the position, or symptoms of illness initially, with information that lead up to this, including causative factors mentioned subsequently. This is a more deductive approach.

In regard to eliciting specific information, comparative data on Chinese and Western (usually Anglophone) doctor-patient interactions reveal the following. Direct questions, e.g. 怎么不好了？ 'What's the matter with you?' is a common opener in Chinese doctor-patient interactions (Gu, 1996, p. 164), and the type of discourse that Chinese and Hong Kong patients prefer from their doctors (where they are presented with a choice between "doctor centred" and "patient centred" approaches) are "doctor centred" directives in which doctors ask for symptom descriptions, explain what is happening, adopt a didactic approach, and do most of the talking through specific questioning (Smith et al., 1999). In Anglophone countries, contemporary models for the doctor-patient consultation, influenced by the development of "patient-centred" approaches, advocate open-ended questions followed by yes-no questions, elicitations on patients' knowledge of illnesses, social and family circumstances and the availability of multiple options to the patient, so that decision-making is entrusted to the patient in a collaborative relationship (Street & Millay, 2001). To be sure, question-asking by the doctor can constitute up to 23% of medical interactions (Li, Desroches, Yum, Koehn, & Deagle, 2007), and West and Frankel (1991) report that doctors initiate 91% to 99% of questions. Physicians are also much more likely to interrupt patients than vice versa (Marvel, Epstein, Flowers, & Beckman, 1999; Barry, Stevenson, Britten, Barber, & Bradley, 2001). Still, patient-participation in the decision-making process is valued and yields higher rates of patient-satisfaction (Gattellari, Butow, & Tattersall, 2001). Such egalitarian doctor-patient relationships are stereotypical examples of "low-context", horizontally organized social relations, mentioned previously.

4.4.1   *Information presentation and elicitation*

We move now to the conversational moves that occur in healthcare interactions and how referential content is exchanged between interlocutors. As outlined earlier, in Chinese, these may be commenced with a direct question such as 'What's the matter with you?', or other direct interrogatives. Li (1999, p. 396) states that in healthcare interactions, "the usual way a Chinese physician greets a patient when s/he comes into the office is: 'So, which part of your body bothers you today?'". Such a question is an example of a 'specific-closed' question. In healthcare interactions in English-speaking countries, a variety of open-ended questions e.g. "How are things with you?", "What can I do for you?" "So, what seems to be the problem?" precede focussed and "yes-no" questions, and elicited information is often responded to with devices such as back-channelling, e.g. "Uh-huh", "Really?", and/or echo-questions "You're feeling pain where?" Table 4.16 shows informants' selections of four scenarios of information presentation and elicitation from a speaker of the other group. The Chinese and English speakers were asked related but different questions: the Chinese speakers were asked about how they relate information that they wished to share; the English speakers were asked about how they elicit information that they wished to gain.

Information elicitation strategies vary according to the perspectives that each group typically adopts in healthcare interactions. Nearly two-thirds of the Chinese speaker informants state that they elicit or present information by asking questions or stating directly what they want to talk about. The following two comments reflect this view:

中国人问问题会比较直接

Chinese people ask for information very directly. (Chi-sp.inf.2)

Table 4.16 Chinese speakers' responses on how they present information to and ask questions of English speakers; English speakers' responses on how they elicit information from Chinese speakers.

	Chi-sp. informants	Eng-sp. informants	
	如果你要同英语人士谈论或询问明确和重要的信息，你会怎么做？ [If you have some specific and important information to talk about with an English speaker or to ask an English speaker, what do you do?]	When I wish to elicit specific information from Chinese speakers:	
等待合适的机会 [I wait for the right opportunity to do so]	28	0	I wait for them to provide it.
我会做些一般性评论，以期对方接着话题往下说[I make some general comments hoping that the other person will pick up on this]	4	0	I make some general comments in the hope that they will provide it.
我会问些一般性、开放式问题，将自己的意图暗示对方[I ask some general, open-ended questions to hint to the other person what I want to talk about]	4	50	I ask general, open-ended questions to elicit this information.
我会直接提问或者表明我想谈论的内容。 [I am direct in asking questions or stating what it is that I want to talk about.]	64	50	I ask specific, yes-no questions to obtain this information.

在中文里，如果你想了解什么，也会直截了当地问

In Chinese when you want to find out something, you state it in a specific and simple manner. (Chi-sp.inf.3)

The strategy of being direct may occur when patients have received a diagnosis and wish to know further information about medication dosage, side effects, after-effects etc. A smaller percentage, 28%, responded that they employed an indirect strategy of 'waiting for the right opportunity'. This strategy may relate to those stages of an interaction in which the doctor supplies information in an advisory or didactic way. The following comment emphasizes attitudinal perhaps more so than rhetorical cues that should accompany information-asking:

问问题，还是乐观幽默一点比较好

    Asking for information, one should be optimistic and humourous. (Chi-sp.inf.6)

But the following comment reminds us that there are typically differences in status and power present in the doctor-patient interaction:

> There is an unbalanced power relationship. The LOTE ['language other than English', i.e. 'Chinese'-] speaker is not in a position to lead the conversation. (Chi-Eng.inter.32. Square brackets added.)

These responses are firstly, not congruent to the "high-context" interpretation of Chinese pragmatic norms which predict that specific questions from patients are less frequent and more marked. Secondly, question asking is not expected to be a prominent feature for a patient who is otherwise believed to be more comfortable with a "doctor-centred" approach (see 3.3.6 and 3.5), that is, an approach that Chinese speakers are believed to adopt more often than others (Bennett, Smith, & Irwin, 1999; Kim, Smith, & Gu, 1999).

    The English-speaking informants were provided with a question relating to information elicitation only as this was seen as the primary communicative strategy that they would employ as healthcare professionals. The responses of the English speakers are characteristic of a patient-centred approach in which information elicitation consists initially of open-ended questions, followed by closed questions to verify, check and exclude information.

> Sometimes I use a direct question or request, but other times less directly. In the healthcare sector, it usually depends on their English-speaking confidence and in some cases how comfortable they are in the settings they find themselves in. (Eng-sp.inf.6)

Interpreters have the same perception about English speakers' information-elicitation strategies as English speakers, but vary somewhat from what Chinese speakers report about themselves. Table 4.17 presents Chinese–English interpreters' responses:

    Responses from Chinese–English interpreters appear to be more reflective of the "general" cultural norms that shape speakers' behaviour than those that may be adopted in a specific healthcare context. In other words, many interpreters report that Chinese speakers tend to 'wait' and make 'general comments' as strategies for information exchange, and that these strategies are practised less so by English speakers. The following comments support this observation.

> My experience is that older Chinese speakers from mainland China tend to speak more obliquely about some things or where etiquette might dictate that they not speak directly. (Chi-Eng.inter.31)
>
> I think that English speakers speak more directly in general. (Chi-Eng.inter.25)

Table 4.17 Chinese–English interpreters' responses on elicitation strategies employed by Chinese and English speakers.

	Chi-Eng interpreters	
	If a person wishes to elicit specific information from another person, how do they do it? 如果一个人想要从另一人那里获取特定信息，通常他们会怎么做？	
	About Chi-speakers	About Eng-speakers
They wait for the other to provide it. 他们等待另一方主动提供	16	3
They make some general comments in the hope that they will provide it 他们会做些一般性评论，以期对方提供相关信息	36	11
They ask general, open-ended questions to elicit this information 他们会问些一般性、开放式问题来引出对方提供相关信息	22	34
They ask specific, yes-no questions to obtain this information 他们会问有针对性的一般疑问句来获取此类信息。	26	51

These two comments mention 'directness', a notion that is explored in greater detail in the following section.

4.4.2 Discursive 'directness'

Notions of 'directness' of speech are, of course, subjective and enactments of 'directness' may primarily be dependent on discourse-internal features rather than cultural ones. Nonetheless, we elicited responses from each group about their views on the other group's perceived directness. A 7-point Likert-scale measure was used, ranging from 'very directly' (1) to 'very indirectly (7), and informants were asked to give a grading indicating their view of the other group's perceived 'directness'. The collated gradings from Chinese speakers about English speakers are given first. These are shown in the fourth row of Table 4.18. These are followed in the last row by English speakers' responses in relation to their perception of Chinese speakers' directness:

The responses from the Chinese speakers show that 57% selected '1' or '2' at the 'very directly' end of the Likert scale to describe the communication features of English speakers. Only 13% made selections on the 'indirectly' side of the scale. From the Chinese speakers we record an overall average rating, with 1 and 7 as the end-points of the scale, of 2.82 to describe the directness of English speakers. The responses from English speakers about Chinese speakers are that they are also direct, although not as direct as how Chinese speakers

Table 4.18 Chinese and English speakers' perceptions of the other group's directness in expressing themselves.

	从 1到 7的不同级别，你认为英语人士表达自己意思的直接程度如何？ [On a scale of 1–7, how directly do English speakers express themselves?]							
	Very directly 在 1–7的级别上 Very indirectly							Rating ave.
	1	2	3	4	5	6	7	
Chi-sp. informants about Eng-speakers	22	35	4	26	4	9	0	2.82
	On a scale of 1–7, how directly do Chinese speakers express themselves?							
	Very directly			Very indirectly				
	1	2	3	4	5	6	7	
Eng-sp. informants about Chi-speakers	4	22	26	30	9	9	0	3.45

perceive English speakers. The most common response (30%) from English speakers about Chinese speakers was a mid-point one (i.e. a '4' grading), followed by responses that Chinese speakers tend to be more direct than indirect. The following English speaker recounts their own experiences which underlie individual differences:

> Sometimes with a direct question or request but other times less directly. In my line of work it usually depends on their confidence and in some cases how comfortable they are in the social setting they find themselves in, which, I think is quite natural.(Eng-sp.inf.20)

Familiarity with others is identified by one English speaker informant as a factor in Chinese speakers' perceived directness:

> In regard to eliciting information, if I have built up a rapport with them from previous interactions, then they usually tell me exactly what they feel without hesitation. Otherwise, they tend to withhold information and not be as direct. (Eng-sp.inf.1)

Following are responses from Chinese–English interpreters on their perceptions of both groups' directness in stating their opinion:

The responses recorded from the Chinese–English interpreters about each group of speakers are more widely distributed across the seven score ratings than

Table 4.19 Chinese–English interpreters' perceptions of both groups' directness in expressing their opinions.

	Chi-Eng interpreters							
	If a person wishes to state their opinion, how directly do you think they do it? 人们在表达个人观点时，你认为他们的直接程度如何?							
	Very directly		在 1–7的级别上		Very indirectly			Rating ave.
	1......2......3......4......5......6......7							
Chi-speakers	4	12	9	25	16	21	13	4.52
Eng-speakers	21	28	15	21	9	3	3	3.53

the responses that both groups of speakers gave about the other group. Chinese–English interpreters view Chinese speakers in general to be more indirect than direct in opinion-stating with an overall average rating of 4.52. One interpreter describes this in the following words:

> 交流方式委婉，期待对方的回复。 They adopt an indirect way to communicate and expect the other party's reply. (Chi-Eng.inter.4)

Another interpreter associates English speakers with the following communicative attributes:

> English speakers talk directly and frankly with rich body language. They speak quickly and in short sentences. (Chi-Eng.inter.29)

Opinion-stating is but one conversational move. We seek to ascertain whether the interpreters also record differences in the perceived directness in the expression of other conversational moves: explanations, answers to questions, requests, complaints/criticisms, and compliments. (This order of speech acts was the one given to informants in the survey.) Table 4.20 presents Chinese–English interpreters' responses in regard to Chinese speakers only.

The rating average column on the right hand side, with a mid-point of 4.0, shows that for four of the five conversational moves, the interpreters respond that Chinese speakers are in general more direct than indirect. In order of perceived directness, starting with the highest perceived level of directness, these are: compliments, explanations, complaints/criticisms. The average ratings for the two remaining moves – answers to questions and requests – are so close to the mid-point that we categorise the overall responses as perceptions that these two conversational moves are enacted in direct, indirect and in 'neither direct, nor indirect' ways. The following comment from an interpreter is congruent to the overall responses regarding requests and complaints/criticisms,

Table 4.20 Chinese–English interpreters' perceptions of Chinese speakers' directness in expressing themselves in five different conversational moves.

	Chi-Eng. interpreters							
	On a scale of 1–7, how directly do Chinese speakers express themselves? 在1–7的级别上，你认为汉语人士表达自己意思的直接程度如何？							
	很直接 Very directly				很委婉 Very indirectly			
	1......2......3......4......5......6......7							Rating ave.
Explanations 解释说明	22	16	19	6	19	19	0	3.41
Answers to questions 回答提问	6	21	18	18	3	30	3	3.94
Requests 提出请求	13	19	13	13	3	27	16	4.06
Complaints, criticisms 抱怨、批评	12	21	15	21	12	9	9	3.64
Compliments 称赞恭维	15	39	15	12	6	6	6	2.97

but expresses an opinion that answers and explanations are not conveyed so indirectly:

> In my opinion, Chinese speakers tend to express complaints/criticism, requests and compliments less directly, while they formulate explanations and answers to questions more directly. (Chi.Eng.inter.15)

The following comment from an interpreter is insightful as it associates perceptions of directness of with the avoidance of face threatening situations, for both Chinese and English speakers:

> Some Chinese speakers may consider that it is to their advantage to be indirect and perhaps convoluted, because they believe that this is the best way to interact with others. At the same time, explanations and responses can sometimes be none other than "it can't be done" or "it's not allowed". It's hard to work out as this can really be a face-saving strategy. In many cases, I think that less direct answers can be part of trying to save face for either person. (Chi-Eng.inter.23)

The following comment relates the relative directness of Chinese speakers to their acclimatisation to and acquisition of Australian English discourse norms:

> Most Chinese-speaking clients describe what they have to say in a straightforward way. Depending on specific situations, some Chinese-speaking clients tend to include unnecessary information, or easily get distracted by

irrelevant information such as chronological events that are hardly related to the subject matter. This all depends on their experience and how long the client has been in Australia. Clients who are familiar with the Australian community and legal/medical systems tend to keep it straightforward and precise. This also depends on personalities etc. (Chi-Eng.inter.16)

Another comment also relates to the length of Chinese speakers' stay in Australia, and that Chinese speakers behave differently in interactions with English speakers than they would with other Chinese speakers:

> In everyday communication with each other, Chinese clients are more introverted or withdrawn and shy in expressing their opinions openly and freely. I think that they change this when they are with English speakers. (Chi-Eng.inter.4)

We focus here on the issue of (health) problems. Information presentation that includes mention of a (health) problem may be accompanied by hesitation, use of euphemism, or circular speech. Stating a problem can also possibly be considered a face-threatening act. We present select answers to the question asked to the interpreters: "How does a Chinese-speaking person report a problem that he or she has?/ '汉语人士如何表述他们所遇到的问题?' We present select comments from the interpreters. In most cases, they cite medical problems as the context, and for this conversational move, there are very many views that express that this is performed by Chinese speakers in an *indirect* way:

> The person will present some sort of an introduction before going into the problem. (Chi-Eng.inter.18)

> 委婉.

>   Indirectly. (Chi-Eng.inter.1)

> Indirectly. They go around the corner before they come to the facts. (Chi-Eng. inter.19)

> 较情绪化，重复，无关信息

>   More emotionally and sentimentally. [They may present] repetitive and irrelevant information.' (Chi-Eng.inter.4)

> Most of the time, patients are inclined to describe their feelings/symptoms rather than directly answering doctors' or nurses' questions. (Chi-Eng.inter.2)

Some report that Chinese speakers give a chronology of events that preceded the problem before coming to the problem itself:

> Chinese speakers often talk indirectly. They talk about how they feel and think . . . and don't raise questions until the end. 他们常常按照时间顺序，前因后果，一一道来，问题在最后提出。

They often recount things in chronological order, listing the causes and effects, and only then is the problem finally raised. (Chi-Eng.inter.29)

It depends on their personality and their ability to condense information. Most Chinese speakers find it difficult to be direct and to the point. Most of those I come across, especially through telephone interpreting, tend to take a historical or very chronological approach. (Chi-Eng.inter.25)

Another comment on the cyclical or metaphorical discourse structures of some speakers is the following:

保持沉默，自己想办法解决，实在不能解决了，再寻求帮助

People will keep silent and find solutions by themselves at first. They will ask for help only if they cannot find any solutions. (Chi-Eng.inter.5)

My experience is that clients normally give a full account of the story, with as much detailed information as they could provide. Sometimes clients tend to give an analogy or give parallel examples to enable better understanding. There are times when clients may even tender their proposed solutions to their own problems. (Chi-Eng.inter.13)

And another observes that responses that are not related to questions are sometimes perceived as 'indirect', when, in fact, misunderstanding of the question may have occurred:

不是委婉，而是说不到点上，没有回答问题。

It is not indirectness. Some of their responses are not to the point, not answering the question. (Chi-Eng.inter.13).

We turn now to the Chinese–English interpreters' perceptions of the directness of English speakers for the same five conversational moves: explanations, answers to questions, requests, complaints/criticisms, and compliments. Table 4.21 presents responses according to a 7-point Likert-scale provided to informants.

Table 4.21 shows a clear pattern of interpreters reporting that English speakers perform all five conversational moves in a generally direct way. In order of directness, these are explanations, answers to questions, requests and compliments, with complaints/criticisms recording some responses that these are expressed indirectly as well directly. One interpreter comments in the following way:

My observation is that English-speaking clients, or say professionals usually put forward their problems, say in some instances, concerns in quite a straightforward way, and ask the other party to comment or respond. Alternatively, if the problem in question is just about something factual, they simply ask for it without any preambles. (Chi-Eng.inter.26)
The English-speaking person is usually the party who is asking the Chinese-speaking clients questions. The English-speaking person is normally very

Table 4.21 Chinese–English interpreters' perceptions of English speakers' directness in expressing themselves in five different speech acts.

	Chinese–English interpreters						
	On a scale of 1–7, how directly do English speakers express themselves? 1–7 的级别上，你认为英语人士表达自己意思的直接程度如何？						
	Very directly 很直接				Very indirectly 很委婉		
	1 . . . . . 2 . . . . . 3 . . . . . 4 . . . . . 5 . . . . . 6 7						
							Rating ave.
Explanations 解释说明	50	34	3	3	6	0	3	1.94
Answers to questions 回答提问	49	27	9	9	3	0	3	2.03
Requests 提出请求	34	38	13	6	6	0	3	2.25
Complaints, criticisms 抱怨、批评	15	24	24	15	12	0	9	3.21
Compliments 称赞恭维	33	39	9	6	6	6	0	2.30

clear and easy to understand. Depending on the profession they have different ways of asking or describing things. Doctors are very subtle and mindful, giving the client plenty of time to answer. (Chi-Eng.inter.16)

Further to these five conversational moves, we present select answers to the question asked to the interpreters: "How do English-speaking people report a problem that they have?/'你认为英语人士会如何讲述他们遇到的问题？'

直接

Directly. (Chi-Eng.inter.1)

很直接

Very directly. (Chi-Eng.inter.8)

明确简单地讲述

They describe things in an explicit and simple manner. (Chi-Eng.inter.25)

很直接，不会拐弯抹角

In a very straightforward way, without digression. (Chi-Eng.inter.15)

首先会很礼貌的开场，然后说出他们的问题，但不一定要"我"帮忙解决。若"他"需要的帮助或做什么，会直接说。

First, there will be a polite start, and then they will speak out their problems, but not necessarily "I" need to help solve. If "he" needs help or needs to do something, he will say it directly. (Chi-Eng.inter.21)

One interpreter observes that the scripts or protocols that English speakers follow allow them to sound succinct and 'to the point', where this may not necessarily be a common feature of the individual speaker's discourse repertoire, or that of the group that they belong to:

> 主要是他们作为professional 会提问，所以很明确。
>
> It is mainly because they are professionals, so they know how to ask and the questions are generally very explicit. (Chi-Eng.inter.10)

One interpreter remarks that expressing oneself directly is one thing, while being clearly understood is another.

> It varies with their education and experience. Most of the English-speaking persons I come across as an interpreter are professionals and can express themselves directly, but they may not take into consideration whether they are being understood or not.(Chi-Eng.inter.24)

4.4.3   Summary of findings

The issue of the 'information gap' is discussed in this section in terms of presentation or elicitation. The implication here is that Chinese speakers both 'have' information (i.e. knowledge of own symptoms, knowledge of medical history) and 'need' information (i.e. a diagnosis, and suggested forms of treatment), and that English speakers both 'need' information (i.e. knowledge of the patient's symptoms, knowledge of their medical history) and 'have' information (i.e. a diagnosis and suggested forms of treatment). We focus on the initial stages of the interaction in which Chinese speakers engage in information presentation, while English speakers typically engage in information elicitation. Information presentation from Chinese speakers is reported, by them, to usually occur in a 'direct way', i.e. via directly posed questions or through plainly stating what the issue is that they want to talk about. For the English speakers, information elicitation occurs either through general, open-ended questions, or specific yes/no ones. These responses are generally congruent to others' findings of patients' and healthcare professionals' discursive habits (Bennett et al., 1999; Kim et al., 1999; Cordella, 2004). The responses from Chinese–English interpreters about English speakers are congruent to those given by the English speakers themselves. However, the interpreters' perceptions of Chinese speakers are that they use a variety of conversational moves, from making general comments, to open-ended questions, to yes-no questions to achieve their interactional goals.

Responses elicited about the perceived directness of the other group yield results that are in line with Gu (1996), Brick (2004), Feng (2011) and Zhu (2017). Chinese speakers perceive English speakers to be direct to very direct, while English speakers perceive Chinese speakers to be moderately direct in their conventions of self-expression. These contrast with the perceptions of Chinese–English interpreters who report that they believe Chinese speakers express, in general, more indirectly than directly, with English speakers employing, in their opinion, a moderately direct style.

Chinese–English interpreters' responses about perceived levels of directness of both groups in regard to the conversational moves reveal the following: Chinese speakers express compliments directly, followed by explanations and complaints and criticisms; English speakers express explanations and answers to questions very directly, followed by requests and compliments also expressed very directly to directly.

4.5   Leave-taking

Leave-takings or closings are culturally specific, both in their obligatoriness and in their structure. For example, Hartford and Bardovi-Harlig (1992) report that Nepalese- and Thai-speakers have minimal "one-part" closings, while English and Hungarian-speakers typically have three- or multiple-part closures. They report that in semi-formal mono-topical interactions and consultations, speakers of American English typically show a resolution of the topic, a preclosing (e.g. "Well, that's your referral organized for you"), opening up the closing (e.g. "I'm sure that the specialist will be able to provide you with a better idea of what your condition is"), shutting down the topic (e.g. "Okay. You're all done"), farewell salutation (e.g. "All the best. Good bye"). Multiple-part closures ensure no loss of face for either interlocutor where sudden or abrupt leave-taking is perceived as face-threatening. Such elaborate closures are perhaps more typical of 'low-context cultures in which the 'horizontal' conceptualization of social relations requires speakers to verbalize what their intentions are, where this cannot be left to context. Brick (2004, p. 84) reports that Chinese leave-takings can range from being rather abrupt to overly elaborate, depending on the relative status of those involved. She observes that it is senior persons who generally initiate leave-taking, whose lead is then followed by others.

It is instructive to consider how Chinese speakers in the role of patients and English speakers in the role of healthcare professionals view their own leave-taking conventions. Table 4.22 contains informants' selections in response to three different means of concluding a healthcare interaction, from single-turn to multiple-turn closings.

While most Chinese speakers and half of the English speakers consider that they conclude healthcare interactions simply and directly, nearly half of the English speakers state that they engage in multiple-part closings as well. Most Chinese speakers report that they take leave in a simple and direct way; half of the English speakers also report doing this. A desire not to take up any more of the doctor's time is a likely motivator for Chinese speakers, while a desire to directly and efficiently disengage with patients is likely to account for English speakers' brevity. At the same time, some Chinese speakers report a number of signals that they provide and a smaller number claim that they employ elaborate leave-taking strategies. No English speakers select the elaborate leave-taking option.

Table 4.22 Chinese and English speakers' responses to how they conclude interactions.

	Chi-sp. informants	Eng-sp. informants	
	你如何与英语人士结束交谈？你如何告辞？[How do you conclude an interaction with an English-speaking person?]	How do you conclude an interaction with a Chinese-speaking person? How do you take leave?	
简单直接。[Simply and directly.]	64	50	Simply and directly.
我会暗示对方我想要结束交谈了。[There are some signals that I give to that show I am ready to conclude the interaction.]	20	50	There are some signals that I give to that show I am ready to conclude the interaction.
我有很多暗示行为和程式化表达来表明自己想要结束交谈了。[There are many signals and some formulaic expressions that I give to show that I am ready to conclude the interaction.]	16	0	There are many signals and some formulaic expressions that I give to show that I am ready to conclude the interaction.

We asked interpreters the same question on their views about leave-taking. The interpreters select responses that are very similar to those for English speakers. However, there is a contrast in the view of the interpreters in regard to Chinese speakers and what this group claims: the interpreters select responses to show that they believe that Chinese speakers employ longer closings. Table 4.23 presents Chinese–English interpreters' responses in regard to both groups' leave-taking conventions.

Overall, the single most common responses from interpreters are that Chinese speakers display some signals to conclude an interaction, while English speakers do this simply and directly. The interpreters' responses about Chinese speakers' leave-taking conventions vary greatly from those of the Chinese speakers themselves, who much more frequently report a direct leave-taking approach. We account for this as there can be variation in the number of steps taken according to the status-relationship of the interlocutors. Brick (2004, p. 84) reports that amongst Chinese speakers, 'upward-directed' leave taking steps (i.e. those initiated by younger or lower-status interlocutors) tend to be more elaborate than 'downward-directed' ones. The interpreters' estimations of English speakers'

Table 4.23 Chinese–English interpreters' responses in regard to leave-taking conventions of both groups.

	Chi-Eng. interpreters	
	How do people conclude an interaction? How do people take leave? 人们如何结束交谈？如何告辞？	
	About Chinese speakers 汉语人士	About English speakers 英语人士
Simply and directly 简单直接	21	50
There are some signals given that show that the speaker is ready to conclude the interaction. 说话人会给出一些暗示以表明自己想要结束交谈了。	50	34
There are many signals and some formulaic expressions to show that the speaker is ready to conclude the interaction. 有很多暗示行为和程式化表达来表明说话人想要结束交谈了。	29	18

leave-taking habits are closely matched to those expressed by that group. Two interpreters come to quite different conclusions:

> English speakers give signals too before concluding an interaction. But a Chinese person is more likely to draw to a close more slowly than an English-speaking person. (Chi-Eng.inter.31)
> I think that with Chinese speakers, and in hospital situations in particular, the ending of a conversation is pretty direct. (Chi-Eng.inter.19)

The responses of all groups of informants can be accounted for through potentially conflicting influences. In terms of Chinese cultural pragmatics, the following influences may pertain: a "high context" interpretation predicts brief doctor-patient leave-takings; the hierarchical asymmetry suggests elaborate recognition of the doctor's expertise and gratitude from the patient; politeness is not so much a face-saving strategy but an expression of closeness which has already been enacted in openers and in the body of an interaction and which does *not* need to be re-stated in an elaborate leave-taking.

In terms of English speakers' cultural pragmatics, the following influences may pertain: a "low context" interpretation suggests more rather than fewer signals because the leave-taking could be face-threatening if it is enacted too abruptly;

time pressures may motivate speakers to restrict themselves to economical fare-wells; the patient-centred approach advocates an 'emancipated' status of the patient to whom formal and empathetic, rather than brief farewells should be accorded.

A combination of features are likely to come to play in leave-taking. A macro-situational one is the paucity of time that healthcare professionals have and the desire of many of them to conclude an interaction as promptly as possible once the overall purpose of the interaction has been fulfilled. Patients, in general, are aware of the time demands that healthcare professionals have, whether or not knowledge of these demands influences their own leave-taking conventions. A micro-situational one is the responsibility of the healthcare professional to ensure that they have performed whichever diagnostic or treatment steps that are appropriate to the patient's situation without risk that diagnostic or treatment error or oversight could have occurred. Leave taking steps amongst English speakers tend to be of similar length (3–5 steps) regardless of age or perceived status. The macro-situational features perhaps predominate which may account for most responses that record a "simple and direct" way that people take leave.

4.6   Metalinguistic awareness and language-transfer features

In contrast to sections 4.2 to 4.5, that focus on various stages of interpreter-mediated (medical) interactions, this section focuses on metalinguistic features, i.e. informants' self-perceptions of their own language, and perceptions of how interpreters render particular conversational moves cross-linguistically. Although communicating via an interpreter, interlocutors may be likely to monitor the form of their language.

We focus here on only one direction of contact between interlocutors and direc-tion of language transfer: from English into Chinese. We elicit Chinese speakers' perceptions of English speakers adapting their own (English) speech and we elicit English speakers' self-perceptions of their own (English) speech. We hypothesise that English speakers may simplify or paraphrase their speech for two reasons: to facilitate the interpreter's comprehension of what they say (especially where the interpreter is a B-language user of that language); some English speakers may believe that certain Chinese speakers have some proficiency in English for them to be able to understand the English speaker directly, alongside interpretation into Chinese provided for them. Table 4.24 presents (self-)perceptions of English speakers' monitoring of their speech.

As Table 4.24 shows, monitoring of English speech is a feature that most Chi-nese speakers suspect that English speakers engage in. Most English speakers also believe that they engage in it. This is an interesting finding as the provi-sion of interpreting services is premised on speakers being able to speak freely in their own language. Speaking freely in an unencumbered way and not being able to understand the language spoken by the other interlocutor also obviates the possibility of linguistic accommodation (Giles & Ogay, 2007). What we mean by linguistic accommodation is the adoption of or convergence towards lexical,

Table 4.24 Chinese speakers' responses to perceived changes in the speech of English speakers and English speakers' responses to perceived changes in their own English speech.

	Chi-sp. informants	*Eng-sp. informants*	
	你认为英语人士和你交谈时会简化或改述他们的用语吗？ [Do you think that English speakers simplify or paraphrase their language when they speak with you?]	Do you simplify or paraphrase the language that you use with Chinese speakers?	
是的 [Yes]	48	50	Yes
可能 [Maybe]	44	43	Maybe
不会 [No]	8	7	No

intonational, rhetorical or other discursive features displayed by the other inter-locutor where both interlocutors seek to 'achieve a common goal' in or through the interaction. What we see here is that English speakers monitor their speech to reduce its complexity (lexical, syntactic, rhetorical or other). As such, this is an example of accommodation in an interpreted interaction.

We hypothesise that this type of accommodation occurs as the English speaker is attuned to the English L2 background of the great majority of Chinese–English interpreters (at least those working in Australia), and the English speaker is pos-sibly attuning their speech to the language level of the Chinese speaker. The Eng-lish speaker cannot communicate effectively with the Chinese speaker without an interpreter, but the English speaker is often reminded that Chinese speakers requiring an interpreter may sometimes use English in initial greetings, in short responses, and attempt to address the English speaker in English, regardless of their proficiency level. In public service interpreting encounters, it is not uncom-mon for speakers to code-switch and/or attempt to communicate directly with speakers of the other language, regardless of whether they are understood by them or not (Angermeyer, 2010).

The same question of English speakers simplifying their speech when inter-acting with Chinese speakers via an interpreter was put to the Chinese–English interpreters. They were also asked whether they thought that Chinese speakers also simplified their language when communicating via an interpreter. Table 4.25 contains their responses to the three selections provided to them.

The responses from the Chinese–English interpreters in regard to English speakers modifying their speech are very similar to the responses from both Chinese- and English -speakers for this same question with an overwhelming number selecting either that it is 'quite likely' or occurring 'sometimes' albeit hard to confirm. In relation to Chinese speakers, nearly half of the interpreters select the response that Chinese speakers do not do this. Only 19% consider this 'quite likely'. The responses relate to perceptions, and it is indeed difficult if not impossible for either Chinese speakers or interpreters to locate evidence of

Table 4.25 Chinese–English interpreters' perceptions of speakers of both groups changing their speech when communicating via an interpreter.

	Chinese–English interpreters	
	Do you think that people generally simplify or paraphrase their language when communicating through an interpreter? 你认为人们在通过译员交流的场合通常会简化或改述他们的用语吗？	
	Chinese speakers simplify or paraphrase 汉语人士	English speakers simplify or paraphrase 英语人士
This is quite likely 这很有可能	19	36
Sometimes. It's hard to tell 有时会，但不一定。	34	60
My experience is that they don't simplify or paraphrase. 我的经验是他们不会简化或改述用语。	47	4

simplification in the speech of English speakers. They may not have regular contact with particular English speakers that allows them to compare how the same English speaker communicates in a situation with another person, and in a different way in a comparable situation with a Chinese speaker via an interpreter. But the English speakers can reflect on their own behaviour and the high incidence (50%) of self-reported simplification or paraphrasing is revealing of the accommodation strategies that they employ in the interpreted interaction.

We return to the Chinese speakers and present their responses to notions of directness in the Chinese interpretations of English source speech in regard to five conversational moves.

The responses from most of the Chinese speakers show that overall, four of the conversational moves are conveyed reasonably directly. In order of perceived directness, these are: requests, explanations, answers to questions and compliments. A majority of the Chinese speakers perceive that only one conversational move – complaints/criticisms – is usually transferred by interpreters in a more indirect than direct way. The responses from the Chinese speakers here pattern in a way strikingly similar to the responses from the Chinese–English interpreters in Table 4.21 in section 4.4.2 that presents their perceptions of the relative directness in the way English speakers express these five conversational moves. With the exception of requests, the rating average of the responses recorded from the Chinese speakers is consistently between 0.3 and 1.0 points higher than the rating average of the Chinese–English interpreters' responses for the four categories: explanations, answers to questions, complaints/criticisms and compliments.

So, what we see here is a general similarity amongst both cohorts' perceptions of English speakers' directness of these conversational moves, with the perception amongst the Chinese speakers that these conversational turns, when interpreted into Chinese, are conveyed in a way that is not quite as direct as the illocutionary force of the English source speech. On the topic of matching the illocutionary force of the source speech with that of the target speech, one interpreter reports on how some Chinese speakers scrutinise the interpreter's interpretations:

> They can be quite critical of the interpreter if they know some English. (Chi-Eng.inter. 13)

Another interpreter makes the comment that their interpretations into Chinese may feature a change in register, and with it, *more direct* illocutionary force, together with a more deliberate re-presentation of the source speech:

> I realised lots of Chinese speaking people are not very educated, so they cannot answer or understand the health professionals' questions in a direct way. With this type of customers, as an interpreter I need to be very patient to explain everything in very simple Chinese. (Chi-Eng.inter.4)

But another Chinese–English interpreter warns against changing the illocutionary force in the target speech. This position invokes notions of accuracy (in the sense of 'equivalence' of the source speech to the target speech), other interlocutors' 'agency' within the interaction, and their own strategies of negotiating intercultural interactions:

> As a general principle I would never condense the message. By relaying the message in full you are empowering the Chinese speaker to deal with the details and the fact of the verbalization of the details in whatever way they wish to (e.g. to gain advantage from the situation, to gain a greater understanding of how English speakers communicate, etc.). You are empowering them to make decisions based on all the "facts", rather than disempowering them by concealing the details/difference in the way things are conveyed. You are inherently conveying a fact of cultural, habitual or contextual difference between an English speaker and a Chinese speaker to the Chinese speaker (which they may already be aware of). In some ways, by condensing the message you are misrepresenting the English speaker by making them sound like a Chinese speaker. You are demonstrating your cultural/linguistic knowledge as against that of the English speaker. (Chi-Eng.inter.20)

Another Chinese–English interpreter recalls how some Chinese-speaking interlocutors respond to her full interpretations of English source speech:

> When I interpret, I normally transfer the entire message to the Chinese speaker without condensing the message. However, it happens every now and then that if the message is quite obvious to them, I am interrupted or stopped by the Chinese speaker while I am delivering this message. (Chi-Eng.inter.30)

Table 4.26 Chinese speakers' perceptions of the directness of Chinese–English interpreters' interpretations into Chinese of five conversational moves.

	Chinese speakers						
	在一个汉英译员在将英语人士的讲话内容翻译成中文时，译员在翻译以下内容时直接程度如何： [When a Chinese–English interpreter is interpreting what the English speaker said into Chinese, how directly does the interpreter formulate the following]:						
	很直接 [Very directly] 很委婉 [Very indirectly]						Rating ave.
	1. . . . . .2. . . . .3. . . . .4. . . . .5. . . . .6. 7						
解释说明 [Explanations]	21	53	16	5	5	0	0	2.21
回答提问 [Answers to questions]	12	53	18	12	6	0	0	2.47
提出请求 [Requests]	29	53	0	6	12	0	0	2.18
抱怨、批评 [Complaints, criticisms]	0	6	31	6	50	6	0	4.19
称赞恭维 [Compliments]	13	47	13	7	20	0	0	2.73

The last sentence of this comment is suggestive of the context being clear to the Chinese speaker and that they perceive an explication of this to be redundant. The following comment about perceptions of the length of interpretations into Chinese is made by an English speaker:

> I'm not always sure that information has been communicated fully. Often I feel that the information I am providing (usually about bowel function, incontinence, ostomy care) is censored or shortened in some aspects. (Chi-Eng.inter.30)

The English speakers were asked an equivalent question in relation to their perceptions of Chinese–English interpreters' interpretations into English and the level of directness expressed in the five conversational moves. Table 4.27 sets out their responses.

Table 4.27 shows that the English speakers view the way that Chinese speakers' conversational moves are interpreted into English by Chinese–English interpreters as being direct. There are no responses for any of the moves that indicate any degree of indirectness in the interpretations into English. These responses are different from those from the Chinese–English interpreters when reporting on the perceived directness of Chinese speakers' source speech in Chinese for the five conversational moves. In Table 4.20 in section 4.4.2 the average ratings given by Chinese–English interpreters to Chinese speakers' directness in expressing the five conversational moves are 0.7 to 2.1 points higher. We can see that Chinese speakers are reported to express these conversational moves in a way which, in

Table 4.27 English speakers' perceptions of the directness of Chinese–English interpreters' interpretations into English of five conversational moves.

	English speakers						
	When a Chinese–English interpreter is interpreting what the Chinese speaker said into English, how directly does the interpreter formulate the following:						
	Very directly				Very indirectly		Rating
	1. . . . . . 2. . . . . 3. . . . . . 4. . . . . 5. . . . . 6. 7						ave.
Explanations	30	25	30	15	0	0	0	2.30
Answers to questions	40	25	20	15	0	0	0	2.10
Requests	40	30	20	10	0	0	0	2.00
Complaints, criticisms	32	21	37	11	0	0	0	2.26
Compliments	42	16	21	0	0	0	0	2.21

general, is slightly direct to neither direct/nor indirect. But the interpretations from Chinese into English that the English speakers receive for these conversational moves are described as being quite direct to very direct. The following is recorded from an interpreter about this:

> To make the message understandable to an English speaker, I might add some words while interpreting. However, I don't provide extra information generally. If the message of the Chinese speaker is 'condensed' and understandable, I would interpret it in that condensed way to keep the original meaning. Any additional wording, as well as any omissions, is what an interpreter should avoid in the course of interpreting. However, it is quite often that clarification or further information is needed in order to make communication efficient. (Chi-Eng.inter.15)

The following contribution was recorded from an interpreter as a general comment about less "elaborate" discursive styles of some Chinese-speaking interlocutors that they have worked with:

> Sometimes Chinese speakers only provide little information with the expectation that the other party should understand the situation, and therefore there is no need to verbalize it in an elaborate way. (Chi-Eng.inter.22)

An interpretation that is based on the form of the source speech would be elliptic. The same interpreter adds the following where the need to provide "clear" target speech suggests that explication of elliptic source speech is the strategy pursued by this interpreter when interpreting into English:

> The interpreter should have a good understanding of what is communicated and be able to provide clear and accurate verbal expression of it. (Chi-Eng. inter.15)

When looking at the four tables 4.20 and 4.21, and 4.26 and 4.27 together, and comparing the responses from Chinese–English interpreters with those of Chinese speakers and English speakers we see a clear pattern: Chinese speech – whether source speech produced by Chinese speakers, or target speech by Chinese–English interpreters – is not perceived as indirect, but it is perceived as *less direct* than English speech. In line with this, by implication this suggests that Chinese–English interpreters' interpretations into both languages are adapted according to the pragmatic norms of directness of each linguistic and cultural group: Chinese–English interpreters may produce interpretations into Chinese that are less direct than the English-language source speech; Chinese–English interpreters may produce interpretations into English that are more direct than the Chinese-language source speech. Further, if this implication is correct, this suggests that Chinese–English interpreters employ *linguistic* means (alongside others) in accordance with intercultural discourse and agency to align the illocutionary force of their interpretations towards the pragmatic norms of the target culture and language. We add here that the responses do not suggest that the illocutionary force of the source speech is overridden by interpreters' adaptations to the pragmatic frames and models of the target language for a particular conversational mode. Instead, there is some evidence for convergence towards the pragmatic frames and models of the target culture.

4.7   Conclusion

This chapter presented data from three groups of informants on five situational features of interpreter-mediated interactions. Looking at the data on introductions, role explanations and pre-interactional briefings on features relevant to intercultural communication presented in section 4.2 we find that all three groups of informants report reasonably high frequencies of introducing themselves. English speakers do this more than Chinese speakers, which is not surprising as this is likely to form part of the opener/greeting that is usually initiated by the English-speaking healthcare professional. Surprisingly, Chinese–English interpreters report the lowest levels of self-introduction. In part, this can be explained by the possibility that some English speakers may do this on their behalf. Interestingly, the other groups report a higher level of the interpreters self-introducing than the interpreters themselves. Role-explanations may be delivered in the same turn as a self-introduction, or they may be identifiable as a separate turn, usually delivered by the interpreters, less often by the English speaker (whose explanation is relayed into Chinese by the interpreter, but with the English speaker remaining the 'principal' of this speech act). The role-explanation is, as argued in 4.2.4, an intercultural frame, as it is a speech act that makes explicit the allophone, procedural and mediated nature of the interaction. Chinese speakers are more commonly the recipient of the role-explanation than English speakers, which suggests that this frame is perceived to be less familiar to them and they are therefore more frequently the recipients of a role-explanation.

Congruent to the higher frequency of reported role-explanations to and for Chinese speakers, we note that Chinese speakers are more likely to receive a briefing that includes mention of intercultural features than English speakers. The Chinese–English interpreter is the key protagonist to provide this and this is confirmed by both groups. Further, both Chinese and English speakers themselves initiate the topic of cultural features at an initial stage of the interaction much less frequently. Chinese–English interpreters infrequently approached either group of speakers to ask them about their knowledge of the other group. It is clear that Chinese speakers view interpreters as experts on the other group's culture; the same cannot be said about the way that English speakers view interpreters. Here, the intercultural agency of English speakers themselves is apparent, where they view interpreters as a group, but not the exclusive group, that possesses intercultural communication skills.

After the interaction has commenced, other features become apparent in interpreter-mediated interactions. The first is physical distance and both Chinese and English speakers report that they do not believe that they alter the physical distance between themselves and their allophone interlocutors. Chinese–English interpreters were asked about speakers of both groups and how close they situate themselves vis-à-vis the interpreter. Chinese–English interpreters report that Chinese speakers tend to position them more closely to the interpreter, while this is not reported for English speakers. There may be logistic features and/or also physiological features (e.g. a Chinese-speaking patient may be hard of hearing and needs to sit closer to the interpreter) that can account for this.

There are differences in the frequency and type of body language displayed by Chinese speakers compared to English speakers. Paralinguistic markers, or in this case body language and kinesics are known to be employed in situations with linguistic discordance (e.g. 'foreigner talk') but we see from all groups' responses that Chinese speakers do not report employing body language as compensatory strategies or accommodation markers to the English-speaking interlocutor whom they may believe use these more frequently. Instead, we record a reported decrease in kinesics and paralinguistic markers used by English speakers who may do so as an intercultural strategy accommodating to their notions of Chinese pragmatics and kinesics.

Information presentation and elicitation depend on a great number of variables – personal, situational as well as cultural ones. The inductive vs. deductive contrast between the discourse norms of Chinese speakers and English speakers was expected to yield different responses to suggestions as to how each informant gives or elicits information. There are mixed responses from Chinese speakers with over a quarter selecting an inductive approach, while nearly two-thirds reported that they use direct yes/no questions or state directly what they wish to convey to others. English speakers all report using direct or targeted means of questioning. Chinese–English interpreters' responses are in line with those of the English speakers, and partly also the Chinese speakers. A more uniform trend and one that is in line with the inductive/deductive contrast is ascertainable in regard to perceptions of both groups of speakers about each other (where a deductive approach to discourse structure is perceived as being more 'direct'). Chinese speakers perceive English speakers as being 'direct' while English speakers perceive Chinese speakers to be 'direct' to 'neither direct/nor indirect'. Chinese–English interpreters also provide a contrastive rating of both groups' discourse norms; their scores describe Chinese speakers as more indirect than direct, and English speakers to be slightly more direct than indirect.

Responses on pragmatic directness were elicited in relation to five speech acts: explanations; answers to questions; requests; complaints/criticisms; compliments. Both Chinese and English speakers were asked about their opinions on the degree of 'directness' that interpreters displayed in their interpretations of these five speech acts into Chinese and English, respectively. Chinese speakers report that requests, followed by explanations are the most directly conveyed speech acts, with complaints/criticisms being the most indirectly conveyed. This conforms with our expectations that complaints/criticisms are face-threatening acts whose illocutionary force is mitigated by indirect or hedging language. English speakers report that requests, followed by answers to questions are the speech acts most directly conveyed. The interpreters also report that for five specific speech acts, compliments are expressed most directly by Chinese speakers, followed by explanations, then complaints and criticisms. English speakers are described by interpreters as being most direct in giving compliments, expressing explanations, and giving answers to questions.

Leave taking is the next feature that we looked at in healthcare interactions. Most Chinese speakers and half of the English speakers claim to take leave "simply and directly". The other half of the English speakers report that there are some signals given before this occurs. This contrasts with the opinions of Chinese–English interpreters who make selections indicating that they believe that Chinese speakers provide more extensive and formulaic signals leading up to disengagement than English speakers do. In regard to the Chinese speakers it is possible that those who provide more elaborate signals do so as they are guided by the concluding turns of the English speakers. These turns may be responses to the three to five steps that English speakers are likely to make to disengage with the patient. The 'low context' culture that most English speakers belong to accounts for this number of turns where a shorter number of turns may be perceived to be face-threatening.

The last feature looked at in this chapter is that of metalinguistic awareness and language-transfer. The interpreter's role is to enable interlocutors to freely communicate with each other, but we were interested to see if Chinese and English speakers adapt, or accommodate their speech to the linguistic repertoires of the two other interlocutors with whom they are communicating – the interpreter, and the speaker of the other language. Interestingly, over 90% of both Chinese and English speakers report simplifying or paraphrasing their language used in interpreter-mediated interactions. It is not surprising that English speakers report doing this, as most Chinese–English interpreters are L2-users of English, and English speakers may do this to ensure that the interpreter has understood and can transfer their speech. But it is less clear why Chinese speakers would report doing this. We hypothesise that this may be an example of an intercultural schema or strategy in which many Chinese speakers are mindful that their source speech will be relayed cross-linguistically into English and therefore often adapt their speech in a way that they believe will make it easier for the interpreter to convey into English, or in a way that they believe is more congruent to how English speakers express themselves. For both groups of speakers, simplification and paraphrasing may be a frequently employed intercultural strategy. Chinese–English interpreters themselves report that this is likely to be a frequent occurrence for English speakers, but not always for Chinese speakers.

This chapter concludes our presentation and analysis of primary and secondary sources. The following chapter summarises the findings presented in Chapters 1 to 4. The following chapter also lists and discusses the implications of these findings for Chinese–English interpreting, and for intercultural communication.

References

Angelelli, C. (2004). *Medical interpreting and cross-cultural communication.* Cambridge, UK: Cambridge University Press.

Angermeyer, P. (2010). Interpreter-mediated interaction as bilingual speech: Bridging macro- and micro-sociolinguistics in codeswitching research. *International Journal of Bilingualism, 14*(4), 466–489. https://doi.org/10.1177/1367006910370914

AUSIT [Australian Institute of Interpreters and Translators]. (2006). *Guidelines for health professionals working with interpreters.* Retrieved from http://ausit.org/AUSIT/Documents/Guidelines_For_Health_Professionals.pdf

AUSIT [Australian Institute of Interpreters and Translators]. (2012). *AUSIT code of ethics and code of conduct.* Retrieved from https://ausit.org/AUSIT/Documents/Code_Of_Ethics_Full.pdf

Austin, J. L. (1975). How to do things with words (2nd ed.). Oxford: Oxford University Press.

Baert, P. (2006). Role. In A. Harrington, B. Marshall, & H.-P. Müller (Eds.), *Encyclopedia of social theory* (pp. 524–526). London: Routledge.

Barry, C. A., Stevenson, F. A., Britten, N., Barber, N., & Bradley, C. P. (2001). Giving voice to the lifeworld: More humane, more effective medical care? A qualitative study of doctor-patient communication in general practice. *Social Science & Medicine, 53,* 487–505. https://doi.org/10.1016/s0277-9536(00)00351-8

Beaulieu, C. (2004). Intercultural study of personal space: A case study. *Journal of Applied Social Psychology, 34*(4), 794–805. https://doi.org/10.1111/j.1559-1816.2004.tb02571.x

Bennett, K., Smith, S., & Irwin, H. (1999). Preferences for participation in medical decisions in China. *Health Communication, 11*(3), 261–284. https://doi.org/10.1207/s15327027hc110308

Bi, J. (1998). *Kuàwénhuà Fēi-yǔyán Jiāojì* [跨文化非言语交际]. Beijing: Wàiyǔ Jiāoxué yu Yánjiuū Chūbǎnshè [外语教学与研究出版社].

Brick, J. (2004). *China: A handbook in intercultural communication* (2nd ed.). Sydney: National Centre for English Language Teaching and Research.

Brown, P., & Levinson, S. (1987). *Politeness: Some universals in language usage* (Vol. 4). Cambridge, UK: Cambridge University Press.

Bührig, K., Kliche, O., Meyer, B., & Pawlack, B. (2012). Explaining the interpreter's unease: Conflicts and contradictions in bilingual communication in clinical settings. In

K. Braunmüller & C. Gabriel (Eds.), *Multilingual individuals and multilingual societies* (pp. 407–417). Amsterdam: John Benjamins. https://doi.org/10.1075/hsm.13.27buh

Calhoun, C. (2002). *Dictionary of the social sciences*. New York: Oxford University Press.

CCEH [Centre for Culture, Ethnicity and Health]. (2014). *Communicating via an interpreter*. Retrieved from www.ceh.org.au/wp-content/uploads/2015/12/LS4_Communicating-via-an-interpreter.pdf

Celce-Murcia, M. (2007). Rethinking the role of communicative competence in language teaching. In E. Alcon Soler & M. Pilar Safont Jorda (Eds.), *Intercultural language use and language learning* (pp. 41–57). Dordrecht: Springer. https://doi.org/10.1007/978-1-4020-5639-0_3

Chen, J. (1987). *Shuōhuà de yìshù* [说话的艺术]. *The art of speaking*. Beijing: Yǔwén chūbǎnshe [语文出版社].

Chesher, T., Slatyer, H., Doubine, V., Jaric, L., & Lazzari, R. (2003). Community-based interpreting: The interpreters' perspective. In L. Brunette, G. L. Bastin, I. Hemlin, & H. Clarke (Eds.), *The critical link 3: Interpreters in the community* (pp. 273–292). Amsterdam: John Benjamins. https://doi.org/10.1075/btl.46.28che

Clyne, M. (1994). *Inter-cultural communication at work: Cultural values in discourse*. Cambridge: Cambridge University Press.

Cordella, M. (2004). *The dynamic consultation: A discourse analytical study of doctor-patient communication*. Amsterdam and Philadelphia: John Benjamins.

Costa, B. (2017). Team effort – Training therapists to work with interpreters as a collaborative team. *International Journal for the Advancement of Counselling*, *39*, 56–69. https://doi.org/10.1007/s10447-016-9282-7

Coupland, J. (2000). Introduction: Sociolinguistic perspectives on small talk. In J. Coupland (Ed.), *Small talk* (pp. 1–25). London: Longman.

Coupland, J., Robinson, J., & Coupland, N. (1994). Frame negotiation in doctor-elderly patient consultations. *Discourse and Society*, *5*(1), 89–124. https://doi.org/10.1177/0957926594005001005

Crezee, I. (2013). *Introduction to healthcare for interpreters and translators*. Amsterdam: John Benjamins.

Dabić, M. (2010). The role of the interpreter in intercultural psychotherapy. *CTIS Occasional Papers*, *5*, 65–80.

Davies, E. (2014). Translation and intercultural communication: Bridges and Barriers. In C. Bratt Paulston, S. Kiesling, & E. Rangel (Eds.), *The handbook of intercultural discourse and communication* (pp. 367–388). Malden, MA: Wiley Blackwell. https://doi.org/10.1002/9781118247273.ch18

De Houwer, A. (2009). *Bilingual first language acquisition*. Bristol: Multilingual Matters.

Feng, H. (2011). Politeness (Keqi): The fragrance of Chinese communication. *China Media Research*, *7*(4), 53–60.

Gadit, A. A. M. (2010). Personal space: Implicaitons in patient-doctor relationship. *Journal of Pakistan Medical Association*, *60*(4), 321–322.

Garrett, P. (2009). Healthcare interpreter policy: Policy determinants and current issues in the Australian context. *International Journal for Translation & Interpreting Research*, *1*(2), 44–54.

Gattellari, M., Butow, P. N., & Tattersall, M. H. N. (2001). Sharing decisions in cancer care. *Social Science & Medicine*, *52*, 1865–1878. https://doi.org/10.1016/s0277-9536(00)00303-8

Giles, H., & Ogay, T. (2007). Communication accommodation theory. In B. B. Whaley& W. Samter (Eds.), *Explaining communication: Contemporary theories and exemplars* (pp. 293–310). Mahwah, NJ: Lawrence Erlbaum.

Grice, P. (1975). Logic and conversation. In P. Cole & J. L. Morgan (Eds.), *Syntax and semantics 3: Speech acts* (pp. 41–58). New York: Academic Press.

Gu, Y. (1990). Politeness phenomena in modern Chinese. *Journal of Pragmatics, 14*, 237–257. https://doi.org/10.1016/0378-2166(90)90082-o

Gu, Y. (1996). Doctor-patient interaction as goal-directed discourse in Chinese social cultural context. *Journal of Asian Pacific Communication, 7*(3–4), 156–176.

Hale, S. (2007). *Community interpreting.* Basingstoke: Palgrave Macmillan.

Hall, E. T. (1976). *Beyond culture.* New York: Random House, Inc.

Hartford, B. S., & Bardovi-Harlig, K. (1992). Closing the conversation: Evidence from the academic advising session. *Discourse Processes, 15*(1), 93–116. https://doi.org/10.1080/01638539209544803

Hlavac, J., Beagley, J., & Zucchi, E. (2018). Application of policy and the advancement of patients' health outcomes through interpreting services: Data and viewpoints from a major public healthcare provider. *The International Journal for Translation & Interpreting Research, 10*(1), 111–136. doi:10.12807/ti.110201.2018.a07

House, J. (2007). What is an 'Intercultural Speaker'? In E. Alcon Soler & M. Pilar Safont Jorda (Eds.), *Intercultural language use and language learning* (pp. 7–21). Dordrecht, The Netherlands: Springer. https://doi.org/10.1007/978-1-4020-5639-0_1

Jones, S. (1971). A comparative proxemics analysis of dyadic interaction in selected subcultures of New York City. *The Journal of Social Psychology, 84*(1), 35–44. https://doi.org/10.1080/00224545.1971.9918518

Kim, M. S., Smith, D., & Gu, Y. (1999). Medical decision making and Chinese patients' self-construals. *Health Communication, 11*(3), 249–260. https://doi.org/10.1207/s15327027hc110307

Kim, R. (2008). California Chinese Pidgin English and its historical connections: Preliminary remarks. *Journal of Pidgin and Creole Languages, 23*(2), 329–344. https://doi.org/10.1075/jpcl.23.2.08kim

Krystallidou, D. (2014). Gaze and body orientation as an apparatus for patient inclusion into/exclusion from a patient-centred framework of communication. *The Interpreter and Translator Trainer, 8*(3), 399–417. https://doi.org/10.1080/1750399x.2014.972033

Leech, G. N. (1983). *Principles of pragmatics.* London and New York: Longman.

Li, H. Z. (1999). Communicating information in convesations: A cross-cultural comparison. *International Journal of Intercultural Relations, 23*(3), 387–409. https://doi.org/10.1016/s0147-1767(99)00003-6

Li, H. Z., Desroches, N. G., Yum, Y.-O., Koehn, C., & Deagle, G. (2007). Asymmetrical talk between physicians and patients: A quantitative discourse analysis. *Canadian Journal of Communication, 32*(3), 417–433. https://doi.org/10.22230/cjc.2007v32n3a1959

Liu, J. (2002). Negotiating silence in American classrooms: Three Chinese cases. *Language and International Communication, 2*(1), 37–54. https://doi.org/10.1080/14708470208668074

Marvel, M. K., Epstein, R. M., Flowers, K., & Beckman, H. B. (1999). Soliciting the patient's agenda: Have we improved? *Journal of the American Medical Association, 281*, 283–287. https://doi.org/10.1001/jama.281.3.283

Mason, I. (2006). On mutual accessibility of contextual assumptions in dialogue interpreting. *Journal of Pragmatics, 38*(3), 359–373. https://doi.org/10.1016/j.pragma.2005.06.022

Mason, I. (2009). Role, positioning and discourse in face-to-face interpreting. In R. de Pedro Ricoy, I. Perez, & C. Wilson (Eds.), *Interpreting and translating in public service settings: Policy, practice, pedagogy* (pp. 177–199). Manchester: St Jerome.

Mason, I. (2012). Gaze, positioning and identity in interpreter-mediated dialogues. In C. Baraldi & L. Gavioli (Eds.), *Coordinating participation in dialogue interpreting* (pp. 177–199). Amsterdam: John Benjamins. https://doi.org/10.1075/btl.102.08mas

Mullamaa, K. (2009). Towards a dynamic role model of liaison interpreters: Self-descriptions of practitioners in Estonia. *New Voices in Translation Studies, 5,* 46–62.

O'Hara, M., & Akinsulure-Smith, A. (2011). Working with interpreters: Tools for clinicians conducting psychotherapy with forced immigrants. *International Journal of Migration, Health and Social Care, 7*(1), 33–43. https://doi.org/10.1108/17479891111176287

Penn, C., & Watermeyer, J. (2012). When asides become central: Small talk and big talk in interpreted health interactions. *Patient Education and Counseling, 88,* 391–398.

Phillips, C. (2010). Using interpreters: A guide for GPs. *Australian Family Physician, 39*(4), 188–195.

Pöllabauer, S. (2015). Role. In F. Pöchhacker (Ed.), *Encyclopedia of interpreting studies* (pp. 355–360). Abingdon, Oxon: Routledge.

Pollard, R. (1998). *Mental health interpreting: A mentored curriculum.* Rochester, NY: University of Rochester.

Ragan, S. (2000). Sociable talk in women's health care contexts: Two forms of non-medical talk. In J. Coupland (Ed.), *Small talk* (pp. 269–287). Harlow: Longman.

Ribeiro, B. T., & de Souza Pinto, D. (2005). Medical discourse, psychiatric interview. In K. Brown (Ed.), *Encyclopedia of language and linguistics* (2nd ed., pp. 658–664). Amsterdam: Elsevier.

Rodriguez-Cuadrado, S., Baus, C., & Costa, A. (2018). Foreigner talk through word reduction in native/non-native spoken interactions. *Bilingualism, 21*(2), 419–426. https://doi.org/10.1017/s1366728917000402

Sarangi, S., & Roberts, C. (Eds.). (1999). *Talk, work and institutional order: Discourse in medical, mediation and management settings.* Berlin: Mouton de Gruyter.

Schneider, K. P. (1988). *Small talk: Analysing phatic discourse.* Marburg: Hitzeroth.

Searle, J. (1969). *Speech acts: An essay in the philosophy of language.* Cambridge: Cambridge University Press.

Searle, J. (1975). Indirect speech acts. In P. Cole & J. Morgan (Eds.), *Syntax and semantics. Vol. 3: Speech Acts* (pp. 59–82). New York: Academic Press.

Setton, R. (2009). Interpreting China, interpreting Chinese. *Interpreting, 11*(2), 109–117. https://doi.org/10.1075/intp.11.2.01set

Setton, R., & Guo, A. L. (2009). Attitudes to role, status and prefessional identity in interpreters and translators with Chinese in Shanghai and Taipei. *Translation and Interpreting Studies, 4*(2), 210–238. https://doi.org/10.1075/bct.32.07set

Sharifian, F. (2011). *Cultural conceptualizations and language* (Vol. 1). Amsterdam and Philadelphia: John Benjamins Publishing Company.

Sharifian, F., & Jamarani, M. (2011). Cultural schemas in intercultural communicaiton: A study of the Persian cultural schema of sharmandegi 'being ashamed'. *Intercultural Pragmatics, 8*(2), 227–251. https://doi.org/10.1515/iprg.2011.011

Smith, D., Dixon, A., Lam, C., & Lam, T.-P. (1999). Patient-centered communication in Hong Kong. *Health Communication, 11*(3), 285–297. https://doi.org/10.1207/s15327027hc110309

Street, R., & Millay, B. (2001). Analyzing patient participation in medical encounters. *Health Communication, 13*(1), 61–73. https://doi.org/10.1207/s15327027hc1301_06

Sun, H. (2004). Opening moves in informal Chinese telephone conversations. *Journal of Pragmatics, 36*(8), 1429–1465. https://doi.org/10.1016/j.pragma.2004.01.007

Sun, J. (2010). Deciphering the Chinese smile: The importance of facial expressions in linguistic communication. *Cross-sections, 6*, 105–120.

Tebble, H. (2013). Researching medical interpreting: An applied linguistics perspective. In E. Winston & C. Monikowski (Eds.), *Evolving paradigms in interpreter education* (pp. 42–75). Washington: Gallaudet University Press. https://doi.org/10.1080/17503 99x.2014.972651

Tebble, H. (2014). A genre-based approach to teaching dialogue interpreting: The medical consultation. *The Interpreter and Translator Trainer, 8*(3), 418–436.

Ting-Toomey, S. (1994). Managing intercultural conflicts effectively. In L. Samovar & R. Porter (Eds.), *Intercultural communication: A Reader* (7th ed., pp. 360–372). Belmont, CA: Wadworth.

Ting-Toomey, S., & Chung, L. (2005). *Understanding intercultural communication*. Los Angeles: Roxbury Publishing.

Tribe, R. (1999). Bridging the gap or damming the flow? Some observations on using interpreters/bicultural workers when working with refugee clients, many of whom have been tortured. *British Journal of Medical Psychology, 72*, 567–576. https://doi.org/10.1348/000711299160130

Tribe, R., & Lane, P. (2009). Working with interpreters across language and culture in mental health. *Journal of Mental Health, 18*(3), 233–241. https://doi.org/10.1080/09638230701879102

Tsai, M.-H. (2005). Opening states in triadic medical encounters in Taiwan. *Communication & Medicine, 2*(1). 53–68. https://doi.org/10.1515/come.2005.2.1.53

Vargas-Urpi, M. (2013). Coping with nonverbal communication in public service interpreting Chinese immigrants. *Journal of Intercultural Communication Research, 42*(4), 340–360. https://doi.org/10.1080/17475759.2013.838985

Wadensjö, C. (2001). Interpreting in crises: The interpreter's position in therapeutic encounters. In I. Mason (Ed.), *Triadic exchanges: Studies in dialogue interpreting* (pp. 71–87). Manchester: St. Jerome.

West, C., & Frankel, R. M. (1991). Miscommunications in medicine. In N. Coupland, H. Giles, & J. M. Wiemann (Eds.), *"Miscommunication" and problematic talk* (pp. 166–193). Newbury Park, CA: Sage.

Wierzbicka, A. (1991). Japanese key words and core cultural values. *Language in Society, 20*(3), 333–385. https://doi.org/10.1017/s0047404500016535

Zhang, Z., & Shang, W. (2002). Enquiry into inquiry: A study of Chinese medical consultation. In C. N. Candlin (Ed.), *Research and practice in professional discourse* (pp. 338–368). Hong Kong: City University of Hong Kong Press.

Zhu, Weihua. (2017). How do Chinese speakers of English manage rapport in extended concurrent speech? *Multilingua, 36*(2), 181–204. https://doi.org/10.1515/multi-2015-0112

5 Findings and implications for intercultural communication and for Chinese–English interpreting

As outlined in Chapter 1, the notion of intercultural communication, as a hypernym, is one that encompasses not only situations in which speakers from two different language backgrounds speak one or the other's language and deal with possible accompanying cultural and discourse-pragmatic transference ('cross-cultural communication') but also situations in which groups of speakers are together, speaking only one person's or even no one's first language and the choice of language and the types of discourse-pragmatic and other features are negotiated locally by all or some protagonists. This book extends this definition further by systematically subjecting features from interpreter-mediated interactions to an analysis of communication patterns across cultures *and* languages. This book looks at and problematizes a distinction that has been made by some of *intercultural competence* referring to the ability to interact in one's own language with people from another culture without requiring knowledge of the target language, while *intercultural communicative competence* is the ability to interact with speakers from another culture in their language. Both attributes are examined in the same interactions as it is both these abilities that interpreters are required to possess in order to interpret effectively and successfully. These attributes are discussed within an approach that describes the positional, situational and discourse-specific features of interpreter-mediated interactions, and the linguistic, pragmatic and inter-cultural knowledge that interlocutors bring to these interactions in a coherent approach, that looks at the interplay between intercultural discourse and intercultural agency in relation to the Inter-Culturality Framework.

The findings that this book focusing on mediated intercultural communication offer for Interpreting Studies and for Chinese–English interpreting in particular are manifold. The 'social turn' in Interpreting (and Translation) Studies from the start of the twenty-first century has resulted in still only few large-scale or qualitative studies that examine intercultural communication as a prominent feature in interpreted interactions. This book addresses a gap that exists in the field of Interpreting Studies such that mediated intercultural communication is the central focus of empirical data about interpreted interactions. Specific to the language pair Chinese–English, the discourse-pragmatic norms and intercultural strategies of Chinese–English interpreters are a vital area of research as the attributes of this group of linguistic mediators have been examined mostly in relation to linguistic message transfer only and aspects of mediated intercultural communication have been looked at in a rather unsystematic way or not at all. Findings are presented employing an Inter-Culturality Framework (ICF) analysis to the data sample. This framework and the in-depth discussion of intercultural features in a hitherto lesser-researched area move a contemporary understanding of mediated intercultural communication forward.

5.1　Summary of findings

This book is primarily about Chinese–English interpreting and intercultural communication. Throughout the book, we have revisited and/or unpacked relevant concepts and perspectives regarding interpreter-mediated interactions involving Chinese and English speakers. The concepts that have been explored include 'language', 'culture', 'interculture and interculturality', 'communication', 'competence for intercultural communication', 'intercultural discourse', involving 'interculatural frames and models', 'intercultural agency', involving 'intercultural schemas and strategies', 'Chinese speakers', 'English speakers', 'intercultural pragmatics', 'non-verbal communication', 'positioning and agency' of an interpreter, and 'changing roles' of an interpreter. Perspectives are mainly concerned with the intercultural perspectives from the Chinese speakers, English speakers, and Chinese–English interpreters. We have conducted extensive data analysis in a number of fields and domains, including conference interpreting, diplomatic interpreting, media interpreting, business interpreting, police, legal and court interpreting, and healthcare interpreting, as well as cultural and intercultural perceptions of respective groups, including sample groups of speakers of both language – Chinese speakers and English speakers – and of Chinese–English interpreters themselves.

In this section, we summarize the major findings of the first four chapters, and in the following section, we explore implications of the findings for Chinese–English interpreting and for intercultural communication.

We commenced this book with an anecdotal account provided by one of our informants, a Chinese–English interpreter, regarding a first-hand intercultural encounter between senior government officials from China on a formal visit to the offices of a senior government official in Australia. This anecdote serves two purposes: setting the scene for this book regarding Chinese–English interpreting and intercultural communication; alerting readers' awareness to what is involved in interpreter-mediated intercultural communication, and strategies to manage and negotiate cultural (mis-)understanding for effective and successful intercultural communication.

One of the points we have made in Chapter 1 is that although people have been communicating inter-culturally for centuries, and research on intercultural communication has been ongoing for decades, it is important to revisit fundamental concepts and perspectives regarding language, culture and interculturality for us to have an in-depth understanding of our day-to-day intercultural communication practices, and in particular, mediated interactions among Chinese speakers and

English speakers through the provision of interpreting services. We are aware of the implicit and fluid nature of such concepts as 'language', 'culture' and 'interculturality'. Therefore, instead of defining or redefining them, we have reviewed and reinterpreted them with the intention to develop a framework that can be sufficiently adopted to interpret the data that we have collected. We have taken an eclectic and holistic approach to the review and reinterpretation of concepts, e.g., the way we approach 'interculture' and 'interculturality' starts from various understandings of such concepts, e.g., interculture refers to a contact situation involving more than on culture or one set of cultural conceptualizations, and interculturality embodies 'transformation' of cultural knowledge and behaviour among people of different linguistic and cultural backgrounds, rather than 'assimilation' or 'transmission' of cultural knowledge and behaviour.

Following earlier research on intercultural communication, e.g., that of Dell Hymes and John Gumperz, regarding the ethnography of communication or culturally distinctive means of communication to place the study of language within the context of culture and society, in particular, the *etic* and *emic* approaches for comparative research across languages and cultures, we acknowledge the seminal works and frameworks that have laid a foundation for understanding our current practices of intercultural communication. Such frameworks include, to name a few, Clyne's (1994) three categories of intercultural communication studies, including contrastive approach, interlanguage approach and interactive intercultural approach; Hall's (1976) high-context versus low-context cultures; Hofstede's (1991, 2011) dimensions of culture; Sharifian's (2011, 2013) cultural linguistics approach to intercultural communication research involving cultural conceptualizations and metacultural competence; and more recently, García (2009), Baker (2011), Li (2011, 2018) and Zhu, Li, and Jankowicz-Pytel (2019) on languaging, translanguaging, and translanguaging space for intercultural encounters and practices.

In light of the review of fundamental concepts, we put forward a framework for continuing intercultural communication research, particularly for mediated intercultural interactions through interpreters from the perspectives of interlocutors and interpreters involved. We name this framework the 'Inter-Culturality Framework' (ICF) because the concept of 'interculturality' captures the dynamics and interactiveness and the changing nature of the interpreter-mediated intercultural communication. This framework enables us to look at such interactions involving interlocutors from different linguistic and cultural backgrounds and interpreters with multiple roles from the dimensions of 'intercultural discourse' and 'intercultural agency'. The former focuses more on broad socio-cultural contexts in which mediated interactions take place, and such contexts consist of implicit intercultural frames and models. As elaborated in Chapter 1, intercultural discourse is about establishing a discursive common ground among interlocutors (including interpreters), and it is a shared discourse of cultural knowledge and experience, which can be co-constructed and re-negotiated. The latter, i.e., intercultural agency, focuses on the cognitive structures of individuals or groups from a cultural perspective through their experiences and perceptions of the world. It involves the awareness of explicit and implicit power and inequality in multi-cultural societies, and the agentive (re-)negotiation of cultural identities, norms and trajectories of actions through various strategies associated with language use and practice. Intercultural agency can be enacted through intercultural schemas and strategies. For detailed elaborations on the four major components of the "Inter-Culturality" Framework (ICF), please see section 1.3 of Chapter 1.

As the book primarily involves mediated intercultural communication among Chinese speakers and English speakers through Chinese–English interpreters, we commenced Chapter 2 by unpacking such concepts as 'Chinese language' and 'Chinese speakers', as well as 'world Englishes' and 'English speakers'. By 'Chinese speakers', we refer to ethnic Chinese speakers, who may be monolingual or who may speak a whole spectrum of Chinese language(s), dialects and Chinese varieties with considerable variation and varying proficiency. By 'Chinese' as a language, we refer to, broadly speaking, Chinese *Pŭtōnghuà* or *Guóyŭ* and *Huáyŭ*, as it is variously labelled in different diasporic regions, and the various dialects and Chinese varieties within Chinese mainland and beyond.

In the case of 'English speakers', it is more complex as, for example, British speakers of (British) English are but one of the many groups of people who use English as their L1 or subsequently acquired language. Therefore, the hypernym 'English speakers' encompasses a vast number of speakers of a whole spectrum of heterogeneous varieties of English, commonly known as 'world Englishes'. The uncommon plural form of 'Englishes', unlike other languages, such as Chinese, French and Spanish, which are not usually referred to in their plural forms, symbolizes the functional and formal variations in the English language and its international spread, use and acculturation over centuries. It is worth noting that the current majority of 'English speakers' are bilingual or multilingual users of English from multicultural speech communities and societies, and they are playing a salient role in determining the change and variation of the English language. This may have implications for mediated intercultural communication through interpreters, as interlocutors, including interpreters cannot assume that speaking English or Chinese will necessarily imply a homogeneous set of norms, conventions, cultural pragmatics, and trajectories.

What both 'Chinese speakers' and 'English speaker' have in common is that they are not homogeneous communities linguistically and culturally across the globe. This, on the one hand, makes intercultural communication, particularly mediated intercultural interactions challenging. It warrants continuing research and practices to deepen our understanding of the changing nature of mediated intercultural interactions. In that respect, the ICF framework helps us put intercultural dimensions of interactions into perspective for effective communication across cultures.

After unpacking 'Chinese language', 'world Englishes', 'Chinese speakers' and 'English speakers' in Chapter 2, we looked at, in particular, intercultural pragmatics concerning Chinese and English speakers. In light of Hymes' SPEAKING acronym, Hall's high-context and low-context culture distinction, Hofstede's cultural dimensions model, and Sharifian's cultural conceptualizations, we introduced the Inter-Culturality framework (ICF) in our analysis of communication practices of Chinese and English speakers. In particular, we looked at areas such as naming practices, terms of address, e.g., kinship terms, honorifics, occupational terms of address, issues of face, and maxims of politeness between Chinese and English. We also looked at communicative events and non-verbal communication, as we are aware that as far as interpreter mediated interactions are concerned, "[p]erceptions of meaning and intent from source messages are conveyed not only in the semantic content of them, but also through context, role, situation, and other paralinguistic features enacted by interlocutors" (Hlavac, Xu, & Xiong, 2015, p. 98). In particular, we looked at major types of paralinguistic practices and non-verbal acts, e.g., kinesic acts. Another main area that we explored in Chapter 2 is regarding the agencies of intercultural interlocutors and interpreters. We argue that it is essential for all parties, including interlocutors and interpreters, to develop awareness of the zone of interculturality and its interlingual and intercultural ramifications at work. It is also essential for all parties involved in mediated intercultural communication to develop awareness of the changing roles of an interpreter, and adjust their intercultural positioning and agency accordingly in mediated intercultural communicative events. Chapter 2 helps us understand the complexity of the wider social and cultural practices concerning Chinese and English speakers, not just because they form the largest numbers of speakers in the world, but also because of the great heterogeneity of their speech interactions, communities and cultural conceptualizations are enormous.

Chapter 3 commenced with an overview of the fields and modes of interpreting and contemporary understanding of the interpreter's role(s). The main findings come from the analysis of data from specific settings: conferences; diplomacy and senior government meetings; media; business meetings; police interviews and courtroom proceedings; and healthcare. In these settings, we analysed data samples of real-life examples of Chinese–English interpreting and applied elements of frameworks outlined in Chapter 1 selectively, including the ICF.

In conference interpreting, the challenges for interpreters are specialist terminology and the formal register used which can include specific and marked rhetorical forms. Interpreters are found to use his/her linguistic resources to recognize and understand forms used in topic-specific idiolects and to reproduce target language forms equivalent to these via intercultural strategies, some of which could be approximation, circumlocution or even foreignizing. At the same time, conference interpreters also recognize and understand the rhetorical features – e.g. inductive vs. deductive argumentative styles, use of metaphor or analogy – which themselves are an intercultural frame that the interpreter manages online via intercultural strategies such as restructuring, paraphrase or 'use of all-purpose words'.

The importance of understanding the illocutionary force of others' source speech and avoiding the possibility of *any* interlocutor losing face is evident in the examples taken from diplomatic and media interpreted interactions. Euphemistic or opaque metaphors may be forms that occur conspicuously in interlocutors' source speech and the interpreters are found to use their knowledge of intercultural schemas to provide target speech forms that capture the illocutionary force, without this offending the face of the recipient of the target speech. Working from Chinese into English, traditional four character phrases are a challenge that interpreters render via sense-for-sense constructions, while retaining the contextual cues reflective of the source culture's socio-political structures. In the same way, in media interpreting, concepts that are more characteristic of the cultural heritage of one language group can posit challenges for the interpreter. Omission is used to avoid the online difficulty of rendering specific concepts, and instead examples of the concept are used as a compensatory strategy.

In business settings, the interpreter's role may sometimes be that of a 'team member' of one of the parties and therefore not impartial and unbiased, i.e. a dual-role mediator. Recalled examples show that commonly used speech acts that interlocutors from both parties employ, e.g. greetings, introductory small talk, welcome speeches, hedging, bluffing or even short move such as a gregarious compliment or a celebratory thank you response are challenges for interpreters. Examples show how interpreters use their knowledge of intercultural discourse and intercultural agency to adopt strategies appropriate to the situation to deal with them.

In interpreted proceedings in the courtroom in mainland China, there are a number of intercultural frames that present challenges to any legal or court interpreter. These challenges are procedural and discourse-related. We see how interpreters at times provide inter-lingual transfer as a *direct recapitulator* and *indirect recapitulator*, which are both relaying roles, but also *narrator* and *principal* (Merlini & Favaron, 2005). Conventions of the interpreter's obligation to interpret and ability to interpret (in a situational sense) differ from court to court, and in some cases, the interpreter is requested to elicit information or to verify something that may be understood but not verbalized by others. That court officials address the interpreter suggests that the interpreter may be seen by them as a fellow inquisitor with bilingual skills, rather than as a non-aligned interpreter. Interpreters do not consistently relay speech into the other language in these given examples, and they appear to subordinate this role to the role of bilingual court official partial to the demands of the presiding judge(s) and/or prosecution.

In healthcare settings in China, interpreters adopt footings that are sometimes similar to those of courtroom interpreters. The situations studied involved in-house interpreters who occupy a dual role as interpreters and as hospital employees. They are found to enact roles congruent to those described in other guidelines for healthcare interpreters such as the 'California Standards for Healthcare Interpreters' (2002) that include 'message converter' and 'message clarifier'.

Chapter 4 presents data from three groups of informants who come to mediated interactions with different perspectives, enacting different roles: Chinese speakers (as consumers of healthcare services); English speakers (as healthcare professionals); and Chinese–English interpreters. The findings from data collected in relation to five situational features reveal a number of patterns. Responses in relation to introductions, role explanations and pre-interactional briefings on features relevant to intercultural communication show that all three groups of informants report reasonably high frequencies of introducing themselves. Chinese–English interpreters perhaps surprisingly report the lowest levels of self-introduction. In part, this can be explained by the possibility that some English speakers may do this on behalf of the interpreter, which the interpreter typically then interprets.

Role-explanations may be delivered in the same turn as a self-introduction, or they may be identifiable as a separate turn, usually delivered by the interpreters, less often by the English speaker which is then interpreted by the interpreter into Chinese. The role-explanation is an intercultural frame, as it is a speech act that makes explicit the allophone, procedural and mediated nature of the interaction. Chinese speakers are more commonly the recipient of the role-explanation than English speakers, which suggests that this frame is perceived to be less familiar to them and they are therefore more frequently the recipients of it.

Chinese speakers are more likely to receive a briefing that includes mention of intercultural features than English speakers. Both groups confirmed, unsurprisingly, that they view the Chinese–English interpreter as the key protagonist to provide this. The Chinese–English interpreter is viewed as an 'authority' to advise on intercultural features and both Chinese and English speakers themselves less commonly initiate discussion on this topic. Responses from Chinese speakers show a high reliance on the interpreter to perform this role. Responses from English speakers are mixed and show that they view the Chinese–English interpreter as *an* authority, but not always the sole source of cultural information relevant to interactions with Chinese speakers. Here, the intercultural agency of English speakers themselves is apparent, where they view interpreters as a group, but not the only group that possesses intercultural communication skills.

Data on proxemics and physical body space were also collected. Neither Chinese nor English speakers reported noticeable changes to their own physical proximity to the speaker of the other language of interpreter. Chinese–English interpreters believe that Chinese speakers position themselves more closely to the interpreter. Situational and logistic features can play a role in this. In regard to paralinguistic markers and kinesics, Chinese speakers do not report employing these as compensatory strategies or accommodation markers to the English-speaking interlocutor whom they may believe use these more frequently. But accommodation is recorded amongst English speakers who record a decrease in kinesics and paralinguistic markers, perhaps as an intercultural strategy accommodating to their notions of Chinese pragmatics and kinesics.

The findings in relation to information presentation and elicitation are mixed, but in part point to differences in the rhetorical and discourse organizational features of Chinese speakers and English speakers. Reporting on themselves, there are few differences between the two groups in regard to whether they use direct or indirect strategies to outline their position – most nominate that they do so directly. Most of these perceptions are shared in a similar way by interpreters, with their perceptions being closer to those of English speakers than Chinese speakers. A more uniform trend and one that is in line with the inductive/deductive contrast is ascertainable in regard to perceptions of both groups of speakers about each other (where a deductive approach to discourse structure is perceived as being more 'direct'). Chinese speakers perceive English speakers as being 'direct' while English speakers perceive Chinese speakers to be 'direct' to 'neither direct/nor indirect'. Chinese–English interpreters also provide a contrastive rating of both groups' discourse norms; their scores describe Chinese speakers as more indirect than direct, and English speakers to be slightly more direct than indirect. These responses are in line with the high-context vs. low-context distinction, advanced by Hall (1976) that describes Chinese as a high-context culture and most English-speaking cultures as low-context, resulting usually in more direct speech patterns.

We see congruence in the responses from Chinese–English interpreters in regard to the way that they view Chinese speakers expressing key speech acts (explanations, answers to questions, requests, complaints/criticisms and compliments) and the way that Chinese speakers 'receive' interpretations from English into Chinese provided for them. What this means is that both groups attach approximately the same levels of rhetorical directness in the expression of these speech acts. We also see similar levels of congruence between Chinese–English interpreters' views about how these same speech acts are expressed in English and English speakers' views about how they 'receive' speech acts interpreted into English from Chinese. This suggests that at the level of rhetorical directness, Chinese–English interpreters are applying their knowledge of intercultural frames and employing intercultural strategies to align the illocutionary force appropriate to the discourse-pragmatic conventions of each language community.

Findings also show that users of interpreting services very often adapt or accommodate their speech in mediated interactions to the interpreter 'receiving' their source speech, but also indirectly to their allophone interlocutor. Simplification or paraphrasing which are both commonly used intercultural strategies are reported to be employed by both Chinese and English speakers. It is not unexpected for English speakers to do this in their English speech for Chinese–English interpreters, most of whom use English as their B-language. But it is surprising that Chinese speakers also report doing this. This points to both groups' awareness of the mediated interaction as a place of intercultural discourse and adaptation or accommodation are practised as intercultural strategies.

5.2   Implications for Chinese–English interpreting

We are informed by the data presented in Chapters 3 and 4 in our discussion of implications, specific and general, for Chinese–English interpreting. There are implications from these two chapters for pedagogy, practice and research. We focus our discussion mainly on interpreter training; there are areas of overlap here with practice and research.

Traditionally, interpreter training has focused on the linguistic skill-base of entrance-level trainees and the development of inter-lingual transfer skills, commencing chronologically with the teaching of short consecutive interpreting, moving to long consecutive interpreting with simultaneous interpreting of seen and then unseen speeches as a typical final point of training. The emergence of public service interpreting in the 1980s led to the development of dialogue interpreting, i.e. usually 'short consecutive' interpreting but working bi-directionally, and to the more widespread teaching of sight translation as a language transfer skill more typical of public service encounters. The technological advances that have occurred since the start of the new millennium have greatly augmented the accessibility of source speeches (in audio or audio/visual form), speech or source text transcripts, and removed barriers to the ease of (self-) recording of target speeches, (self-)monitoring of target speeches, and the distribution and sharing of source and target speeches amongst interpreter trainers, trainee interpreters and further afield.

The 'social turn' in Interpreting Studies, which coincided roughly with the aforementioned technological advances ushered in an opening up of the discipline to other areas of the social sciences, e.g. discourse studies, sociolinguistics, anthropology, sociology, politics, international relations and social work. There has been a broadening of the thematic areas and settings in which interpreter training is conducted so that it commonly encompasses educational, welfare, health and legal settings, as well as conference, scientific, business or diplomatic ones. The emergence of intercultural communication as a discipline area over the last 20 years has been acknowledged within Translation Studies generally (Katan, 1999), but the 'cross-fertilization' between the two areas has perhaps not been as rich as one might have expected (cf. Kearns, 2008). Schäffner (2003) identifies a difference in approach evident in the two disciplines: intercultural communication focuses on naturally occurring interactions amongst people who do not share the same cultural-linguistic background; Translation Studies (and within it Interpreting Studies) focuses on enabled communication via the intervention and addition of a key protagonist who performs mediation as his/her primary role.

Chapter 3 offers a number of implications for interpreter pedagogy. The first is a general one stated clearly by Setton (2009): the differences in conceptualization of social organization and social categories in Chinese society compared to English-speaking societies, with commensurate non-equivalence of categories and terms cross-linguistically as not only an over-arching cultural feature, but as something reflected in each language's typological categories. A second implication relates to the notion of role. In predominantly Anglophone countries such as Australia, the United Kingdom and the United States, guideline documents such as the AUSIT Code of Ethics and Code of Conduct conceptualize the contemporary interpreter as an impartial, autonomous and independent (freelance) professional who interacts with others on the same level, providing and expecting reciprocal treatment from parties with whom s/he works. While this conceptualization is not specific to Western or Anglophone countries, the conventions of (self-)introduction, role explanation and briefing may be enactments more typical of interpreters working in predominantly Anglophone countries and the way that Chinese–English trainee interpreters acquire, practice and perform these steps may differ cross-linguistically. Enactment of another role alongside that of an interpreter (e.g. hospital employee, business team member, civil servant within the Ministry of Foreign Affairs) typically influences his/her interpreting performance such that impartiality or unbiasedness cannot usually be maintained. The way an interpreter presents him-/herself when occupying a dual-role function needs to address notions of interpreter independence and impartiality held by Chinese and English speakers. Where these differ, the trainee interpreter needs to practise providing this type of information to both groups of speakers in regard to role.

The different settings offer a number of features, many of them 'inter-cultural' referring to the 'moving' between Chinese and English cultures, but many of them relating to the specific 'culture' of the setting itself, i.e. the 'culture' of a formal conference, the 'culture' of a meeting of senior government officials or the 'culture' of a public press conference. Here, intercultural communication is a hypernym encompassing contact not only between Chinese speakers and English speakers, but contact between the 'culture' of a formal conference held in China (in Chinese), and the 'culture' of a formal conference held in an English-speaking country (in English). This means that the trainee interpreter is not only moving between two languages and linguistic cultures, but between two different sets of 'conference culture'. The data and examples presented in sections 3.3.1 to 3.3.3 show how Chinese–English interpreters working in conference, diplomatic and media settings in predominantly Chinese-speaking countries enact interpreter roles according to the setting-specific culture of the respective Chinese-speaking country. This has a commensurate effect on the use of face-saving strategies, use of honorifics, mitigating strategies, and knowledge and use of geo-political terms. Business meetings are another good example of the differences that exist in the 'culture of business meetings' in China which features up to 16 different stages and the 'culture of business meetings' in Britain which features only six stages. The more 'horizontal' structure of British meetings has a commensurate effect on the number of stages and the likely discourse of protagonists hosted in that country.

There are features presented in the excerpts of interpreted courtroom proceedings in mainland China that differ from those recorded in interpreted courtroom proceedings from studies in Australia (Hale, 2004) or America (Berk-Seligson, 2002). In the same way, the footings enacted by in-house hospital interpreters presented in section 3.3.6 in a Chinese hospital differ from those recorded from in-house hospital interpreters in predominantly Anglophone countries (Angelelli, 2004; Hsieh & Kramer, 2012).

Looking at Chinese–English interpreting in general and focusing on non-conference and non-business settings, particularly in bi-directionally interpreted interactions we see that these often take place between speakers with different status, educational and world-view profiles. There are other or additional features such as differences in register, rhetoric, proxemics or shared knowledge that place demands on the interpreter's skill levels. Current descriptions touch on features relevant to intercultural communication. However, these descriptions stop short of describing how cognitive activity relates also to the interpreter exercising intercultural agency in his/her interpretations. Gile's (1995) effort model and other descriptions of interpreting, (e.g. Seleskovitch, 1978; Moser-Mercer, 1996; Moser-Mercer, Frauenfelder, Casado, & Künzli, 2000; Nolan, 2005) do not identify intercultural communication as a specific feature of the interpreted event.

At the same time, other descriptions include it as a specific feature (e.g. Cokely, 1992) or as an embedded one (Hale, 2007). The implications of this book for interpreter training are that features of intercultural communication are prominent in practice and research and intercultural communication needs to be integrated in interpreter training programs.

This means that situated learning and practice in interpreter training has a 'dual' conceptualization: how a particular setting is enacted in a Chinese-speaking country and how the same setting is enacted in an English-speaking country. It calls also for the briefing and preparation of protagonists in simulated interactions to have clear notions of their roles, so that trainee interpreters encounter not only different thematic areas but also different procedures, hierarchies, turn-taking conventions and registers of speech not only in both languages, but according to the socio-cultural conventions of Chinese and English speakers. This kind of approach to training was one advocated by Heinz Göhring, a T&I educator, researcher and practitioner based at the Institute for Applied Linguistics and Cultural Studies in Germersheim (now part of University of Mainz). His books, including *Interkulturelle Kommunikation* 'Intercultural Communication' (Göhring, 2002) were influential in the development of interpreter training in Germany and Austria, and interpreter training in these two countries (particularly at the undergraduate level) features intercultural communication strongly.

Chapter 4 shows us that there are a number of situational features in public service interpreting that are relevant to interpreter training which can be included as features of classroom training and/or interpreting performance testing for students in the Chinese–English language pair. These include: naming practices and the role of titles or honorifics, use of first or family names, informal or familiar designations and use of personal pronouns or address forms, role explanation (in both languages) and pre-interactional briefings (in one or both languages). They also include: awareness of the use of proxemics, phatic language, kinesics and haptics and their function in the respective language cultures and how these features are negotiated and reflected in trainee interpreters' verbal and non-verbal performance; rhetorical styles, discursive practices, inductive vs. deductive communicative approaches and theme/rheme structure at the sentence level. The last three points are relevant to trainee interpreters and how they consider delivery into the target language which may include re-organization of or digression from the source language speech. Lastly, the trainee interpreter needs to consider the performance of common and frequent speech acts and their 're-presentation' in the target language, as well as how small talk and other typically formulaic moves such as leave taking are performed in Chinese as well as in English.

5.3   Implications for intercultural communication

The previous section presented implications of our research findings for Chinese–English interpreting. In this section, we suggest relevant implications for intercultural communication. We have discussed various types of competence in Chapter 1, e.g., linguistic competence, communicative competence, intercultural competence, multi-dialectal/multi-varietal competence, symbolic competence, performative competence, meta-cultural competence, and trans-languaging competence.

We have suggested three steps that intercultural interlocutors, including interpreters, may consider taking (Xu, 2017, p. 711), i.e., acknowledging paradigm shifts; anticipate intercultural differences and variations in conceptualizations and practices, and acquiring new competence for effective intercultural communication. These steps may imply that when we enter the zone of interculturality, we may acknowledge that the paradigms surrounding Chinese and English have shifted as both languages have largely become heterogeneous in terms of their forms, functions, norms, uses and users, and they are both increasingly used as regional and global lingua francas. In the meantime, we anticipate different cultural conceptualizations, norms and cultural traditions and practices that are associated with languages and speech communities as heterogeneous as Chinese, English, Chinese speakers and English speakers. In terms of acquiring new competence for effective interpreter-mediated intercultural communication, our research findings show that interlocutors and interpreters acquire sufficient exposure to mediated intercultural communicative events and increasing familiarity with different fields and domains of interactive and interpreting practices, and sufficient knowledge of intercultural discourse (including frames and models) and intercultural agency (including schemas and strategies) as well as effective use of strategies to (co-)construct and (re-)negotiate meaning across cultures.

References

Angelelli, C. (2004). *Medical interpreting and cross-cultural communication.* Cambridge, UK: Cambridge University Press.

Baker, C. (2011). *Foundations of bilingual education and bilingualism.* Bristol, New York and Ontario: Multilingual Matters.

Berk-Seligson, S. (2002). *The bilingual courtroom: Court Interpreters in the judicial process.* Chicago and London: University of Chicago Press.

California Healthcare Interpreters Association. (2002). *California standards for healthcare interpreters ethical principles, protocols, and guidance on roles & intervention.* Retrieved from www.chia.ws/standards.htm

Clyne, M. (1994). *Intercultural communication at work: Cultural values in discourse.* Cambridge and New York: Cambridge University Press.

Cokely, D. (1992). *Interpretation: A sociolinguistic model.* Burtonsville, MD: Linstok Press.

García, O. (2009). *Bilingual education in the 21st century.* Oxford: Wiley Blackwell.

Göhring, H. (2002). *Interkulturelle kommunikation.* Tübingen: Stauffenburg.

Gile, D. (1995). *Basic concepts and models for interpreter and translator training.* Amsterdam and Philadelphia: John Benjamins.

Hale, S. (2004). *The discourse of court interpreting.* Amsterdam and Philadelphia: John Benjamins.

Hale, S. (2007). *Community interpreting.* Basingstoke: Palgrave Macmillan.

Hall, E. T. (1976). *Beyond culture.* New York: Random House, Inc.

Hlavac, J., Xu, Z., & Xiong, D. Y. (2015). Intercultural pragmatics at work: (Self-)perceptions of intercultural behaviour of Chinese and English speakers and interpreters in healthcare interactions. *Intercultural Pragmatics*, *12*(1), 91–118. https://doi.org/10.1515/ip-2015-0004

Hofstede, G. (1991). *Cultures and organizations: Software of the mind*. London: McGraw-Hill.

Hofstede, G. (2011). Dimensionalizing cultures: The Hofstede model in context. *Online Readings in Psychology and Culture*, *2*(1), 1–26. https://doi.org/10.9707/2307-0919.1014

Hsieh, E., & Kramer, E. M. (2012). Medical interpreters as tools: Dangers and challenges in the utilitarian approach to interpreters' roles and functions. *Patient Education and Counseling*, *89*, 158–162. https://doi.org/10.1016/j.pec.2012.07.001

Katan, D. (1999). *Translating cultures: An introduction for translators, interpreters and mediators*. Manchester: St. Jerome.

Kearns, J. (2008). *Translator and interpreter training: Issues, methods and debates*. London and New York: Continuum.

Li, W. (2011). Moment analysis and translanguaging space: Discursive construction of identities by multilingual Chinese youth in Britain. *Journal of Pragmatics*, *43*(5), 1222–1235. https://doi.org/10.1016/j.pragma.2010.07.035

Li, W. (2018). Translanguaging as a practical theory of language. *Applied Linguistics*, *39*(1), 9–30. https://doi.org/10.1093/applin/amx044

Merlini, R., & Favaron, R. (2005). Examining the 'voice of interpreting' in speech pathology. *Interpreting*, *7*(2), 263–302. https://doi.org/10.1075/bct.9.08mer

Moser-Mercer, B. (1996). Quality in interpreting: Some methodological issues. *The Interpreters' Newsletter*, *7*, 43–55.

Moser-Mercer, B., Frauenfelder, U., Casado, B., & Künzli, A. (2000). Searching to define expertise in interpreting. In G. Englund Dimitrova & G. Hyltenstam (Eds.), *Language processing and simultaneous interpreting: Interdisciplinary perspectives* (pp. 107–131). Amsterdam: John Benjamins. https://doi.org/10.1075/btl.40.09mos

Nolan, J. (2005). *Interpretation: Techniques and exercises*. Bristol: Multilingual Matters.

Schäffner, C. (2003). Translation and intercultural communication: Similarities and differences. *Studies in Communication Sciences*, *3*(2), 79–107.

Seleskovitch, D. (1978). *Interpreting for international conferences* (S. Dailey & E. McMillan, Trans.). Leesburg, VA: Pen & Booth.

Setton, R. (2009). Interpreting China, interpreting Chinese. *Interpreting*, *11*(2), 109–117. https://doi.org/10.1075/intp.11.2.01set

Sharifian, F. (2011). *Cultural conceptualizations and language. Chapter 1: On cultural conceptualizations*. Amsterdam and Philadelphia: John Benjamins Publishing Company.

Sharifian, F. (2013). Globalisation and developing metacultural competence in learning English as an international language. *Multilingual Education*, *3*(7), 1–11. https://doi.org/10.1186/2191-5059-3-7

Xu, Z. (2017). Developing meta-cultural competence in teaching English as an international language. In F. Sharifian (Ed.), *Advances in cultural linguistics* (pp. 703–720). Switzerland: Springer. https://doi.org/10.1007/978-981-10-4056-6_31

Zhu, H., Li, W., & Jankowicz-Pytel, D. (2019). Translanguaging and embodied teaching and learning: Lessons from a multilingual karate club in London. *International Journal of Bilingual Education and Bilingualism*, 1–16. https://doi.org/10.1080/13670050.2019.1599811

Index

Printed in Great Britain
by Amazon

82176363R00129